Cognitive Behavioural Therapy Workbook

FOR

DUMMIES®

2ND EDITION

by Rhena Branch and Rob Willson

WILEY

John Wiley & Sons, Inc.

Cognitive Behavioural Therapy For Dummies,® 2nd Edition
Published by
John Wiley & Sons, Ltd
The Atrium
Southern Gate
Chichester
West Sussex
PO19 8SQ
England
www.wiley.com

For general information on our other products and services, please contact our Customer Care Department within the U.S. at 877-762-2974, outside the U.S. at 317-572-3993, or fax 317-572-4002.

For technical support, please visit www.wiley.com/techsupport.

Wiley publishes in a variety of print and electronic formats and by print-on-demand. Some material included with standard print versions of this book may not be included in e-books or in print-on-demand. If this book refers to media such as a CD or DVD that is not included in the version you purchased, you may download this material at http://booksupport.wiley.com. For more information about Wiley products, visit www.wiley.com.

British Library Cataloguing in Publication Data: A catalogue record for this book is available from the British Library

ISBN: 978-1-119-95140-7 (pbk); ISBN 978-1-119-95381-4 (ebk); ISBN 978-1-119-95383-8 (ebk); ISBN 978-1-119-95382-1 (ebk)

Printed and bound in Great Britain by TJ International Ltd., Padstow, Cornwall.

10 9 8 7 6 5 4 3

About the Authors

Editors: For a book with one author, do not include the author's name as a heading. For more than one author, start a paragraph with the author's name in bold, as shown here.

Rhena Branch MSc, Dip CBT, is an accredited CBT practitioner and qualified clinical supervisor. She has co-written several books in addition to those in the *For Dummies* series. Rhena teaches and supervises on the MSc in CBT at Goldsmiths, University of London and runs a private practice in central London.

Rob Willson, BSc, MSc, Dip SBHS, currently divides the majority of his work time between private practice and conducting research on Body Dysmorphic Disorder at the Institute of Psychiatry, London. Previously he spent twelve years working at the Priory Hospital, North London where he was a therapist and therapy services manager. He also trained numerous CBT therapists over a seven-year period at Goldsmiths, University of London. Rob's main clinical interests are anxiety and obsessional problems, and disseminating CBT principles through self-help. He has made several TV appearances including in the BBC documentary 'Too Ugly for Love'.

Authors' Acknowledgments

Many researchers, fellow therapists and authors have influenced our understanding and practice of CBT over the years and therefore the content in this book. Founding fathers, Albert Ellis and Aaron T. Beck, of course merit special mention. Others include (in no specific order): Ray DiGiuseppe, Mary-Anne Layden, Jacqueline Persons, David A. Clarke, Adrian Wells, Stanley Rachman, Paul Salkovskis, Christine Padesky, Michael Neenan, David Veale, David M. Clark, David Burns, Kevin Gournay and many more. Special thanks goes to Windy Dryden for his extensive writings and for teaching us both so much.

Finally, a genuine thank you to all our clients (past and present) for allowing us to get to know you and learn from you.

Publisher's Acknowledgments

We're proud of this book; please send us your comments at http://dummies.custhelp.com. For other comments, please contact our Customer Care Department within the U.S. at 877-762-2974, outside the U.S. at 317-572-3993, or fax 317-572-4002.

Some of the people who helped bring this book to market include the following:

Acquisitions, Editorial, and Vertical Websites

Project Editor: Simon Bell

Commissioning Editor: Kerry Laundon

    (Previous Edition: Alison Yates)

Assistant Editor: Ben Kemble

Development Editor: Kathleen Dobie

Copy Editor: Kate O'Leary

Technical Editor: David Kingdon

Proofreader: Anne O'Rorke

Production Manager: Daniel Mersey

Publisher: David Palmer

Cover Photo: Kristy-Anne Glubish/Design Pics/Corbis

Cartoons: Rich Tennant (www.the5thwave.com)

Composition Services

Project Coordinator: Kristie Rees

Layout and Graphics: Carrie Cesavice, Erin Zeltner

Proofreader: Melissa Cossell

Indexer: Potomac Indexing, LLC

Publishing and Editorial for Consumer Dummies

    Kathleen Nebenhaus, Vice President and Executive Publisher

    Kristin Ferguson-Wagstaffe, Product Development Director

    Ensley Eikenburg, Associate Publisher, Travel

    Kelly Regan, Editorial Director, Travel

Publishing for Technology Dummies

    Andy Cummings, Vice President and Publisher

Composition Services

    Debbie Stailey, Director of Composition Services

Contents at a Glance

Table of Contents

Introduction

. . . .

Welcome to the *Cognitive Behavioural Therapy Workbook For Dummies*, 2nd Edition. Cognitive behavioural therapy, or CBT, is a form of psychotherapy found scientifically to be effective with depression, anxiety, and many other types of problems.

Quite often people accept a physical illness or accident that impairs their daily functioning but may fail to accept that they have become mentally unwell. Every human being regardless of culture, creed, class, background, race or any other distinguishing characteristic is likely to experience some form of emotional or mental disturbance during the course of their lives. The good news is that it's totally normal to become psychologically disturbed and it's absolutely possible to recover. CBT can really help.

We've written this book to bring the types of CBT exercises we use in our work with troubled clients to you. We know that CBT works because we've seen it work! And we want it to work for you too. Whatever your problem, we hope that you'll find this book useful and informative.

About This Book

This book gives you an arsenal of skills and tools to help you beat a range of psychological problems. We try to give you just enough theoretical information to enable you to do the exercises contained in each chapter. All the worksheets and tasks in this workbook are indicative of the types of work we do with our clients in one-to-one CBT therapy.

You can use this workbook on your own to help you to basically become your own CBT therapist. Alternatively, you can use it alongside a course of CBT treatment with a qualified professional. Unfortunately we can't cover every type of psychological difficulty in depth in this book or it would turn out to be encyclopedic in length! So we've endeavoured to touch on the most common disorders that CBT has been proved effective at resolving. You can use this book as a jumping-off point to better understand your particular problems and how to battle them. If you think that you need some additional professional input then don't hesitate to get it!

Yep, it's a workbook, and that means it involves – you guessed it – work. But if you really put your energy into doing the work and regular practice, you'll get benefits. Is it worth it to you to sweat and struggle in order to feel and function better? If so, roll up your sleeves, do some preliminary stretches, put on your sweatbands and hurl yourself into the process!

A Serious Note About Humour

Embarking on a course of self-help can be daunting. Learning a bunch of new techniques designed to help you overcome your psychological problems is hard work, no question about it. In an attempt to lighten the mood we inject a bit of humour and irreverence into our writing. Please understand however, that we do take psychological disturbance very seriously and we know that feeling bad isn't funny. Hopefully our writing style will make this book entertaining and accessible. Laughter can indeed be good medicine. But most of all our aim with this book is to give you some seriously useful advice and practice opportunities to help you get well and stay well.

How To Use This Book

Like most *For Dummies* books, you don't need to read this book in order from start to finish. You can dip in and out of it, going to the chapters that seem most relevant to you. We've made efforts to cross reference a lot so that you're guided to other chapters which complement or more fully explain concepts or exercises. The following table shows where to find information on specific issues CBT can help with, and you can use the Table of Contents at the front of the book and the Index at the back to locate the information you want as well.

Characteristics of CBT and relevant chapters	
CBT Characteristic	*Chapter Number(s)*
Helps you develop flexible, self-enhancing beliefs and attitudes toward yourself, others, and the world around you	16
It is goal-directed	8
Offers skills and strategies for overcoming common problems such as anxiety, addictions, depression and more	9, 10, 11, 12, 13
Addresses your past with a view to understanding how it may be affecting your present day beliefs and behaviours	16, 17
Focuses on how your problems are being perpetuated rather than searching for a singular reason or root cause	2, 7
Encourages you to try things out for yourself and practice new ways of thinking and acting	4, 5
Highlights relapse prevention and personal development	18, 19, 20

Please use this book to write in, make notes and work! That's what it's written for! You've got our express permission to mess it up as much as you like; after all it's your book and you're the one who'll benefit by using it.

What Not to Read

Don't read anything that you don't want to read. This book is for you. Read whatever you think will be most helpful to you. Perhaps you've had enough of this introduction chapter. Fair enough, move on. Ideally we'd like you to read the whole thing (if we're honest) but that's because we wrote it and we think that every chapter has something of value to offer. But hey, it's up to you and you certainly don't have to agree with us (or our egos . . .).

Anything in this book that is relevant to you and helps you with your individual problems is what you should be reading. Focus on that. If it bores you, confuses you, or doesn't seem to apply to you – give it a miss.

Foolish Assumptions

We assume that if you've bought this book then you're interested in using CBT techniques on yourself. We're guessing that you've heard of CBT before or had it recommended to you by a friend or professional. We're also guessing that you've got one or two psychological problems that you'd like to be free from.

But even if our assumptions are completely wrong (or indeed foolish), this book may be of interest to you. You may have a friend or family member who you're concerned about and want to learn more about CBT treatment. You may be feeling okay but still have an interest in CBT and how it may be able to further your enjoyment of life. So we assume, foolishly or not, that you'll get something of use out of this book whatever your reasons for buying it.

How This Book Is Organised

The *Cognitive Behavioural Therapy Workbook For Dummies* has five parts.

Part I: Pinpointing Primary Principles

This part of the book gives you the groundwork for understanding your problems in relation to the CBT framework. Chapter 1 gives you an idea of what CBT is all about and how it applies to common problems. In Chapter 2 we show you how to recognise your problemtatic thinking patterns. Chapter 3 is all about how to get on top of toxic thinking and finding better alternative ways of thinking for the future. In Chapter 4 we show you how to act like a scientist in the interest of improving your emotional and mental health. We get a bit new age in Chapter 5 by introducing mindfulness and other techniques for directing your focus of attention.

Part II: Pinning Down Problems and Giving Yourself Goals

The chapters in this part are devoted to helping you to define your problems in specific terms and to choosing specific goals with regard to your identified difficulties.

Chapter 6 explains the CBT view of healthy and unhealthy negative emotions and gives you the chance to get to grips with your own emotional responses. Chapter 7 shows you how some of the ways in which you try to cope with problems may be in themselves problematic. In Chapter 8, we really focus on getting to grips with appropriate goals.

Part III: Putting CBT into Practice

The chapters in this part are all about putting CBT into practice on specific problems like anxiety, depression and low self-opinion. Chapter 9 deals with anxiety problems, Chapter 10 looks at exercises for overcoming addictions, and in Chapter 11 we deal with common body image problems. Chapter 12 covers tips for dealing a blow to depression, and Obsessive Compulsive Disorder is addressed in Chapter 13. In Chapter 14 we look at ways to lift low self-esteem. Chapter 15 is all about improving interpersonal relationships.

Part IV: Forging into the Future

In this part Chapter 16 helps you to look at long standing beliefs and ways of thinking that may affect you in the present. We include a lot of worksheets to help you challenge old and unhelpful beliefs about yourself, others and the world at large. Chapter 17 deals with techniques to make your new beliefs more permanent. In Chapter 18 you get the chance to focus on further personal development. Relapse is a real possibility and in Chapter 19 we give you a chance to plan and trouble shoot for possible problem resurgence. Chapter 20 is about helping you to live in a positive way even after you've largely defeated your initial problems.

Part V: The Part of Tens

This part contains handy top ten tips for working with professionals, getting some sleep, and renewing your motivation to get better. Sometimes readers may like to start at the part of tens and then go on to other chapters and parts in the book!

Case Examples Used in This Book

All the characters used in case examples throughout this book are entirely fictional. However, the types of problems we use them to typify are very common and based on our clinical experience with real clients over the years. Our hope is that you'll be readily able to identify with aspects of these made-up character's experiences and relate them to your own difficulties.

Icons Used in This Book

We use icons throughout this workbook to bring different types of information to your attention and to clearly guide you through the book.

This icon signposts a case example and completed sample worksheet.

You'll see this icon next to blank worksheets. It indicates your chance to put the work into workbook.

This alerts you to additional useful information that may help you to better understand a concept or to complete an exercise.

 This icon is used to emphasise information worth bearing in mind throughout your CBT self-help work.

 This icon is an alarm! It denotes possible pitfalls, common errors, or potential dangers.

Where to Go from Here

This workbook is designed to be a hands-on practical approach to using CBT. It contains lots of exercises and tasks to get you moving along the road to recovery. Because it's a workbook we don't go into great depth about theoretical CBT concepts and principles. It's a book focused more on action. For more about background CBT theory you're recommended to get the companion book, *Cognitive Behavioural Therapy For Dummies*, 2nd Edition (Wiley). It also has a section that suggests other useful CBT-based books to add to your library. *Boosting Self-Esteem For Dummies* (also written by us) has a lot of very useful CBT tips and techniques designed to help you learn to appreciate yourself more fully. We also recommend getting the *CBT Journal For Dummies* (we did this one, too), which is a valuable adjunct to all other CBT-based *For Dummies* books. You may also want to get *Personal Development For Dummies All-in-One*, edited by Gillian Burn (Wiley), which has a CBT section as well as sections based on other useful *For Dummies* self-help books.

Part I
Pinpointing Primary Principles

The 5th Wave   By Rich Tennant

"I'm tired of letting everyone pull my strings."

In this part . . .

You'll get the groundwork for understanding your problems in relation to the CBT framework. We show you what CBT is all about and how it applies to common problems. We show you how to recognise your problematic thinking patterns, how to get on top of toxic thinking and how to find better alternative ways of thinking for the future.

You also get to act like a scientist in the interest of improving your emotional and mental health, before we come over a bit new age by introducing mindfulness and other techniques for directing your focus of attention.

Chapter 1

Exploring the Basics of CBT

. . . .

. . . .

*U*sually people respond to negative, difficult, or downright bad life events with negative emotions such as sadness or anger (to name but two). It is both natural and normal to feel distressed when bad things happen. The degree of distress you feel depends partly on the severity of the bad event. But the key word here is 'partly'. Often the meanings you attach to given events can take a bad situation and make it worse. The way you *think* about aspects of your current life or past experiences can move you from healthy, normal distress to more problematic psychological disturbance. Feelings of depression, anxiety, rage, or guilt, for example, are painful and can lead to further difficulties in your life.

Fortunately, the situation's not all doom and gloom! You can learn to recognise how your thoughts, beliefs, and attitudes impact on your feelings. Once you understand this principle, you can then work on changing your thinking and behaviour to help you take bad situations and make them better.

In this chapter we introduce the main theoretical stuff you need to know about Cognitive Behavioural Therapy – CBT for short – to get you started.

Understanding the Nuts and Bolts of CBT

As the name implies, CBT is a form of psychotherapy that focuses on *cognition* – your thoughts – and on *behaviour* – your actions. One way of summing up CBT is to say 'you feel the way you think'. But CBT also looks closely at behaviour, since the way you act is often determined by how you feel. Furthermore, the way you act can have either a positive or negative influence on your feelings. Without necessarily realising it, you may be acting in ways that are actually fuelling your bad feelings.

The interaction between thoughts, feelings, and behaviours is at the core of CBT. Therefore CBT looks closely at how you think and act in order to help you overcome both behavioural and emotional difficulties.

Blinding you with the science of CBT

CBT practitioners are interested not only in helping people to *feel* better in the short term but also in using scientifically verified strategies to help people *get* better and stay better in the long term. CBT has been tested and developed through many scientific studies. With continued research it is likely that more will be learnt about which techniques work best for specific types of problems. Because of CBT's scientific basis, it invites you to take a more scientific approach to both understanding and resolving your problems.

A big component of CBT involves helping people become their own therapists through the continued use of specific techniques. This self-directed element is probably one of the reasons people who have had CBT relapse less frequently than those treated using other psychotherapeutic approaches or medications without CBT.

Okay. So here might be a good place to clarify a few terms. Like many professions, psychology and psychotherapy use a lot of jargon. Sometimes in this book we use weird words and other times we use more everyday words, but *weirdly*. The following definitions help to make your reading more straightforward:

- ✔ **Cognitive:** Refers to your thoughts and anything else that goes through your mind including your dreams, memories, images, and your focus of attention.

- ✔ **Behaviour:** Includes everything that you do and all the things you choose *not* to do – such as avoiding situations or sulking instead of speaking.

- ✔ **Therapy:** Describes a method of treating a problem – physical, mental, or emotional. We use it mainly to refer to *talking therapies* such as CBT and other types of psychotherapy.

- ✔ **Belief:** Refers to your personal thinking styles and your way of understanding the world and your experiences. It also means your personal rules, codes, and attitudes for living.

- ✔ **Consequence:** Describes the result or outcome of an event of some kind. In this book we mainly refer to behaviour and emotional consequences (basically the kind of results produced by ways of acting or from specific emotions).

- ✔ **Distress:** Refers to normal negative human emotions that, though uncomfortable and unpleasant, don't cause you long-term problems.

- ✔ **Disturbance:** Refers to more extreme, intense negative emotions that can cause long-term problems and interfere significantly in your life.

- ✔ **Experiment:** No, we're not talking about test tubes and chemistry. What we mean are exercises that you devise and try out to see what sort of effect they have on your feelings.

- ✔ **Exposure:** Refers to action on your part to expose yourself to feared or avoided situations in order to help yourself recover from your problems. Note that we're not referring to the kind of exposure that could get you arrested!

- ✔ **Healthy:** Refers to appropriate and constructive behaviour, thoughts, or emotions.

- ✔ **Unhealthy:** Refers to inappropriate and destructive behaviour, thoughts, or emotions.

Linking thinking and feeling

You may generally conclude that if something happens to you, such as your car breaking down, that it is the actual event that makes you feel angry or anxious. Makes sense, right? Well, not entirely actually, no. According to CBT, what determines the quality and intensity of the emotion you experience are your *thoughts* about the event.

So whilst events contribute to your emotional and behavioural reactions (sometimes significantly), it is your *beliefs,* or the meaning you give to events, that lead you to feel healthy distress or unhealthy disturbance.

The more negative the event, the more distressed you probably feel. So if you lose your job, get mugged, or are involved in a serious accident you are very likely to feel intensely distressed. Intense distressed feelings in response to very negative events are still considered healthy because they're appropriate to your experience. But you can avoid becoming disturbed even in the face of very challenging life situations if you monitor your thinking.

Attaching meaning to events

Positive events normally lead to positive emotions and negative events to negative emotions (rather obviously). But the personal meanings you assign to events in your life sometimes may lead to unhealthy and problematic emotional reactions. Sometimes your thinking can lead you to attach extreme meanings to relatively minor events. For example, you may decide that your husband working late means that he's about to leave you for another woman. Some of the meanings that you give to events may be unrealistic, inaccurate, and fundamentally unhelpful.

When you attach a faulty meaning to an event, you're very likely to experience an unhealthy negative emotion, such as extreme guilt as Coral does in the following example. However when Coral attaches a fair and accurate meaning to the event, she experiences the healthy negative emotion of intense disappointment.

We also use the words *distressed* and *disturbed* to refer to healthy and unhealthy negative emotions. The difference between distress and disturbance is in the *quality* of the emotion you experience. This is an important concept that we go over more fully in Chapter 6.

- ✔ **Disturbed** refers to inaccurate or rigid ways of thinking about events that lead you to experience extreme unhealthy negative emotions.

- ✔ **Distressed** refers to accurate and balanced ways of thinking about events that lead you to experience appropriate healthy negative emotions.

Coral was putting her young children to bed but they just wouldn't settle down. After several minutes of trying to get them to sleep she lost her temper, shouted, and threw a cuddly toy across the room. Worksheet 1-1 shows the disturbed meaning she gave the event.

Worksheet 1-1	Coral's Unhealthy Personal Meaning Page
Event:	Losing my temper with my children
Personal meaning	I should never get that angry around the kids. This means that I am a terrible mother.
Emotion	Guilt

The extreme meaning Coral attaches to her loss of temper leads her to feel guilty. Guilt is likely to feed further self-downing and is unlikely to help Coral to make it up to her kids. Worksheet 1-2 shows a more healthy evaluation.

In CBT, we use the term *self-downing* to mean extreme self-criticism or putting yourself down on the basis of your actions. In Chapter 12 we discuss the healthy alternative to self-downing, which is self-acceptance.

Worksheet 1-2	Coral's Healthy Personal Meaning Page
Event:	Losing my temper with my children
Personal meaning:	I wish I hadn't got so angry with the kids. This means that I did a bad thing but I am still a pretty good mum overall.
Emotion:	Disappointment

Because Coral attaches an appropriate and fair meaning to her temper tantrum, she experiences a healthy negative emotion. Disappointment helps Coral to condemn her behaviour but not herself as a mother. She may now look more closely at her beliefs that led her to become so angry in the first place and make some changes.

Take a recent event from your own life in which you got yourself into a unhealthy emotional state. Use the Personal Meaning Page in Worksheet 1-3 to reassign a different meaning to the event and see if you can end up feeling a healthier emotion. Try to think differently about the event. Perhaps the personal meaning you're giving the event is overly negative and extreme. Try taking a more compassionate and objective view of yourself within the context of the negative event. You may find it useful to use these questions as a guide to filling out the worksheet:

✔ What happened exactly? What did you or someone else do? Record this as the event.

✔ What does the event mean about you? About other people? The world or life conditions? This is your personal meaning.

✔ How do you feel inside? Record your emotion.

✔ Is your personal meaning accurate, fair, and balanced? Or is it inaccurate, biased, and rigid?

✔ In order to be distressed about the event instead of disturbed, what new meaning could you give to the event?

You can use two pages as we did in Coral's case if you want to see a clear distinction between your personal meanings. If you're having trouble coming up with words for your feelings, take a look at Chapter 6, which covers emotions in depth.

Worksheet 1-3	My Personal Meaning Page
Event:	
Personal meaning:	
Emotion:	

Checking How CBT Can Work for You

CBT is growing in popularity as an effective treatment for a host of common psychological problems. A lot of research into CBT has focused on its use for the treatment of anxiety and depression in particular, and the results are encouraging. More and more doctors are recommending CBT because research shows that it helps people to stay well longer.

CBT is used to treat a wide range of psychological problems. Chances are good that whatever emotional or behavioural problem you're experiencing, this workbook can help get you going in the right direction. Worksheet 1-4 offers a checklist of some of the problems you may experience that CBT can help you overcome.

Even if you think that your problems are too severe for a self-help book like this one to be enough, CBT may still work for you. You may benefit most from seeing a therapist who can offer you additional support and guidance. Chapter 21 offers lots of advice on working with a therapist.

Worksheet 1-4   Problem Clarification Checklist

- ❑ Anger problems
- ❑ Anorexia
- ❑ Binge eating or over-eating
- ❑ Body dysmorphic disorder
- ❑ Bulimia
- ❑ Chronic fatigue syndrome
- ❑ Chronic pain
- ❑ Depression
- ❑ Excessive use of alcohol
- ❑ Excessive use of non-prescription or 'street' drugs
- ❑ Feelings of low self-worth
- ❑ Gambling and on-line gambling
- ❑ Obsessive-compulsive disorder
- ❑ Ongoing feelings of guilt or shame
- ❑ Panic attacks
- ❑ Personality disorders
- ❑ Post-traumatic stress disorder
- ❑ Social phobia
- ❑ Specific phobias
- ❑ Spending excessive amounts of money
- ❑ Worrying all the time

Don't be alarmed if you find that you have ticked two, three, or more items on the list; problems often overlap. In fact, for people to have more than one problem at a time is the norm, not the exception. An example of problem overlap is depression and anxiety – people frequently experience both at the same time. You can also make yourself feel guilty about your depression or ashamed about your social phobia, depending on what meanings you give to your original problems. CBT calls this overlap of two or more problems a *meta-emotional problem* or a *secondary emotional problem*. Luckily the strategies that you use to work on your primary problem usually work on your secondary ones too. So take heart.

Ranking your problems

Taking stock of the areas of your life you want to target for change before you get started can be useful. Your doctor or psychiatrist may have given you a diagnosis, or you may not be clear about what your problem actually is.

Putting your problems down on paper can help you to see how your problems may be interacting with each other. Writing them down also gives you a clearer starting point for overcoming them. Sometimes problems don't fall into neat and tidy categories or they overlap somewhat. You can use the Problem Clarification Checklist in Worksheet 1-6, later in this chapter, to help you put your finger on your problems.

Consider what problems you have and how they impact on different areas of your life. Work, home life, relationships, physical health and study are some areas your problems may impact. Review your list and look for any overlapping symptoms. An example of problems overlapping may be decreased ability to concentrate at work due to sleep disturbance.

Meg has arthritis and is very rarely pain free. Some days are better than others but the pain is getting her down. Lately, Meg has been drinking more in the evening to help her sleep. How she ranks her problems is shown in Worksheet 1-5.

Worksheet 1-5	Meg's Problem Ranking Worksheet
Rank: Problem	*Description of Effects*
First ranking problem: Chronic pain from arthritis	Aches in elbows, wrists, and knees. I'm not able to do activities that I used to really enjoy. My sleep is disturbed because pain often wakes me up. My mood is poor.
Second ranking problem: Depression	I don't feel like seeing friends or spending time with my family. I find housework and daily shopping overwhelming. I spend too much time dwelling on my thoughts and feelings. I drink wine to numb pain and depressed feelings.
Third ranking problem: Alcohol use	Sometimes a lot of wine can help me sleep but I wake up feeling worse. I don't like the idea of needing to rely on alcohol to cope. I've read that alcohol is a depressant, so I suppose that it may be worsening my depression.

In Meg's example, you see that her feelings of depression stem from chronic pain but that her use of alcohol is actually making her depression worse. From examining her Problem Ranking Worksheet, Meg can choose to intervene at several points. Now use Worksheet 1-6 to rank your own problems.

Worksheet 1-6	My Problem Ranking Worksheet
Rank: Problem	*Description of Effects*
First ranking problem:	
Second ranking problem:	
Third ranking problem:	

You may wish to continue the sheet to include a fourth or fifth ranking problem. However, be careful not to make things seem worse than they are! Try to stick to ranking your *main* problems and realise that a lot of other feelings you may be having, such as irritation or loneliness, are often problem *effects* (or in CBT terms, *emotional consequences*).

Breaking down your behaviours

Disturbed emotions tend to lead to destructive and self-destructive behaviours. Destructive behaviour rarely aids effective problem solving. On the contrary, it often creates further problems or worsens existing ones. Worksheet 1-7 is yet another checklist to help you to identify different types of big, bad, and ugly behaviours that you may sometimes recognise yourself doing.

Worksheet 1-7	Checklist of Bad Behaviours

Self-destructive behaviours:

❑ Drinking excessively

❑ Eating poorly (too much or too little)

❑ Engaging in high-risk sexual activities

❑ Gambling

❑ Lashing out verbally or physically

❑ Spending money compulsively or recklessly

❑ Sulking

❑ Taking risks when angry (such as reckless driving)

❑ Using illegal drugs

(continued)

Mood-lowering behaviours:

- ❑ Isolating yourself from friends and family
- ❑ Letting daily chores mount up
- ❑ Neglecting your hygiene
- ❑ Not asking others for help or support
- ❑ Not engaging in activities you usually enjoy
- ❑ Repeatedly calling in sick at work
- ❑ Sleeping too much or too little
- ❑ Staying in bed all day
- ❑ Staying indoors most of the time
- ❑ Stopping taking your medication

Avoidance behaviours:

- ❑ Avoiding exercise
- ❑ Doing other unrelated tasks rather than doing what actually needs to be done (such as tidying your desk rather than writing an essay)
- ❑ Engaging in superstitious behaviour in an attempt to ward off feared events
- ❑ Not answering the phone
- ❑ Not opening post (such as bills)
- ❑ Not speaking much in social gatherings
- ❑ Putting off tasks
- ❑ Staying away from situations that you find threatening (lifts, busy places, parties, and so on)
- ❑ Using rituals to help quell anxious thoughts and feelings

Now, as human beings and therefore given to making mistakes, many people exhibit some of the types of behaviours in the list from time to time. However these types of behaviours are very frequently linked to psychological problems. The more items you've ticked off on the checklist, the more probable it is that you're experiencing emotional disturbance. In turn, your 'bad' behaviours are almost certainly making things worse.

Stewie has social phobia and feels very anxious in social settings. Worksheet 1-8 shows his top five bad behaviours.

Worksheet 1-8	Stewie's Top Five Bad Behaviours

1. Keeping quiet in social settings until I'm absolutely certain what I want to say.

2. Avoiding going to parties where I don't know everybody.

3. Eating lunch on my own at work.

4. Spending too much time indoors.

5. Only going to the shops during quiet periods.

Stewie's big five fall under the Avoidance Behaviours category on the checklist in Worksheet 1-7. He may feel better in the short term because he's trying so hard to avoid situations in which he feels anxious. In the long term, however, Stewie is keeping his anxiety alive because he doesn't give himself the chance to discover that he can survive social awkwardness.

The big checklist of bad behaviours in Worksheet 1-7 can serve as a guideline for identifying your top five behaviours that may be perpetuating your problems. We offer space to identify your own bad behaviours in Worksheet 1-9.

Worksheet 1-9	My Top Five Bad Behaviours
1.	
2.	
3.	
4.	
5.	

Connecting Emotion, Thinking, and Behaviour

To put everything from this chapter together, start by selecting an emotion to investigate. This is your target emotion. In Worksheets 1-10 and 1-11 Margot chose depression as her target emotion and Tom selected anxiety. You get to choose your target emotion in Worksheet 1-12.

Next consider how your target emotion is affecting your thoughts. Margot's depression-based thinking includes ideas that socialising is pointless and she puts herself down for being a 'misery guts'. Tom's anxiety-based thinking leads him to conclude that he's helpless in the face of his fears and unable to cope with the discomfort of anxiety.

Now examine how your target emotion and feeling-based thinking are leading you to act. Think about what your target emotion makes you feel like doing. You can include past, present, or even potential future actions. Margot's depressed thoughts lead her to isolate herself, and Tom's anxious thinking tells him to continue avoiding public transport.

Finally, examine how your feeling-based behaviour is effecting your target emotion. By isolating herself from her friends, Margot actually makes her depression worse. Tom eases his anxiety in the short term by refusing to get on the bus, but his avoidance makes him even more fearful of using public transport.

Worksheet 1-10	Margot's Behaviour Effect Analysis
Target emotion:	Depression
Feeling-based thinking:	Going to see a film with my friends is pointless. I don't enjoy socialising anymore and nobody wants to be around a misery guts like me anyway.
Feeling-based behaviour:	Declining invitation to go to see film. Staying indoors and avoiding phone calls from friends.
Effect of behaviour on target emotion:	I end up lonely and isolated. I give myself a hard time for neglecting my friends. I seem to end up feeling even more depressed.

Worksheet 1-11	Tom's Behaviour Effect Analysis
Target emotion:	Anxiety
Feeling-based thinking:	Using public transport is too uncomfortable and scary. I'll only panic if I try to use the tube. It's just too painful to even try going on the bus.
Feeling-based behaviour:	Walking instead of using public transport. Only going to places I can drive to.
Effect of behaviour on target emotion:	The longer I avoid going on tubes and buses, the more anxious I feel about it. Lately I feel anxious even if I go near a tube station or bus stop. Ultimately I feel my anxiety increasing.

Worksheet 1-12	My Behaviour Effect Analysis
Target emotion:	
Feeling-based thinking:	
Feeling-based behaviour:	
Effect of behaviour on target emotion:	

After completing your own Behaviour Effect Analysis, you may realise that some of your actions are perpetuating your problems, even though they seem to make sense based on your feelings. We look more closely at this concept (and ways to overcome it!) in Chapters 7, 9, and 12.

Picturing Your Problems as a Simple A-B-C

By this stage you can see that:

✔ Your thoughts, beliefs, or personal meanings affect how you feel

✔ Your feelings affect how you behave

✔ Your behaviour also affects how you feel

Also note that your emotional state can further affect how you think and how you view the world around you. For example, if you're depressed then you tend to have more depressed thoughts and the world may seem bleak, dangerous, and joyless. You may notice bad things in the news and focus much more on negative aspects of your own life. Whereas when you're not depressed the world looks much brighter even though very little in your personal circumstances has actually changed.

The diagram in Figure 1-1 shows how life events, thoughts, emotions, and behaviours interact and potentially influence one another. We include this figure here as a visual recap on what has been introduced in this chapter. In the figure:

✔ **Events** include all your past and present experiences plus things that may happen in the future. Events can be global, personal or involve other people in your life.

✔ **Thoughts** include anything that goes on in your mind. Philosophies you live by, personal standards and morals, plus the way you think about yourself, others, and the world all fall into the *Thoughts* category.

✔ **Emotions** include feelings of anger, guilt, sadness, and so on. In Chapter 6 we show you the difference between functional distressed feelings and unhelpful disturbed feelings.

✔ **Behaviour** basically includes anything that you do. Your actions and deliberate inaction are both types of behaviour. As with emotions, it's possible to have both constructive and destructive behavioural responses to events.

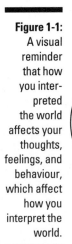

Figure 1-1:
A visual reminder that how you interpreted the world affects your thoughts, feelings, and behaviour, which affect how you interpret the world.

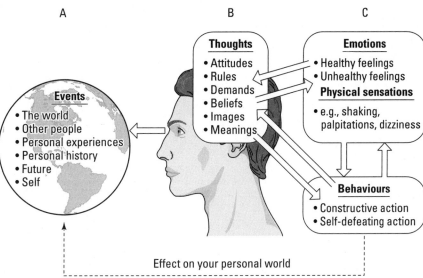

A   B   C

Events
• The world
• Other people
• Personal experiences
• Personal history
• Future
• Self

Thoughts
• Attitudes
• Rules
• Demands
• Beliefs
• Images
• Meanings

Emotions
• Healthy feelings
• Unhealthy feelings
Physical sensations
• e.g., shaking, palpitations, dizziness

Behaviours
• Constructive action
• Self-defeating action

Effect on your personal world

It is our intention to keep things simple but sometimes we muddy the waters. And we do appreciate you bearing with us. If you've read this chapter and done the exercises (at least some of them), then you're well on your way to using CBT!

Following are two examples of what we mean by this and a chance for you to apply it yourself.

The A-B-C format is the main method CBT uses to formulate or chart problems. We go into the A-B-C format in much more detail in Chapter 3 but Worksheet 1-13 shows basically how it works.

Worksheet 1-13	Simple A-B-C Chart	
A (Activating Event)	**B (Belief/Thought)**	**C (Emotional and Behavioural Consequences)**
Failing an important test	I'm a total idiot for failing	Emotional: Depression
	I should not have failed!	Behavioural: Decide resitting the exam is pointless

In essence, the Simple A-B-C Chart is very similar to Worksheet 1-3. However Worksheet 1-14 shows the format you most often see used in CBT books like this one.

Worksheet 1-14	My Simple A-B-C Chart	
A (Activating Event)	**B (Belief/Thought)**	**C (Emotional and Behavioural Consequences)**
		Emotional:
		Behavioural:

Chapter 2

Recognising Problematic Thinking Patterns

In This Chapter

▶ Making thinking mistakes and thinking corrections

▶ Getting intimate with your thinking errors

*W*e all jump to conclusions, make a crisis out of nothing, or take events personally from time to time. Thinking in unhelpful ways is a pretty normal human thing to do. In fact thinking errors are *so* common that clinicians and researchers have been able to sort them into clear categories. But *common* doesn't mean *harmless*. As we discuss in Chapter 1, the way you think has a definite impact on how you end up feeling. So if you often think in unhealthy ways then you're more likely to experience emotional problems. A central technique of CBT is helping you to recognise more readily when you are thinking in a skewed way. In this chapter we assist you in doing just that, plus show you ways to question and readjust your thinking.

Getting to Grips with Common Thinking Errors

In this section, we outline some of the most common thinking mistakes human beings tend to make. You probably don't regularly make all of these thinking errors, but to help you better understand them, we invite you to imagine thinking in the ways described in the examples here. If you identify with a particular thinking error then you'll probably benefit from doing the corresponding worksheet. So there's no need for you to complete every worksheet unless you think it applies to you.

Catastrophising is when you take a relatively minor event and imagine all sorts of terrors and nightmare scenarios resulting from it. Another way of describing this thinking error is 'making a mountain out of a molehill'.

Imagine that you say something to offend your future mother-in-law. From this you conclude that she'll turn your fiancé against you, the wedding will be off, your parents will be mortified, and nobody will ever want to go out with you again.

You can use the set of questions in Worksheet 2-1 to view your catastrophic thoughts more critically.

Worksheet 2-1	De-catastrophising Your Thoughts
What, if any, hard evidence supports my conclusions:	
What, if any hard evidence disproves my conclusions:	
Can I adopt a more accurate perspective on the event?	
What are some less terrible conclusions I can make about the event?	
What practical steps can I take to deal with the situation?	

All or nothing thinking – also called 'black or white' thinking – involves assuming that a situation is either entirely good or entirely bad, leaving no in-between or grey areas.

Say you went to a job interview and answered one question poorly. If you're thinking in an 'all or nothing' manner, you may decide that the entire interview was a complete wash out based on your one hiccup.

Find a point between the extremes by asking yourself the questions in Worksheet 2-2.

Worksheet 2-2	Thinking between Extremes
Am I focusing on only one aspect of the overall event?	
Am I giving one aspect of the event too much importance?	
What is a fair and accurate rating to give this aspect of the event on a scale of one to ten?	

What are some other aspects of the event that can help me to view things more realistically?	
Taking all aspects of the event into account, what is a more balanced rating to give the event?	

Just to be clear, *making demands* is a *big* thinking error. Albert Ellis, who founded one of the very first cognitive-behaviour therapies, puts an individual's demands at the very core of emotional and psychological problems.

When you *make demands* you are expecting yourself, others, and the world to follow your rules and to never break them. We all hold attitudes, values, standards, ideals, and beliefs about how the world and everyone in it ideally should act. And holding those opinions is all fine and well as long as we can be flexible and allow room for error and deviation. But if you start *demanding* that everyone and everything sing to your tune, you'll be emotionally disturbed when things don't go your way.

Imagine that you have a preference to be treated politely. So you tell yourself something like, 'I want to be treated politely but I don't absolutely have to be treated this way. I can stand a bit of impolite behaviour.' Now imagine that you turn this *preference* into a *demand*. So you tell yourself something like, 'I must be treated politely and I can't stand it if I am not!' Can you see how the preference allows you to deal with impolite behaviour from others without leading to unhealthy anger? Can you see how the demand may give rise to unhealthy anger and other negative emotions?

Make your life better by being more flexible in your thinking; Worksheet 2-3 helps show you how.

Worksheet 2-3	**Thinking Flexibly**
What kind of language am I using in my head? Am I using terms such as 'must' or 'have to'?	
Am I accepting that other people have their own rules and use their own free will?	
Is it possible for me to have my own standards but to *also* allow myself and others to fall short of these standards?	
Is my demand realistic?	

(continued)

Is my demand ultimately helping me?	
How can I keep my standards and ideals but turn my demands into *preferences*?	

With *fortune-telling* you make predictions about the future and firmly believe that your prophetic visions are correct. The trouble is that many of your predictions are likely to be negative and may stop you from taking goal-directed action.

You want to approach your boss for a pay rise but predict that he'll say 'no' and be unpleasant about it; if you listen to your fortune-telling thoughts, you may never just take your chances and ask!

Challenge your predictions for the future by submitting them to some empirical tests and answering the questions in Worksheet 2-4.

Worksheet 2-4	Thinking without Your Third Eye
My prediction:	
How can I test out my prediction?	
What can I gain by risking taking action despite my negative prediction?	
What events from my past may be influencing the way I expect this future event to unfold?	
What action can I take to help myself adjust to a poor outcome? What steps can I take to try and resolve potential problems?	

Oh, how we do love to guess what others are thinking! But, when you *mind-read,* you often assume that others are thinking in judgemental and disapproving ways about you. These assumptions can lead to all sorts of difficulties such as social anxiety and relationship ruptures.

Imagine that you go to a party with a friend and you don't know anyone there. Some people talk to you but then move on to talk to other people they seem to know. You are on your own for a time and notice other people glancing at you. You assume that they're thinking 'who is *she*?', 'who invited *her*?', 'what in the world is *she* doing here?'.

Try questioning your mind-reading before letting your thoughts run riot; Worksheet 2-5 can help.

Worksheet 2-5	**Resisting Mind-Reading**
What are some alternative explanations for my assumptions?	
Is it possible that my mind-reading may be wrong?	
What can I do to test out my mind-reading and gather more information?	

Emotional reasoning is when you decide that your strong feelings are a true reflection of what is actually going on in reality. Because you *feel* a certain way you decide that your feelings must be correct. You may then fail to take in other information that contradicts your feelings.

You feel very jealous about your partner's attention to another person. Because you *feel* so jealous, you may assume that your partner is definitely having an affair. Or if you wake up in the morning *feeling* very anxious, you may assume that there must be something to be afraid of and look for a reason to be worried.

If emotional reasoning is one of your personal thinking errors, practice looking beyond your feelings. Consciously and deliberately put your feelings to one side and use your observation skills to take in the reality of the situation. Your feelings are more likely to reflect your thoughts about what an event *means* to you than to reliably describe what is *actually* going on. Separate fact from feeling by being more sceptical; using Worksheet 2-6 can help.

Worksheet 2-6	**Favouring Facts over Feelings**
What is the event or situation?	
What emotion am I experiencing?	

(continued)

How might my feelings be leading me to distort the facts?	
What facts may I be ignoring because of my strong feelings?	
If I give myself time for my feelings to subside *before* drawing conclusions , how do I view the situation when I'm feeling calmer?	

Do you find yourself thinking in terms of 'never' or 'always'? As in 'things *never* go my way' or 'I *always* screw up important meetings'? Or perhaps you think in global terms like 'people can't be trusted' or 'the world is unfair'? Or maybe you conclude that you're a totally bad parent, partner, employee, or whatever based on one or more of your actions. If so, you are probably *over-generalising* and making widespread judgements about yourself, others, or the world on the strength of one or two particular features.

This tendency is also called making the part/hole error; that is, you judge the whole on the basis of one or more of its parts. Doing so can lead you to make some pretty rash and harsh judgements and to hold a pretty unforgiving attitude.

It's easy to allow a few bad things to cloud your judgement about an overall event or situation. Instead of deciding that something is all bad because of a few hiccups, try reminding yourself to keep the good stuff in sight.

You've recently started a new job. On your third day at work your boss presents you with a list of objectives, some of which you think are a bit unrealistic. You try to run the list past a few of your colleagues for some feedback but they're all too busy to talk. You find yourself thinking that you *always* end up with totally unreasonable bosses, the job is *terrible,* and *everyone* you work with is unsupportive. You *never* get the good jobs.

Sort out over-generalising by being highly specific about the negative aspects of a particular situation, as Worksheet 2-7 helps demonstrate.

Worksheet 2-7	**Specific Thinking**
What is the *specific* thing I am basing my judgements on?	
Am I making a *total* judgement of myself, others, or a situation based on this one *specific* aspect?	
What other aspects of myself, others, or the situation am I ignoring?	

Can I suspend *total* judgement and instead judge only the *specific* aspect of myself, others, or the situation	
How might I benefit from being more specific in my judgement?	

So you call yourself, other people, and the world nasty names, do you? Well, you're in the *labeling and rating* club – and it's an ugly place to be. If you call yourself 'useless' every time you screw up, or the world 'cruel' every time it deals you a blow, or others 'no good' when you're treated impolitely, then you're in danger of feeling a lot of really toxic emotions.

Your friend has recently had a bereavement. You don't go to visit her on Friday night because you have prior plans. When you next speak to her she sounds very low and a bit annoyed with you for failing to visit. You then label yourself as a totally selfish person and a rubbish friend because you didn't put her needs first on Friday night.

Try giving up the rating game. Use the questions in Worksheet 2-8 to see yourself and others as more complex than your labels may suggest.

Worksheet 2-8	**Resisting the Urge to Rate**
Label I apply to myself or others:	
Am I being fair when I apply this label?	
Am I allowing for varying degrees of goodness or badness in myself, others, or the world?	
What are some other more complex aspects of this person, me, or the situation that I may be overlooking when I apply a label?	
Is it possible for me to label the *specific action* or *event* instead of the whole person, myself, or the world?	

With *mental filtering* you only let information through that fits with what you already believe about yourself, others, or the world. So if you think of yourself as a failure you only process information that points to you failing; if you believe that your boss is an ass, you only see evidence to support that view; and if you think the world is unsafe.

then you only acknowledge scary and dangerous news about the world. This filtering process can lead you to have a very biased and negative view of yourself and your environment.

Pretend for a moment that you believe that the world is a dangerous and unpleasant place. You pick up the newspaper and focus on the situation in Iraq, terrorist attacks, and shootings in your city. You fail to take in articles about successful recycling initiatives, crime reduction in major cities, and elderly people being entertained by youth groups.

Tackle this thinking error by letting in additional information that contradicts your viewpoint; Worksheet 2-9 helps you organise your thoughts.

Worksheet 2-9	Thinking without Filters
What is my particular filter?	
What information is my filter stopping me from considering?	
How might I think and behave if I were to remove my filter?	

Disqualifying the positive is very similar to mental filtering. Imagine, for example, that you believe that you are unlikable and unacceptable socially. Your mental filter only lets you notice information that supports your negative self opinion. If any positive information does sneak through your filter, you quickly discredit or disqualify it and throw it back out.

So you believe you are fundamentally unlikable. Someone asks you to go for a drink after work. Instead of seeing the invitation as evidence *against* your idea that you're unlikable, you may think that they're only asking you because nobody else was available or because they feel sorry for you.

The questions in Worksheet 2-10 help you counteract this thinking bias by deliberately and consistently gathering positive data.

Worksheet 2-10	Thinking Positively
How do I respond to positive cues from others and my environment?	
Do I acknowledge positive feedback and respond to it?	

What positive information and experiences can I write down? (I can look at my positive data log when I find myself thinking negatively.)	
How can I practise taking a compliment graciously?	
How will acknowledging positive information from others help me?	

Having *low frustration tolerance* (*LTF*) is about deciding that *uncomfortable* equals *unbearable*. Basically, if you have LFT you're likely to give up striving toward your goals whenever the going gets too tough or painful.

The adage that anything worth having requires effort and is worth the blood, sweat, and tears really does hold true. A lot of good things in life don't come easily.

Imagine you want to improve your health by losing a few pounds and getting fit through exercise. But as soon as you're offered a cream cake you tell yourself that resisting it is too painful and the deprivation is unbearable. You go to the gym but as soon as your muscles begin to ache you decide that you just can't take the discomfort and exercise is too much like hard work. So you go home, order a pizza, and flake out in front of the telly.

Overcome low frustration tolerance by challenging your attitude toward discomfort and by fostering high frustration tolerance; Worksheet 2-11 offers some questions to ask yourself.

Worksheet 2-11	**Heightening Your Frustration Tolerance**
Is what I'm experiencing really *intolerable* and *unbearable*?	
Is what I'm experiencing really just *difficult* to tolerate or to bear?	
What are some of the reasons that make bearing this discomfort worthwhile?	
What evidence exists to support the idea that I can tolerate this discomfort?	
What other things worth doing can I push myself to do, even if they're uncomfortable or unpleasant?	

Personalising involves taking random events and making them a personal issue. You tend to make everything that happens around you *about* you, even if reality indicates otherwise. This tendency can lead you to assume inappropriate responsibility for events and/or to feel unhealthy emotions in response to events that have little or nothing to do with you.

You plan a barbeque and invite your neighbours. Unfortunately a freak thunderstorm rolls in just as the burgers are on the grill. Several women rush home because their clothes are sodden. One couple starts arguing. In the end the remaining guests and your family sit down to potato salad in your kitchen whilst the barbeque pit outside gently smolders. You think that the weather is out to get you, the women are holding you to blame for their ruined outfits, and clearly your aborted barbeque has resulted in the impending divorce of the rowing couple.

Worksheet 2-12 demonstrates that you can remove yourself from the centre of the universe and take things less personally by challenging your thoughts.

Worksheet 2-12	Thinking More Objectively
What else has contributed to the outcome of the situation other than you?	
Are you taking personal responsibility for things that are not within your control?	
What are some additional reasons that may account for the way people around you are responding?	
Are you really the only person affected by specific events and conditions or are others affected too?	
Is what has happened really all about you?	

Listing Your Personal Favourites

All humans occasionally think erroneously. Chances are that you make some thinking mistakes more often than others. If you make a list of the errors described in this chapter that you tend to make most, you can increase your chances of catching yourself in the act. The sooner you notice faulty thinking, the sooner you can strive to correct it. Use Worksheet 2-13 to list your main thinking errors.

Worksheet 2-13	My Main Thinking Errors

Knowing Where and When You Think Your Way to Trouble

After looking at the main thinking errors and listing the ones that you tend to make the most often, you can use the Worksheets 2-14 to 2-17 to chart and correct them.

You'll find that certain situations give rise to your thinking errors. We call these *triggers*. Getting to grips with your personal triggers and your problematic thinking patterns can help you to readjust your thinking and increase your chances of feeling healthy negative emotions.

 Martha is nominated for employee of the month. She is delighted about the nomination but it turns out that another worker, Spencer, actually wins the award. Martha gets very unhealthily sad/depressed about not winning. She tells herself that she's a useless employee. She decides that her boss obviously thinks she's inadequate and feels hurt that all her hard work is for naught.

Martha pinpointed four thinking errors she was making about the event of failing to win the work award. She then challenged her thinking and changed her unhealthy sadness/depression and hurt to healthy sadness and disappointment. You may not always be making as many thinking errors as Martha did. Sometimes only one thinking error can easily be spotted. The important thing is to use the worksheet to help you think in a more helpful and balanced way – so that you can avoid emotional disturbance and act in your own best interests!

Worksheet 2-14	Martha's Thought Record	
Situation/Event (What happened? When? Where? Who else was involved?)	**My Thoughts** (What went through your mind at the time?)	**Outcome** (What was your feeling/emotion? What did you do?)
- Spencer won the award instead of me. - It happened Friday at work - My boss and supervisor decided who would win the award	- I have to win or it means I'm not a good worker - My boss and supervisor think I'm bad at my job - I never get recognised for hard work	- I felt depressed and hurt - I pretended to be okay, but I didn't go out to celebrate with Spencer

Worksheet 2-15	Your Thought Record	
Situation/Event (What happened? When? Where? Who else was involved?)	**My Thoughts** (What went through your mind at the time?)	**Outcome** (What was your feeling/emotion? What did you do?)

Worksheet 2-16	Martha's Thought Correction Sheet	
Thinking Error (List the types of thinking errors I made)	**Thinking Corrections** (Record an alternative way of thinking for each error)	**New Outcome** (How do I feel and act differently after correcting my thinking?)
– Demand making – All or nothing thinking – Disqualifying the positive – Over-generalising	– I was demanding that I win the award, not preferring to win but realising that winning isn't essential. I can still be a good worker without winning the award. – I decided that the situation was awful on the basis that I didn't win. But in fact it was a fun work event and I could have enjoyed the celebrations even though I lost to Spencer. – I ignored the fact that I was nominated in the first place and this is evidence that my work is adequate. – It obviously is not true that I never get recognised for hard work because I was nominated even if I didn't win.	– I still feel sad about losing to Spencer but not depressed – I recognise that my work is good and is appreciated by my bosses – I feel both disappointed about losing and pleased about being nominated – I will be able to go out next Friday with my friends from work and feel okay – I will ring Spencer and congratulate him

Worksheet 2-17	My Thought Correction Sheet	
Thinking Error (List the types of thinking errors I made)	**Thinking Corrections** (Record an alternative way of thinking for each error)	**New Outcome** (How do I feel and act differently after correcting my thinking?)

Chapter 3

Taking Toxic Thinking In Hand

*T*he main point in this chapter is that when you think in more balanced and constructive ways, you reduce emotional and behavioural problems. The way you think about specific events in your life, and the meaning you give to these events, determines how you feel and act in response to them.

This chapter helps you to link your thinking to your emotions and behaviours. We introduce you to negative automatic thoughts (NATs) and how to catch yourself thinking in unhelpful ways. The A-B-C Forms aid you in breaking down your problems and changing unhealthy thinking in order to change how you feel for the better.

Noticing Your Negative Thinking

Negative automatic thoughts, or *NAT*s for short, are thoughts that seem to just pop into your head without warning or welcome. That's why we refer to these thoughts as *automatic*. Frequently, NATs are extreme, distorted, and unhelpful ways of interpreting an event or situation, which is why we refer to them as *negative*. NATs can also be examples of common thinking errors. (See Chapter 2 for more in-depth information on the different types of thinking errors.) However, NATs don't always take the form of typical thinking errors and can therefore be harder to spot. Most people don't notice their negative automatic ways of thinking in response to negative situations. If you do happen to notice your NATs, you may not question the truth and usefulness of them very often.

Noticing your NATs can increase your chances of managing your emotions by allowing you to correct any unhelpful thoughts you may be having about an event. NATs are shortened versions of your beliefs and noticing them more readily helps you better understand how your beliefs are leading to specific emotions about a given situation. The A-B-C Form we introduce later in this chapter helps you to change unhelpful beliefs and NATs in order to overcome your emotional problems.

According to CBT, an event doesn't directly or solely *cause* you to experience an emotion. Rather, the *meaning* that you assign to the event (your thoughts, beliefs, and attitudes about what happened) determines how you ultimately end up feeling and behaving.

The NAT form helps you to identify a trigger situation, by which we mean an event that triggers your NATs and lead you to experience a particular negative emotion. It also gives you a chance to record your NAT's and link them to how you ended up feeling in the trigger situation.

A *trigger* can be an actual event, a memory, an image, a past event, a future event, a physical sensation, or your emotions and behaviours.

Nick is rather shy, in fact you might even say that he's a touch socially anxious. He doesn't like to draw attention to himself in public or social situations and often worries about looking foolish. Nick arrives at a pub to meet a few close friends. On his way in he trips on the doormat and nearly falls over. Worksheet 3-1 shows how Nick used the NAT form.

Worksheet 3-1	Nick's NAT Form
NAT Form Questions	*Nick's Answers*
What was the trigger?	I tripped over at the door of a very busy pub when going to meet some friends. A lot of people noticed and a few asked if I was okay.
What were your negative automatic thoughts?	Oh no, everybody has seen me trip and will laugh at me. This is just typical of me; I'm such a clumsy idiot. I can't stand the feeling of all these people looking at me and judging me. The whole evening is ruined now. I'll never be able to relax in here after being so clumsy.
What emotions did you experience?	I felt very self-conscious and anxious.

Natasha's mother died of a terminal illness two years ago. Unfortunately her death came rather suddenly and Natasha didn't get a chance to say goodbye properly. Natasha and her mother argued a few days before her death and because of this Natasha didn't visit her mother on the day she died. Last night Natasha was watching TV and was reminded of her mother by a scene in the programme of a son sitting by his father on his deathbed. Natasha used the NAT form in Worksheet 3-2 to write down her negative automatic thoughts.

Worksheet 3-2	Natasha's NAT Form
NAT Form Questions	*Natasha's Answers*
What was the trigger?	A scene on TV of a father on his deathbed, with his son looking after him. I had a strong memory of arguing with mum just a few days before she died.
What were your negative automatic thoughts?	I absolutely should not have had an argument with mum when she was ill. I should have visited her the day she died. I'm a bad daughter and a selfish, horrible person for treating mum so poorly.
What emotion did you experience?	I felt guilty.

You can see from the preceding examples that by stopping to think about and record NATs, both Nick and Natasha are more likely to link their thoughts to their extreme and unhelpful emotions.

Triggers aren't limited to actual events that occur in the outside world. They also include internal events such as dreams, heart palpitations, or feelings like depression. Notice that Nick's troublesome thoughts are triggered by an *actual* event – tripping on a doormat. Natasha's toxic thinking is triggered by an *internal* event – the *memory* of arguing with her mother and being unable to make it up before she died.

Try using the NAT form in Worksheet 3-3 to note down your immediate thoughts in response to a trigger event. You can also use the form to make sense of a recent or past event when you experienced an extreme negative emotion. Picture the scene in your mind and try to recall how you felt and thought at the time.

If you're having difficulty describing and naming your feelings, have a look at Chapter 6, which explains more about healthy and unhealthy emotions.

Worksheet 3-3	My NAT Form
NAT Form Questions	*Your Answers*
What was the trigger?	
What were your negative automatic thoughts?	
What emotions did you experience?	

Being Sceptical about Your Negative Automatic Thoughts

Unhealthy thinking very often leads to unhealthy negative emotions such as depression, guilt, or rage. Other ways of putting this idea include saying that thinking distortion leads to emotional disturbance and that thinking badly leads to feeling badly. Additionally, NATs distort the facts, impede problem solving, and are very often just plain wrong. So don't believe everything you think! Instead, we encourage you to review your thoughts, put them through a battery of tests (or at *least* one test!) and decide whether they're fair and accurate reflections of reality. You can then formulate a healthier way of thinking if you discover that your NATs are causing you emotional and behavioural problems.

When you think in rigid and extreme ways you don't leave any room for human error. So if you believe 'I must not fail at important tasks!' then you deny the possibility that you may fail at an important task despite your *desire* not to do so. You're also going to be very depressed if you do fail. A more flexible and balanced way of thinking is to say 'I really don't want to fail at important tasks but the reality exists that I may fail'. This attitude encourages you to meet your desire to succeed but also allows you to accept the possibility of failing. If you do fail, you're likely to feel appropriately sad instead of depressed.

Chapter 6 is all about healthy and unhealthy negative emotions. Unhealthy feelings like depression stem from rigid and unbalanced thoughts and beliefs. These types of feelings tend to lead to destructive behaviors like avoidance and giving up. Healthy negative emotions like sadness are still uncomfortable but they tend to lead to constructive behaviors like confronting problems and trying to solve them.

When deciding whether or not your thought is true and accurate, ask yourself the following questions:

- ✔ Does my thought leave room for error or does it demand that I always meet certain criteria at all times?
- ✔ Does my thought reflect what can actually happen in reality or does it deny reality?
- ✔ Does my thought fairly and accurately sum up the situation or is it biased against me?

Have a look at Natasha's cognition correction quiz in Worksheet 3-4, in which she corrects her answers to the NAT form in Worksheet 3-2.

Worksheet 3-4	Cognition Correction Quiz
My negative automatic thought:	I absolutely should not have argued with mum just before she died and I am a horrible and selfish daughter/person for doing so.
Can I prove that my thought is true?	Well, it's true that I argued with mum but I can't prove that I absolutely shouldn't have. I suppose that if I insist that I shouldn't have argued with mum then I'm sort of denying reality. It is true that arguing with a dying person is sort of selfish, but I suppose it isn't true that I'm a totally horrible and selfish person just because of this one act.
Is my thought extreme/rigid or balanced/flexible?	My thought is pretty extreme/rigid because I'm putting a demand on myself to have made up with my mum before she died. I'm also being quite extreme in deciding that I'm horrible and selfish.
Is my thought leading to healthy feelings and behaviours?	I feel terribly guilty and I keep replaying mum's last few days in my mind and berating myself. When I feel this guilty I avoid visiting mum's grave and I avoid phone calls from my father in case he mentions her.

How am I likely to feel and act if I continue thinking in this way?	I'll probably go on feeling guilty about mum and I may even get depressed. My guilt means that I avoid people that could offer support. I also spend a lot of time focusing on how bad I feel about not making up with mum rather than remembering the rest of her life. I don't think I'll allow myself to grieve for mum properly if I keep thinking in this way.
Would I encourage a friend to think in this way?	No, I wouldn't. I'd try to get a friend to be more compassionate and forgiving with herself.
What evidence can I find against my thought?	Mum was very irritable toward the end of her life and I suppose she had some responsibility for the argument too. I did a lot for mum during her illness and I spent a lot of time with her. I do lots of things for other people in my life so I suppose that shows that I'm not that horrible and selfish a person. Mum died suddenly and I had no way of knowing that our argument would be the last time I had with her.
How would I need to change my thought in order to feel better and act more constructively?	I would need to accept that I did argue with mum just before she died and forgive myself for doing so.
How would thinking in a more balanced/flexible way help me?	Well, I certainly would feel better. I might be able to feel sad about mum's death without beating myself up so much. I could be more comfortable about spending time with my father. Perhaps I would be able to focus on other things instead of ruminating on mum's death every time something reminds me of it.
My healthy new thought:	I wish I hadn't argued with mum before she died but I did. Arguing with her was unfortunate and I may have behaved selfishly but it doesn't make me a horrible daughter/person.

Try using the cognition correction quiz in Worksheet 3-5 to challenge and change your NATs.

You can look at your NAT form in Worksheet 3-3 again to remind you of the negative automatic thoughts you identified. Use the cognition correction quiz in Worksheet 3-5 as many times as you need to until you have challenged all your unhelpful thoughts related to your trigger.

Worksheet 3-5	My Cognition Correction Quiz
My negative automatic thought:	
Can I prove that my thought is true?	
Is my thought extreme/rigid or balanced/flexible?	
Is my thought leading to healthy feelings and behaviours?	
How am I likely to feel and act if I continue thinking in this way?	
Would I encourage a friend to think in this way?	
What evidence can I find against my thought?	
How would I need to change my thought in order to feel better and act more constructively?	
How would thinking in a more balanced/flexible way help me?	
My healthy new thought:	

You may want to visit Chapter 2 for a comprehensive list of thinking errors and specific questions you can use to challenge each different type of thinking error.

Working with A-B-C Forms

Getting to grips with recognising and testing your NATs can help you find the A-B-C Forms much more straightforward.

The A-B-C Form is probably the tool most commonly used by CBT therapists. We've devised two versions of this useful form:

- ✔ Form I helps you to record trigger events, your thoughts, feelings, and behaviours.

- ✔ With Form II, you can challenge and correct your unhelpful thinking. Using A-B-C Forms can really help you to break down a problem situation. The form can help you to identify your thoughts and beliefs that are leading you to feel unhealthy negative emotions and behave in non-constructive ways.

Beware of becoming befuddled! As the most common CBT tool, you may encounter many different versions of the A-B-C Form. We do our best to provide you with a simple and user-friendly version of the form here. But other versions of the form are okay, too. If you've read other CBT books or been shown a similar form by a CBT therapist, just remember that the same stuff applies to any type of A-B-C Form. And you can use whatever version of the form you find the most useful.

Filling out Form 1

A-B-C Form I helps you to see the problem – namely an activating event or trigger – and your resulting problematic thoughts, feelings, and behaviours. You may wish to take note of the following explanations before you start. In the A-B-C Form I:

- ✔ **A** is for activating events, or triggers, which are situations past, present, or future that trigger off your thoughts and beliefs.

- ✔ **B** stands for belief and represents your thoughts and beliefs. These include the meanings you attach to your trigger and how you think about yourself in relation to the trigger. Your B determines how you ultimately feel and act in response to your trigger.

- ✔ **C** is for consequences of your behaviours and emotions. They are what you do and feel in response to your trigger (A) *because* of your thoughts and beliefs (B).

Worksheet 3-6 shows Natasha's completed A-B-C Form I, in which she records her activating event, writes down how she feels and what she did based on those feelings, and identifies her negative thoughts.

Because people tend to notice their emotions more readily than the thoughts that produce them, you may find it easier to record your feelings and behaviours (C) prior to recording you thoughts and beliefs (B). For that reason, the A-B-C worksheets ask you to describe consequences (C) before your beliefs (B).

Worksheet 3-6	Natasha's A-B-Cs Catching Up With Her

Date _____

Activating Event/Trigger	Beliefs/Thoughts	Thinking Error
TV programme reminded me of arguing with mum just before she died.	I absolutely should not have argued with mum just before she died and I'm a horrible and selfish daughter/person for doing so.	Demand making Labelling Over-generalising

Consequences

- I felt guilty and kept replaying our argument in my mind
- I avoided answering dad's phone calls in case he mentioned something about mum.

Use the information you've gathered from the previous worksheets in this chapter to complete your own Form I in Worksheet 3-7.

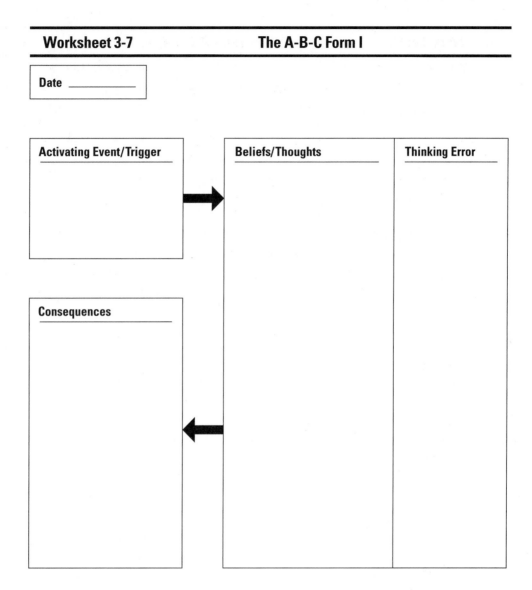

Worksheet 3-7 **The A-B-C Form I**

Date _____

Activating Event/Trigger

Beliefs/Thoughts

Thinking Error

Consequences

Finishing off with A-B-C Form II

Now you're ready to use A-B-C Form II to help you correct thinking errors, change NATs, and thereby give yourself a chance to feel a healthier negative emotion and act constructively. But before you attempt this next step, here are some explanations for a bit more jargon in case of any confusion:

✔ **D** stands for *Disputing* or questioning the validity of your thoughts, NATs, and beliefs about your trigger and looking for ways to correct your negative thinking.

✔ **E** stands for the *Effect* of challenging and changing your thinking on both your feelings and actions.

✔ **F** stands for your *Functional new thought* or your new way of thinking about the trigger and how it moves you forward.

Worksheet 3-8 gives you a peek at Natasha's second A-B-C Form.

Worksheet 3-8	Natasha's A-B-C Form II	
Dispute	*Effect*	*Functional New Thought*
What are some reasons I can generate to question my unhealthy thoughts? My thoughts are too extreme and I end up feeling very guilty. I'm not solely responsible for the argument with mum. I wouldn't encourage a friend to be so extreme in their thinking about the same situation. How can I correct my thinking errors? I can prefer but not demand that I hadn't argued with mum. I can recognise that I'm still an okay person even if I didn't make up with mum before she died. I can stop labeling myself as horrible and self-ish on the basis of this unfortunate and regrettable act.	How do I feel after challenging my thoughts? I feel remorseful but not guilty about arguing with mum prior to her death. How might I act differently as a result of challenging my thoughts? I am able to focus more on her life rather than on the details of her death. I could probably go to visit her grave. I can answer dad's phonecalls and see him more often because I'm not feeling guilty.	How can I express my new thought in my own words? I really wish/prefer that I hadn't argued with mum before she died, but I did. This may mean that I did a selfish thing but doesn't make me a horrible or selfish person overall.

Try putting your own problem through the paces of the A-B-C Form II, using Worksheet 3-9. The questions in Worksheet 3-5 are designed to help you complete the Dispute section of this form.

Worksheet 3-9	My A-B-C Form II	
Dispute	*Effect*	*Functional New Thought*
What are some reasons I can generate to question my unhealthy thoughts?	How do I feel after challenging my thoughts?	How can I express my new thought in my own words?
How can I correct my thinking errors?	How might I act differently as a result of challenging my thoughts?	

One of the benefits of the A-B-C Forms is that you can carry them with you as handy tools for quickly jotting down the nuts and bolts of any unpleasant triggers and your resulting troublesome emotions. You may find that you're able to do a lot of thought challenging in your head after working through the other worksheets in this chapter. You are then in the position of being able to note down shorter versions of your questioning in the dispute section of the second form. The A-B-C Forms are also useful because they include nearly all of the steps involved in overcoming emotional disturbance.

Trying Out Alternative Thoughts

Disputing your less than helpful thoughts and coming up with new, different, and sometimes exciting alternative ways of thinking is a great start. Yes, that's right, we said *start* – there's much more: More fun, more games, and more forms! Why? Well, come on . . . it *is* a *workbook*, after all. If you've been thinking in an unhelpful and slightly skewed manner for a long time, cementing in new and better ways of thinking takes some effort. And one of the best ways to really consolidate your new beliefs and thoughts is to *act on them*. Give them a good test run. Consider your functional new thought from Worksheet 3-9 and ask yourself how you can try out this alternative.

Natasha has been making herself feel guilty by thinking in guilt provoking ways for two years. She wisely understands that changing her guilty thinking for good will require some practice. Worksheet 3-10 shows some of her ideas for trying out her new alternative functional thoughts.

Worksheet 3-10	Natasha's Acting on Alternative Thoughts Form
What is my functional new thought?	I really wish/prefer that I hadn't argued with mum before she died, but I did. This may mean that I did a selfish thing but doesn't make me a horrible or selfish person overall.
How can I put this new thought to the test?	Well I can try deliberately thinking my new thought every time I'm reminded of mum's death. I can even try bringing up the memory of arguing with mum whilst holding this new functional thought. I can try looking at photos of mum and practising this new thought before, after, and during looking at the photos. I can try rehearsing this new thought several times every day, even if I'm not reminded of mum's death. I can recall memories of mum's final days and remind myself of all the reasons that my new thought is both accurate and helpful.

Natasha has come up with several good ways of trying out her alternative healthy belief about arguing with her mother in the days before her death. She increases her chances of overcoming her guilt and engaging more with her healthy grief by doing so.

Use the following worksheet to think up ways to try out your new functional alternative way of thinking about your own trigger event.

Worksheet 3-11	My Acting on Alternative Thoughts Form
What is my functional new thought?	
How can I put this new thought to the test?	

Helping Yourself with Homework

In CBT we use homework as a way of helping you to further your therapeutic gains. Homework is often a dreaded word, conjuring up images of teachers and reports. But don't think of homework in that way now. Rather, think about tasks you can set yourself to help you surmount any emotional or behavioural difficulties you may have. Better still, you can choose your own assignments! You probably know better than anyone else what type of homework you need to do in order to help you bed down better ways of thinking and acting.

Natasha is here again to help illustrate the point we are making about homework. She has done her best to try out her new alternative functional thoughts. Now she's taking things one step further by identifying ways of really pushing herself to hold onto her new helpful way of thinking about her mother's death. Check out her efforts in Worksheet 3-12.

Worksheet 3-12	Natasha's Homework
What is my functional new thought?	I really wish/prefer that I hadn't argued with mum before she died, but I did. This may mean that I did a selfish thing but it doesn't make me a horrible or selfish person overall.
What homework can I give myself to help me enforce this new thought?	I can push myself to tell others about my argument with my mother prior to her death and still think in the new way about it, no matter how they react. I can bring up mum's death with my father and think myself out of guilt. I can go to visit mum's grave and tell her my new way of thinking or at least rehearse it while I'm there. I can rent films that have themes or scenes of parents dying and practise thinking my new thought about mum's death. I can act according to this new thought by refusing to replay the argument but instead choosing to focus on other aspects of mum's life and death.

Perhaps you can think of other homework assignments Natasha can set herself to help her overcome her guilty thoughts and feelings. Or maybe you can devise some homework for yourself to help you to consolidate your conviction in your new functional way of thinking about your trigger event.

Try setting yourself some healthy belief strengthening homework by using the same worksheet. Remember to build on and make more strenuous those tasks you may have created for yourself in Worksheet 3-13.

Worksheet 3-13	My Homework
What is my functional new thought?	
What homework can I give myself to help me enforce this new thought?	

Chapter 4

Experiencing Experiments

. . . .

In This Chapter

▶ Designing and conducting behavioural experiments

▶ Gathering evidence to learn more about your thoughts, predictions, or assumptions

▶ Doing surveys, data collection, and storing your results

. . . .

*T*reating your thoughts, predictions, assumptions, and beliefs as theories or hunches about reality rather than as facts is a cornerstone of CBT. Doing an experiment to check out whether a painful thought that has entered your head fits reality, or whether an alternative thought might fit the facts better is a key to moving from understanding things in your head to 'feeling' them in your gut.

Seeing Things Like a Scientist

When presented with a theory about the world, a scientist asks 'what's the evidence that supports that view?' When presented with the data from an experiment, a scientist goes on to wonder 'is that a valid conclusion from the data?' and 'could these results be explained in any other way, by another theory?' To further understand the validity of competing theories, a scientist would want to know how to find out more; how to gather more data to see which theory fits the facts best, which would lead to another experiment.

Using CBT resembles being your own personal scientist, trying to see whether your conclusions (your theories) about yourself, the world, or other people, drawn from your personal experiences (your data) are valid or accurate, or whether an alternative conclusion might be more accurate. And just like a scientist, you may need to conduct further experiments to compare two or more theories to see which one best fits the facts.

You can use experiments to help yourself check out many different kinds of thoughts, from an automatic thought that 'pops into your head' to a core belief that you have held for a very long time.

Some theories are hard to give up, and you may sometimes have to repeat experiments to gather enough data to reduce your conviction in an old theory and build your conviction in a new one.

Executing excellent experiments

Use the checklist in Worksheet 4-1 to help make sure that your behavioural experiments are effective.

Worksheet 4-1	Experiment Checklist
❑	Have you identified the thought you want to test in a clear, testable fashion?
❑	Have you formulated an alternative theory or thought?
❑	Have you been specific about how, where, when, or with whom you will conduct your experiment?
❑	Is your experiment sufficiently challenging to help test your prediction?
❑	Is your experiment realistic and manageable?
❑	Have you considered what might interfere with the results of your experiment (such as safety behaviours, subtle avoidance, escaping from the situation), and planned to overcome them (such as by purposefully dropping a safety behaviour)? (See Chapter 7 for more on safety behaviours and other problematic coping strategies.)
❑	Is your experiment sufficiently long to gather the evidence you need to test out your thoughts? (For example, it would take, at the very least, 20 minutes to discover that your anxiety reduced within a situation.)
❑	Have you considered whether you need to carry out another experiment?

Putting predictions to the test

At the risk of stating the obvious, seeing something for yourself makes it far easier to believe it's true. A behavioral experiment should help you to do exactly that – see for yourself whether a prediction comes true or not. To conduct your own behavioural experiment, follow these steps:

1. **Describe the problem.**

   For example, Sheila is afraid that she won't be able to cope with colleagues' questions about why she's been off sick for three months suffering from depression.

   Whatever your problem, describe it specifically.

2. **Identify the prediction you want to test in your experiment.**

   State your problem as a hypothesis, using the classic if/then structure. Sheila's hypothesis is 'I won't be able to cope if people ask me questions about being off sick. If they do, I'll get too anxious and feel so ashamed that I'll have to run out of the office, and then it will be even harder to get back to work.'

3. **Formulate an alternative prediction.**

   Instead of your worst fear, think of milder, less drastic circumstances that are as likely to be realised as your fears. In the example, Sheila's alternative may be something like, 'I suppose it might not be as bad as I think, and I can give superficial answers and stress that I'm happy to be fit enough to return to work.'

4. **Specify how you will test your predictions.**

   Write down the specific actions you can take to prove whether your predictions are correct. Sheila can test her predictions by returning to work on Wednesday so that her first week back isn't too long. She can plan to greet colleagues she feels will be welcoming first off and turn to them for support if need be.

5. **Write down the results of your experiment.**

Record your feelings and reactions as well as other people's behaviour and reactions. Sheila's results look like this: 'I felt really nervous as I walked into the office, but everyone seemed quite pleased to see me. The office was really busy and I think they were far more interested in having me back than where I'd been. I got the impression my boss was concerned that I didn't overdo it, but *no one* probed about my illness!'

6. **Analyse the results of your experiment.**

Look at your predictions from Steps 2 and 3 and evaluate how accurate they were. Sheila's analysis is, 'I still need to recognise that the way I think is being dragged into negativity a bit, since the way I thought things might go was far worse than reality. But I guess feeling worried about going back to work is pretty normal and that might have made me catastrophise that bit more. Still need to keep putting my negative thoughts to the test!'

You may wish to use the thought record sheet from Chapter 2 (Worksheet 2-15) to help you note and organise some of the negative predictions that tend to enter your mind.

You can use Worksheet 4-2 to design experiments to test out your own thoughts.

Worksheet 4-2	**My Prediction Sheet**
Describe the problem:	
Identify the prediction you want to test:	
Formulate an alternative prediction:	
Specify how you will test your prediction:	
Write down the results of your experiment:	
Analyse the results of your experiment:	

You may still have some reservations about whether your old or alternative prediction is most accurate and choose to conduct another experiment in order to learn more.

Finding out which theory works best

Some problems create thoughts that can't be proven or disconfirmed. This outcome is particularly true of obsessive-compulsive disorders and anxiety problems. In these instances you can experiment with seeing how treating your problem as if it is a psychological problem, and use CBT to tackle it, even if you're not yet convinced your problems are the product of your thoughts and behaviours. You can then be guided in your next step by how this strategy works.

For example, you can treat intrusive thoughts of causing harm as if they are the product of excessive worry rather than as if they are the product of you being bad or dangerous.

Moray uses Worksheet 4-3 to record the results of his experiment to determine how it works if he treats his fears of having a heart problem as if they are a worry problem.

Worksheet 4-3	Moray's Health Anxiety Prediction Sheet
Describe the problem:	I'm worried that my heart pounding is a sign of a heart problem and even though I've seen three doctors I can't be convinced that there's nothing wrong with me.
Identify the prediction you want to test:	Treating my problem as if it's an anxiety problem will make no difference. What I really need is better proof that my heart is okay.
Formulate an alternative prediction:	Treating my problem as if it's an anxiety problem and reducing my self-monitoring and checking will help me become less anxious.
Specify how you will test your prediction:	I'll keep a frequency chart for my checking behaviours and deliberately resist seeking reassurance, checking my body, and monitoring my heart rate. I'll also stop using the Internet to search for an answer as to what my problem might be or to reassure myself that there's nothing wrong.
Write down the results of your experiment:	After a week I have noticed that I have fewer really anxious days and my worries about my heart are not on my mind quite as much as they were.
Analyse the results of your experiment:	That it makes sense to keep reducing my checking, but I'm not yet convinced my problem is 'just' anxiety.

You can sometimes learn even more about the effect of a strategy such as checking, reassurance seeking, trying to control your thoughts, or trying to resist anxiety by comparing a 'usual' level of such a strategy against a day of really increasing that strategy. Repeating this experiment a couple of times should give you a clearer understanding of the effect of a coping response. Many people find that once they discover for themselves that a coping strategy actually makes them feel worse, they feel far more determined to cut that strategy out.

Conducting a self-help survey

The people with clipboards seeking your opinion on a new brand of mayonnaise can actually be an inspiration for change! Surveying friends and family members about their experiences can be especially valuable in helping you realise that you are not alone in experiencing a particular kind of thought, feeling, or bodily sensation. This knowledge in turn can help you feel more normal and reduce feelings of anxiety and shame. The trick here is to be very clear about the kinds of information you ask for.

Multiple choice questions can help as they add clarity about what you're looking for. For example, ask a question such as: Do you have unwanted thoughts about hurting someone a) never, b) once or twice a year, c) about once a month, d) about once a week, e) daily. You can combine these with more open questions like 'Please describe the most upsetting unwanted thought that popped into your head in the last month'.

Moray used Worksheet 4-4 to increase his understanding of how anxiety can affect people's bodies by conducting a survey on friends about their bodily sensations when feeling scared.

Worksheet 4-4	Moray's Survey Behavioural Experiment
Describe the problem:	I'm worried that my heart pounding is a sign of a heart problem and even though I've seen three doctors I can't be convinced that there's nothing wrong with me.
Identify the prediction you want to test in your experiment:	That other people don't get such strong feelings of their heart pounding if they feel anxious, which means there must be something physically wrong with me.
Formulate an alternative prediction:	That some people might also have strong bodily sensations when they feel anxious.
Specify how you will test your prediction:	I'll ask ten people about how their body reacted the last time they felt really scared or anxious. I can use a couple of friends, my dad, who used to suffer from anxiety, and some of the people from the anxiety management group I belong to.

(continued)

Write down the results of your experiment:	I got round to speaking to eight people in total. Seven reported strong bodily sensations — heart pounding, feeling hot, wobbly legs — and one guy from the group described feeling really unreal and distant from his surroundings when anxious.
Analyse the results of your experiment:	I guess when people say it's 'just' anxiety they don't always realise how much of a physical experience it can be. It doesn't prove that there's nothing wrong with me but does confirm that very strong, and even strange bodily sensations can be caused by anxiety.

Take care to use surveys to gather useful new information, rather than as reassurance to try to eliminate any doubts. Reassurance at best brings you very temporary relief and ultimately fuels your worries.

Acting as an observer

Sometimes throwing yourself into the deep end of confronting your fears can prove too difficult. A creative solution to this dilemma is to get someone else to jump in for you! This scenario really can be a meaningful stepping stone in learning that what you are afraid will happen may not actually come true. By having someone act out the experiment you fear, with you acting as observer, you can see how accurate your predictions are about what will happen.

Ray was very afraid that he would have a panic attack in a public place and collapse. He feared doing so would be terribly humiliating and cause massive inconvenience to the people around him. This fear meant that Ray limited going far from home as much as possible and escaped from any public situation as fast as he could if he felt himself start to feel panicky. Ray enlisted some help to tackle his panic and avoidance, using Worksheet 4-5.

Worksheet 4-5	Ray's Pride Paralysis Prediction Sheet
Describe the problem:	Panic attacks.
Identify the prediction you want to test:	That if I collapse in a supermarket everyone will stop and stare, and if there turns out not to be anything seriously wrong with me the people working in the shop will hate me.

Formulate an alternative prediction:	I can't imagine things going any other way.
Specify how you will test your prediction:	My friend Zac has agreed to pretend to collapse in the supermarket, and I'm going to watch and make note of what happens from a few feet away.
Write down the results of your experiment:	When Zac pretended to collapse a couple of people noticed, and one man stopped to see if he was okay. Most people just carried on shopping. A shop assistant brought him a chair and suggested calling paramedics, but Zac reassured them he was fine and set off again after a couple of minutes.
Analyse the results of your experiment:	Zac found the whole thing quite funny, and he certainly wasn't freaked out. The people seemed mostly indifferent or quite nice. It really has made the possibility of collapsing seem a bit less scary.

You need to see the experiment for yourself because you'll probably discount what someone reports if they just tell you about it later. But keep in mind that observing someone else may not be a substitute for ultimately putting your predictions to the test yourself.

You can also use observation without setting up an experiment. For example, a woman who thought she was being ignored observed how much eye contact people in the street made with each other made and found she was really over-estimating how often people look at others.

Writing Down Your Results

To make good use of the data you collect, keeping written records of your experiments is helpful. Doing so can help you to reflect on all of your hard work, and build a portfolio of evidence to help challenge unhelpful thoughts and build up your conviction in more helpful alternatives. Use Worksheet 4-6 to record the results of your experiment.

Worksheet 4-6	My Behavioural Experiment Record Sheet		

Date: _____

Prediction or Theory	Experiment	Results	Conclusion/Comments
Outline the thought, belief, or theory you are testing. Rate your strength of conviction 1–100%.	Plan what you will do (including where, when, how, with whom), being as specific as you can.	Record what actually happened including relevant thoughts, emotions, physical sensations, and other people's behaviour.	Write down what you have learned about your prediction or theory in light of results. Re-rate your strength of conviction 0–100%.

Guidance on carrying out a behavioural experiment: 1. Be clear and specific about the negative and alternative predictions you are testing. Rate your strength of conviction in the prediction or theory you are testing or evaluating. 2. Decide upon your experiment, and be as clear as you can be as to how you will measure your results. 3. Record the results of your experiment, emphasising clear, observable outcomes. 4. Evaluate the results of your experiment. Write down what these results suggest in terms of the accuracy of your predictions, or which theory the evidence supports. 5. Consider whether a further behavioural experiment might be helpful.

Carrying out behavioural experiments is a no-lose proposition. Whatever the outcome, you'll have more information about the nature of your problem, which you can use to inform your solutions.

Chapter 5

Where's Your Head At? Controlling Your Concentration

*W*hilst a large part of CBT involves dealing with the content of your thoughts, CBT also recognises more recent developments in areas such as mindfulness meditation. Basically, times exist when your thoughts are best left alone. Mindfulness and other similar techniques emphasise *accepting* unwelcome thoughts and essentially allowing them to play themselves out without any interruption or intervention on your part. This strategy can be very useful for dealing with unpleasant thoughts, images, or physical sensations. If you're able to accept your thoughts as *just thoughts* rather than interpreting them as *facts*, you can lessen their emotional impact. In this chapter we introduce some basic exercises that you can use to help you better manage troublesome thoughts, irksome images, and fearsome physical feelings.

Aiming Your Attention

Particularly if you suffer from anxiety or depression, you're likely to have a lot of threatening or pessimistic thoughts (or both). Not a lot of fun. Harnessing the ability to *not* pay attention to your thoughts can be very useful in these circumstances. Concentrating on anxious or depressed thinking can further lower your mood or heighten your anxiety. With practice you can learn to dis-attend to your thinking and focus your attention on the outside world instead.

Turning your attention *away* from your thoughts and mental images – *dis-attending* – is not the same as thought suppression. Suppression involves attempts to deny, control, or stop unwelcome mental activity. Thought suppression tends to have a paradoxical effect so that the more you try to stop thinking certain things, the more you tend to produce the exact sort of thoughts that you mean to avoid! In essence, suppression is the opposite of *accepting* the presence of unpleasant thoughts and images. You accept your mental activity, however unpleasant, but then *choose* to aim your attention away from it.

One way to pay less attention to or dis-attend from depressing and anxious thoughts is by regarding them as background noise. When you put the TV or radio on between channels you tend to get static. Try imagining that your unhelpful negative thoughts are like interference on the radio or the muzak you hear played in lifts or when you're on hold on the telephone. These sounds can be annoying but we tend to ignore them rather than focusing on them.

The Attention Analysis Worksheet is devised to help you note where you focus most of your attention, on the outside world or on your internal thoughts and feelings. It also aids you in seeing the benefits of changing your focus of attention.

Matt has been suffering from an episode of depression for the past few weeks. (See Chapter 10 for more information about overcoming depression.) Increasingly he is staying indoors and withdrawing from other people. Matt often has thoughts about how bad he feels and how bleak the future seems. Because these thoughts feel very intense and important, Matt focuses on them a lot. When he does venture outdoors Matt feels very uncomfortable and detached from the world around him. He then tends to dwell on how odd and uncomfortable he feels. Matt often appears to be in a bit of a daze because he's so absorbed in his own thoughts and feelings.

Matt used the Attention Analysis guidelines in Worksheet 5-1 to better understand and re-aim his attention.

Worksheet 5-1	**Matt's Attention Analysis**
Where is my attention mainly focused? On the outside world around me or on my internal thoughts, images, and feelings?	My attention is mainly focused on my internal world. I pay a lot of attention to how low and tired I'm feeling and search for possible reasons for my depression. I also focus on bleak images of the future and how bad I feel compared to other times in my life. I realise that I also spend a lot of time stuck in a cycle of thinking the same sorts of things over and over, normally about my lack of energy and motivation to do daily tasks.
When I do focus my attention on the outside world, what external information do I tend to notice?	When I go out of the house I focus on how weird and detached I feel. I also look at other people and notice how normal and content they look in comparison to me. Sometimes I focus on how little I enjoy activities that I used to like or how difficult I find everyday tasks such as food shopping and going to the bank. I dwell on how I once found these tasks simple and ordinary and how they now seem like such a big deal.

What external things might I focus on to help me stop paying attention to my internal thoughts and feelings?	I could focus more on the task at hand rather than on how difficult I'm finding it. I could also take more time to experience the sounds, smells, and sights around me. I could pay more attention to how other people look and act and try to interact with shopkeepers and other people more often. I could try to focus on what other people are saying and doing rather than comparing myself to them.
What are some additional practical strategies I can use to help me refocus my attention away from unhelpful thoughts and feelings?	I can turn on the radio in the kitchen when I am getting myself ready in the morning and listen to a soothing or interesting programme. I can make a phone call or go out to meet a friend rather than allowing myself to get stuck indoors thinking the same depressing thoughts each day. I can surf the Internet, play a computer game, do a puzzle or crossword, or do something physical such as gardening, housework, or some DIY — anything that requires a degree of concentration and draws my attention away from my bad feelings and negative thoughts.
What are the effects of refocusing my attention? (Complete this section after at least three days of deliberately aiming your attention away from your internal thoughts and feelings.)	After a few days of deliberately and consistently focusing my attention on tasks and my environment I noticed a slight lift in my mood. I also am more able to get on with the day and override my depressed feelings if I don't pay them too much attention. When I'm out of the house, I notice that by focusing on other people and the world around me, I feel less weird and detached.

Your anxious or depressed thoughts can be very compelling. Be prepared for your attention to return to unhelpful negative thoughts and feelings. Simply redirect your attention onto more benign activities each time it wanders into gloomy territory. Gaining greater control over your attention and concentration takes practice.

Sue is anxious about lots of things but in particular she suffers from anxiety in social situations. (See Chapter 9 for more about how to combat anxiety.) She often worries about what people think of her when she is out socially. Sue often plans conversations in her head prior to speaking in hope that she'll appear interesting and clever. After Sue returns home from a party or an evening out with friends, she'll often review the evening and look for any possible social faux pas that she may have committed.

Worksheet 5-2 shows the results when Sue used the Attention Analysis Worksheet to get a better idea of what she was focusing on during social interaction and the effects of changing her attention focus.

Worksheet 5-2	Sue's Attention Analysis
Where is my attention mainly focused? On the outside world around me or on my internal thoughts, images, and feelings?	I mainly focus on my anxious feelings and on how I appear to the other people present. I focus a lot on what to say next and wonder how people will react to whatever I say and do. Sometimes I get distracted by my thoughts about not fitting in with other people or about how uncomfortable I feel socially. I also monitor myself for blushing, shaking, or other signs of social awkwardness which others might notice and consider odd.
When I do focus my attention on the outside world, what external information do I tend to notice?	I tend to look for signs of people reacting badly to what I say or looking bored when I'm talking. I monitor other people for subtle signs that they either like or dislike me. I also focus on how easily others seem to make social chit chat in comparison to myself.
What external things might I focus on to help me stop paying attention to my internal thoughts and feelings?	I could focus on what people are saying rather than on planning what to say next. I could take in the environment more by focusing on the music, atmosphere, décor, and so on.
What are some additional practical strategies I can use to help me refocus my attention away from unhelpful thoughts and feelings?	I can resist the urge to replay social interactions and look for social errors that I may have made. Instead I can focus on the enjoyable aspects of the event. I can also deliberately resist monitoring myself for signs of anxiety such as blushing and shaking. Instead of focusing my attention on trying to stop my hands from trembling, I can focus on tasks like paying for a drink. I can also switch my attention from seeking signs of whether or not people like me and focus my attention on what my impressions are of them.

What are the effects of refocusing my attention? (Complete this section after at least three days of deliberately aiming your attention away from your internal thoughts and feelings.)	When I pay more attention to the conversation and stop preparing what to say, things tend to flow more naturally. I feel less anxious and awkward when I focus my attention on the environment but do not monitor others for their reactions to me.

Whether you're having depressed or anxious thoughts and feelings, or are experiencing unwelcome images and unwanted thoughts of a different nature (such as those experienced in Obsessive Compulsive Disorder – see Chapter 13), redirecting your attention may be helpful.

Worksheet 5-3 gives you the chance to try using the Attention Analysis worksheet yourself and see if it has a positive effect.

Worksheet 5-3	**My Attention Analysis**
Where is my attention mainly focused? On the outside world around me or on my internal thoughts, images, and feelings?	
When I do focus my attention on the outside world, what external information do I tend to notice?	
What external things might I focus on to help me stop paying attention to my internal thoughts and feelings?	
What are some additional practical strategies I can use to help me refocus my attention away from unhelpful thoughts and feelings?	
What are the effects of refocusing my attention? (Complete this section after *at least* three days of deliberately aiming your attention away from your internal thoughts and feelings.)	

Training Yourself in Task Concentration

The purpose of task concentration exercises is to help you get better at *choosing* what you concentrate on rather than allowing your attention to wander. Everyone has the ability to focus their attention and to concentrate on a task whilst filtering out extraneous stimuli. Some people are better at doing this than others, possibly as a result of practice. Imagine a busy, open-plan office with a lot of people doing different jobs and talking on phones. Although a lot of background noise and activity is happening, the employees learn to concentrate on their task and to tune out distractions. Or imagine that you're trying to negotiate a tricky driving situation – you probably turn your attention to the task of driving and fail to notice songs on the radio as much. You too can get better at concentrating more on tasks and the environment and less on yourself, your thoughts and feelings. If you're suffering from an emotional problem, then you're probably spending more time than you realise focusing on unhelpful thoughts and sensations.

Start by making a list of five situations that you find relatively *non-threatening* (situations in which you experience little or no anxiety or distress). Then make a list of five more *threatening* situations (situations that you may be avoiding because they make you feel anxious or distressed). Start from the least anxiety provoking and progress to the most anxiety provoking situation. Have a look at how Sue did this in Worksheet 5-4.

You can use this technique to better monitor the effects of task concentration on your mood and physical sensations. Doing so also gives you a chance to work on strengthening your attention muscles.

It's generally easier to dis-attend from unhelpful thoughts in situations where you're pretty comfortable than in those that provoke anxiety or low mood. By listing both threatening and non-threatening situations, you can practise deliberately directing your attention where you want it to go in situations where you feel okay and eventually do the same in less comfortable situations.

Try these steps to help you get behind the steering wheel of your attention:

1. Focus on your internal feelings and thoughts for a few minutes (you can time yourself if you like). Note any unpleasant physical sensations, negative thinking and images.

2. Now interrupt those thoughts and turn your attention to your environment and other people. Keep your attention on the outside world for a few minutes (time yourself if you like) and make mental notes of what you see going on around you.

3. Now switch your attention back and forth between your internal world and the external world.

4. Try keeping your attention on the external environment for longer periods, pulling your attention away from your internal thoughts and feelings should it wander.

5. After you've gotten used to turning your attention to what you decide to focus on- try doing the same in situations you typically find threatening.

6. Work your way through your threatening situations starting from the easiest to the hardest like Sue does in Worksheet 5-4.

Don't give up or become disheartened if you find this exercise difficult to master at first. It takes time and practice.

Worksheet 5-4	Sue's Situations

My five non-threatening situations:

1. Going to the cinema with my best friend.

2. Having dinner at my parents' house with just the family.

3. Travelling on the train during quiet times.

4. Going to the local pub with my best friend and her boyfriend.

5. Walking my dog in the park.

My five threatening situations (starting from easiest to hardest):

1. Going out for a drink with colleagues from work.

2. Having something to eat in a busy cafe on my own.

3. Travelling on the train during really busy periods.

4. Going to a different pub to meet several friends or people I don't know well.

5. Going to a party where I only know one or two people.

Sue used her five non-threatening situations as opportunities to practise switching her attention focus back and forth between herself and tasks or the environment. Once she felt that she'd mastered this skill, Sue pushed herself into her list of threatening situations and practised concentrating on tasks and the environment rather than on her anxious thoughts and feelings.

Now make your own list of situations using Worksheet 5-5.

Worksheet 5-5	My Situations

My five non-threatening situations:

1.

2.

3.

4.

5.

My five threatening situations (starting from easiest to hardest):

1.

2.

3.

4.

5.

Now you can practise yo-yoing your attention between yourself and the outside world in your non-threatening situations until you feel you're ready to give the process a go in the more personally threatening situations on your second list.

Worksheet 5-7 provides an opportunity to make a record of your efforts. Use the worksheet to record the details of a specific event in which you deliberately focused your attention and concentration onto the outside world plus particular tasks. Make sure that you clearly record strategies that helped you to reduce negative feelings and thoughts. By recording what you learnt through the exercise you'll better remember the benefits next time round. You can use Worksheet 5-7 as many times as needed.

Sue used Worksheet 5-6 to record the results of her task concentration training.

Worksheet 5-6	Sue's Task Concentration Record
Where was I?	At a work event held in a banquet hall.
What was I doing?	I was at a manager's leaving party. I was mingling with other guests and serving myself food and drink.
Who was I with?	About 60 other employees were there. Three women that work in my office were there but otherwise I didn't really know anyone else.
What methods did I use to keep concentrating on the task and the external environment?	I concentrated on getting some food and ordering a drink. I watched people dancing and tried to make eye contact with other people. Instead of sitting hidden in a corner, I forced myself to stand in a more central position in the room. I made small talk with several people I vaguely knew rather than sticking like glue to the three women from my office. I even danced to a few songs with a group of people, even though I didn't really know them.
What did I learn from this exercise?	At first I felt really self-conscious and anxious but after about half an hour I started to feel okay. Pulling my attention away from myself and resisting monitoring myself for blushing and shaking took a lot of effort. But it really helped to focus my attention on watching other people and to concentrate on tasks such as eating and getting a drink. I noticed that by making eye contact and standing in the middle of the hall many people approached me to make small talk. I actually managed to enjoy myself.

As Sue noted, focusing on the external environment and tasks rather than on herself wasn't easy! This process may sound simple but mastering it takes a lot of persistence and determination. Don't be tempted to give up too readily. Stick with it!

Recording results of any behavioural changes you make can be useful. You can look back at your records to remind yourself of the benefits of changing aspects of your behaviour should you experience a resurgence of your original problems. Keeping a record also allows you to clearly see what specific strategies worked.

Now's your chance to use the Task Concentration Record Sheet to record your learning and observations using Worksheet 5-7.

Worksheet 5-7	My Task Concentration Record
Where was I?	
What was I doing?	
Who was I with?	
What methods did I use to keep concentrating on the task and the external environment?	
What did I learn from this exercise?	

Finding Your Focus

Hopefully the exercises in the preceding sections have given you a good idea of where you tend to aim your attention and the positive effects of changing your focus to tasks and the environment around you. Using a simple pie chart is another quick and effective way of monitoring the focus of your attention and recording how you divided your attention or concentration in a given situation.

Sue used the pie chart method to make a more visual record of her attention focus whilst at the work party. Sue's chart is shown in Worksheet 5-8.

Worksheet 5-8	Sue's Pie Chart
What was the situation?	A leaving party in a banquet hall for a manager who was moving on to another job. About 60 other employees present, three of whom I knew reasonably well.
How was my attention divided during the majority of the time that I remained in the situation?	*(Pie chart showing Task/Environment shaded and Self unshaded)* ■ Task/Environment □ Self

You can probably see from Figure 5-1 that Sue focused roughly 70 per cent of her attention on tasks and other people/environment. Only about 30 per cent of her attention was focused on herself, her thoughts and feelings for the majority of the party.

If you're experiencing anxiety, depression, or other troublesome emotional problems, you're likely to benefit from focusing as much of your attention as possible on others/environment and concentrating deliberately on tasks. In short, the less attention you pay to yourself and your internal world, the better for you!

Have a go at using the blank pie chart in Worksheet 5-9. Simply record the situation and shade in segments of the pie that represent your attention focus on others/environment. Leave the segments that represent attention focused on yourself (thoughts, feelings, images, and physical sensations) unshaded.

Worksheet 5-9	My Pie Chart
What was the situation?	
How was my attention divided for the majority of the time that I remained in the situation?	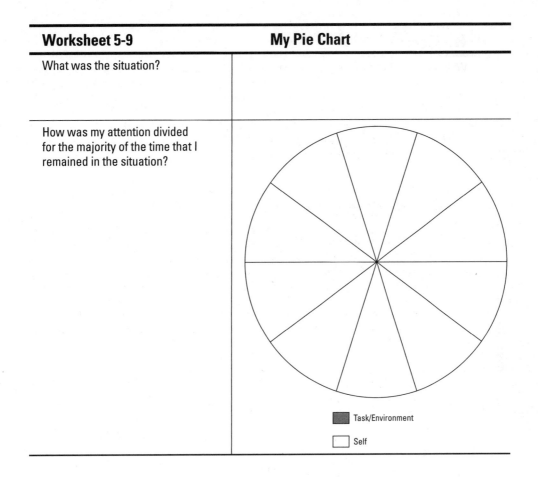

Task/Environment

Self

Making Your Mind More Mindful

Mindfulness meditation is gaining in popularity because this approach seems to help people manage stress, depression, and other conditions such as chronic pain. We don't profess to be able to adequately explain this entire practice here; we just offer you a taster version.

The whole experience of mindfulness resembles looking at the world with fresh eyes, free from judgement or comment. The idea is to hold your attention in the present moment and to focus as much as possible on the here and now.

The techniques described in the following sections may sound very simple or even a bit facile. In practice, though, these techniques for managing your thoughts are very difficult to master. People spend years practising various forms of meditation, so be prepared to find the process difficult at first.

Living in the present

This technique isn't dissimilar to concentrating on tasks. Instead of allowing your mind to wonder into worry territory or to planning your next move, focus as much as you can on whatever you are currently *doing*.

Even if you are brushing your teeth or sitting in a chair near a window, focus your attention on the *actual experience* of brushing your teeth or on what you can *see* out of the window and how your body *feels* in the chair.

Suspending judgement

Most of the time you make snap judgements about your experiences without even being wholly aware that you're doing so. Depending on the value you assign to your experiences, you label them as good, bad, or neutral. Mindfulness meditation is about becoming more able to suspend judgement and to simply *accept* experiences.

Try to focus your attention on whatever you're *doing* – be it gardening, waiting in a queue, or eating a meal. Instead of judging the event as good, bad, boring, or satisfying, try to experience the moment fully without making any value judgements about it.

Suspending judgement can be very useful for dealing with unwelcome thoughts and feelings. Rather than judging your thoughts and feelings as bad or as indications that you're unwell, try to accept their presence and don't attach any value or meaning to them.

Getting off the thought train

Another technique for managing unhelpful thoughts involves allowing your thoughts to pass by. Rather than trying to stop unwelcome thoughts or getting involved in thinking more *about* unwelcome thoughts, just *observe* them.

Imagine your thoughts and feelings as carriages on a train. Instead of engaging with your thoughts, watch them pass through the station and carry on down the track. Resist the urge to jump on the thought train and instead just let it chug on by.

Identifying when to ignore yourself

Many of the negative thoughts you experience when you're having emotional problems are likely to be inaccurate, biased, and distorted perceptions of reality (see Chapter 2 for more about thinking errors). Thus in addition to challenging and changing your thinking (which we talk about in Chapter 3), ignoring or disregarding many of the thoughts you generate when you're emotionally disturbed is best.

Matt became aware of recurring themes to his thinking when he was feeling very depressed. He made a note of these themes and decided to regard these thoughts as symptoms of his depression rather than as factual, true, or accurate. Worksheet 5-10 shows the results.

Worksheet 5-10	Matt's Thematic Toxic Thoughts
What is my main emotional problem?	Depression.
What are some of the typical thoughts I have when I feel this way?	I'll never be normal again. What's the point of life anyway? How did I get this depressed? Everything is difficult and nothing is enjoyable. I'm a real disappointment to everyone in my life and to myself. The world is a terrible place.
What good reasons exist for disregarding these thoughts?	These are just typical things I tend to think when my mood is low. If I were feeling better I'd see things more positively and very differently. These thoughts are just a by-product of depressed feelings and don't accurately represent my future or reality.
What effect does ignoring/ disregarding these thoughts have on my mood?	If I really make an effort to consider these thoughts as just an unpleasant part of depression, I tend to feel a bit better. I can choose to turn my attention away from this type of thinking and then I notice that the thoughts often fade away.

You can use Worksheet 5-11 to help identify troublesome themes to your thinking. See if you can pinpoint when you are best off ignoring yourself!

Worksheet 5-11	My Thematic Toxic Thoughts
What is my main emotional problem?	
What are some of the typical thoughts I have when I feel this way?	
What good reasons exist for disregarding these thoughts?	
What effect does ignoring/disregarding these thoughts have on my mood?	

Mindfully mundane

All the little things that you do as part of your everyday routine you can probably start to do more mindfully if you *put your mind to it*. Consider this approach to be another way of strengthening your attention muscles and increasing your control over your concentration. Often people hurry through various tasks in an attempt to get them over and done with. Instead, you can take a little time to focus on the subtle aspects of each of your daily duties. For example, focus on the feel of the water when you're washing up, the taste of the glue from the back of a stamp you've just licked, the whirring of the washing machine that you've just switched on, and the taste and feel of the toothpaste on your tongue as you brush your teeth.

Use Worksheet 5-12 to make a list of daily tasks that you can do more mindfully in a deliberate effort to practise controlling and redirecting your attention.

Worksheet 5-12	My List of Daily Duties
What are some everyday tasks that I can do more mindfully?	

Part II
Pinning Down Problems and Giving Yourself Goals

The 5th Wave   By Rich Tennant

"This position is good for reaching inner calm, mental clarity, and things that roll behind the refrigerator."

In this part . . .

The chapters in this part are devoted to helping you to define your problems in specific terms, and to choosing specific goals with regard the difficulties you identify.

We cover healthy and unhealthy negative emotions and give you the chance to get to grips with your own emotional responses. We also show you how some of the ways in which you try to cope with problems may be in themselves problematic. Finally, we really focus on getting to grips with appropriate goals.

Chapter 6

Getting Emotional

. . . .

. . . .

Many CBT therapists make a distinction between two types of negative feeling states or emotions – healthy and unhealthy. *Healthy emotions* are those feelings you have in response to negative events that are appropriate to the event, lead to constructive action, and don't significantly interfere with the rest of your life. *Unhealthy emotions* are feelings you have that are out of proportion to the event in question, tend to lead to self-destructive behaviours, and cause problems in other areas of your life.

One of the aims of this workbook is to help you to experience healthy negative emotions more often. In this chapter we introduce you to different ways of identifying your feelings in the first place, show you ways of discerning between the two types of negative emotions, and give you a chance to put your finger on your problematic emotions.

Expanding Your Emotional Vocabulary

So you know that you're feeling *something*. Yes, an emotion's definitely going on in there, but what on earth *is* it? And what shall you call this churning internal experience?

Putting a name to your feelings isn't always easy. Psychologists can use lots of different words to describe subtly different emotions because they deal with that kind of thing all the time. But you may be more accustomed to using vague terms to articulate how you feel inside. Perhaps you use words such as 'upset', 'worked up' or 'bad'. These words give an indication that you're in a negative emotional state but they don't really provide much more information beyond that.

The advantages of applying a specific label or name to your feelings are threefold:

✔ It is easier for others (and even for yourself) to understand the precise nature of what you're feeling.

✔ It makes it easier for you to work out whether what you're feeling is a healthy or unhealthy negative emotion.

✔ It becomes easier for you to select an alternative healthy negative emotion as a goal.

One way of giving a name to your feelings is to begin by noting what triggered your feelings. By *trigger* we mean the event, potential event, or thought that starts your emotional juices flowing. Next, look closely at how your emotion leads you to act, or want to act (whether you actually do so or not) – we call these *action tendencies*. Your *actual behaviour* includes what your actions are in response to your emotion. Your *emotional guess* is your attempt to unravel what you're feeling and to decide on what label or name to give to your emotional experience. The name you decide best describes your internal feelings is your *emotional label*. Following are examples of what we mean.

Horace's wife of ten years moved out of the family home and has asked him for a divorce. His wife's decision was unexpected and seemed to come from out of the blue. Horace knows that he feels very upset but he's having trouble describing what he's feeling. Worksheet 6-1 shows how he uncovers his basic emotion.

Worksheet 6-1	Horace's Feeling Fact File
Trigger:	My wife has left me.
Actual behaviour:	Crying a lot.
	Avoiding people who may ask me questions about my wife and our marriage.
	Searching my mind for possible ways this could have been avoided.
	Eating less.
	Looking at pictures of my wife and crying.
Action tendencies:	I want to stay in bed all day, although I do drag myself to work.
	I don't want to talk to anyone about what has happened in my marriage.
	I don't want to look after myself or my home anymore.
Emotional guess:	Looking at what I've been doing and feeling like doing, I think I may be feeling very sad and possibly depressed. If I saw a friend of mine responding this way to the same event, I'd probably say that they were feeling depressed.
Emotional label:	Depressed

Lois has a friend who repeatedly cancels their dates to meet. Sometimes her friend has a plausible excuse for breaking their arrangements but more often she seems to have found another option that is more attractive to her. This scenario often leaves Lois with no alternative plans for the evening. On this occasion Lois's friend has cancelled a long-standing agreement to attend a concert. Lois is now left with a spare ticket and no companion. Lois's efforts to get to her real feelings about this situation are shown in Worksheet 6-2.

Worksheet 6-2	Lois's Feeling Fact File
Trigger:	My friend cancelled for the concert at the last minute.
Actual behaviour:	I didn't say much to her on the phone but was quite sulky. I tore both the tickets up and put them in the bin. I thought about how badly she treats me and what a good friend I am to her.
Action tendencies:	I will not call her again and will wait for her to call me. I will not make any attempt to go out with her and will try to make her say sorry for treating me so badly.
Emotional guess:	I feel angry with my friend for letting me down again. I can't believe the way she treats me. Doesn't she realise that I'm now left all on my own? I guess that I'm angry with her, but more than that I'm very upset that she's let me down so many times. I just don't deserve that kind of treatment. I guess that my feelings are more hurt than angry.
Emotional label:	Hurt

Both Horace and Lois are able to give a name to their emotional experience by looking more closely at what their behaviours actually are and how they feel like behaving, or plan to behave in the future. See if you can give a name to your emotion by using the same method and completing Worksheet 6-3.

Worksheet 6-3	My Feeling Fact File
Actual behaviour:	
Action tendencies:	
Emotional guess:	
Emotional label:	

Hopefully you find the feeling fact file useful in helping you identify your basic emotion. But if you still find the process difficult, don't worry. Sometimes what you need are more feeling words at your fingertips. Following is a list of common human emotions. You can use this list as a springboard to finding other words that describe variations on the same basic feelings. You will then have more feeling labels to choose from and use to describe emotions. You can use a thesaurus or dictionary to find more feeling words.

- ✔ Anger
- ✔ Anxiety
- ✔ Concern
- ✔ Depression
- ✔ Disappointment
- ✔ Embarrassment
- ✔ Envy
- ✔ Fear
- ✔ Grief
- ✔ Guilt
- ✔ Hurt
- ✔ Jealousy
- ✔ Regret
- ✔ Remorse
- ✔ Sadness
- ✔ Shame

Bear in mind that this is by no means a definitive list! Feel free to add as many emotion words as you like. In the rest of this chapter we show you ways of determining whether your emotions are in the healthy or unhealthy camp, whatever you choose to call them.

Understanding the Anatomy of Emotions

Feelings don't exist in a self-contained bubble. Human emotions exist in *context*. Confused? Fear not. Horace and Lois in the previous section show how behaviours are a fundamental aspect of emotions. All human emotions – whether positive or negative, healthy or unhealthy – are comprised of four dimensions. These dimensions interact and reinforce one another. Figure 6-1 shows this relationship.

Noting what is going on in the four dimensions of your emotion offers important clues to the type of emotion you're experiencing – healthy or unhealthy. See how Horace does this with Worksheet 6-4.

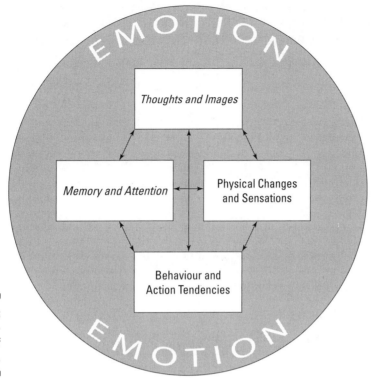

Figure 6-1:
The dimension of emotions.

Worksheet 6-4	Horace's Four-dimensional Emotion
Emotion:	Depression
Thoughts and images:	I keep thinking about what I might have done to drive my wife away. I have thoughts about how miserable and hopeless my future is going to be. I have images of my wife in the arms of another man. I imagine myself being alone in my old age.
Physical sensations and changes:	I have a gnawing pain in the pit of my stomach almost all the time. I burst into tears easily. My appetite has disappeared and I'm losing weight.

(continued)

Memory and attention:	I've been searching my memory for clues that my wife was planning to leave me, things that I should have picked up on.
	I keep remembering how in love we were when we were first married.
	I keep noticing couples in the street looking happy.
	I keep hearing love songs on the radio and noticing romantic films on TV.
Behaviour and action tendencies:	Crying a lot.
	Not making myself meals.
	Poring over pictures of my wife.
	Avoiding conversations about my marriage.
	Wanting to stay in bed all day.
	Avoiding friends and family.

Having broken down his emotion of depression into these four dimensions, Horace makes the realisations about his feelings shown in Worksheet 6-5.

Worksheet 6-5   **Horace's Realisations**

I can see by analysing my Four-dimensional Emotion Worksheet that I am blaming myself for the breakdown of my marriage and telling myself that I should have seen the signs and prevented my wife from leaving. I can also see that my avoidance behaviour is stopping me from sharing my feelings with friends and family who may be able to offer support. Also looking at photos and dwelling on the happy times we had together is making my depression worse. Focusing my attention on happy-looking couples is also leading me to compare my situation with theirs and lowering my mood further.

Use Worksheet 6-6 to break down your identified emotion into the four dimensions.

Worksheet 6-6   **My Four-dimensional Emotion**

| Emotion: | |
| | |

Thoughts and images:	
Physical sensations and changes:	
Memory and attention:	
Behaviour and action tendencies:	

Now you can use the space in Worksheet 6-7 to record any realisations you have about your emotional experience.

Worksheet 6-7   **My Realisations**

_____

_____

_____

_____

Working Out Whether Your Feelings Are Healthy or Unhealthy

As you may already realise, your thoughts, attention, focus, behaviour, and even some of your physical sensations are ways of determining whether you're in the grip of an unhealthy or a healthy emotional experience. These four aspects or dimensions of emotional experience are different depending on the type of feeling you're having. For example, the action tendencies associated with healthy sadness tend to be constructive. They help you to accept and adjust to a negative event or situation. The action tendencies associated with unhealthy depression tend to be destructive because they prevent you from accepting the negative event and moving forward. In general, healthy negative emotions are less intensely uncomfortable than their unhealthy counterparts. Even if you're extremely sad you're likely to feel less intense discomfort or emotional pain than if you're unhealthily depressed.

Taking note of your thinking

Rigid thinking is a surefire sign that you're feeling something unhealthy. *Rigid thinking* involves demanding that you, others, and the world play by certain rules – your rules. This attitude is troublesome because you leave no room for deviation or error. So when your demands aren't met (and they frequently won't be), you're likely to become emotionally disturbed.

The alternative to rigid/demand-based thinking is *flexible/preference-based thinking*. Here, you hold preferences, standards, and ideals for how you, others, and the world perform. But – and the *but* is crucial – you also accept the possibility of your preferences not being met. So when you fail to live up to your personal standards, others behave in undesirable ways, or the world refuses to fall in with your plans you may feel emotionally distressed, but not unduly disturbed.

When you hold demands that aren't met, you're also at risk of putting yourself or others down harshly. Doing so can lead to more emotional pain and more practical problems too.

Look out for words and phrases such as 'should', 'must', 'it's essential', 'have to', 'got to', and 'ought to' in your thinking and self-talk. These are often signals that you're thinking rigidly.

Samantha is very sensitive to criticism from others. She often senses that she's being criticised when someone makes even a slightly negative comment. Samantha's husband sat down for dinner and mentioned that the pasta was overcooked and that he didn't much like the meal she'd prepared. Samantha was very angry about her husband's comments and threw quite a tantrum, screaming at him for being so ungrateful and smashing things around in the kitchen. She and her husband went to bed without speaking.

You can use a Thought Test to see if your thinking about a given event or situation is rigid/demand based or flexible/preference based. The outcome is the acid test for knowing whether your emotion is a healthy or unhealthy one. Have a look at Samantha's Thought Test in Worksheet 6-8.

Worksheet 6-8	Samantha's Thought Test
Thought:	My husband must not criticise my cooking and he's totally ungrateful for doing so.
Is my thought flexible/ preference-based?	No, it isn't. I guess if I say that he must not criticise my cooking, then I'm not leaving room for the possibility that he may do so.
Is my thought true/does it fit with reality?	I guess if it were true that he must not criticise my cooking, then it must mean that he's lacking free will. The reality is that he did say that the pasta was overcooked and that the meat sauce was insipid. So I guess this goes to show that there's no reason that he must not be critical about the meal I prepared.

Is my thought helpful?	Well, I did get pretty angry and say a lot of vicious things. I also did smash rather a lot of china whilst freaking out at him. We went to bed without speaking and the evening was pretty unpleasant. So I guess that my thought wasn't very helpful all in all.
Is my thought leading me to put myself down?	Not at first. But I feel pretty down on myself now for getting so angry with my husband.
Is my thought leading me to put other people down?	Oh, yes. And how. I really think he's despicable for being so ungrateful.
Based on all this, is my thought leading to a healthy or an unhealthy emotion?	Unhealthy.

Samantha's example shows that her rigid thinking led her to become unhealthily angry with her husband. If she had held a flexible preference such as 'I really prefer that my husband not criticise my cooking but there's no reason why he must not do so' she may have felt healthily angry or annoyed about his unflattering remarks.

Now it's you turn! Recall a recent event when you think that you may have been experiencing an unhealthy emotion. Use the Thought Test in Worksheet 6-9 to find out whether your thinking at the time was flexible or rigid and your emotion healthy or unhealthy.

Worksheet 6-9	**My Thought Test**
Thought:	
Is my thought flexible/ preference-based?	
Is my thought true/does it fit with reality?	
Is my thought helpful?	
Is my thought leading me to put myself down?	

(continued)

Is my thought leading me to put other people down?	
Based on all this, is my thought leading to a healthy or an unhealthy emotion?	

If you find, like Samantha did, that your thought is resulting in an unhealthy negative emotion, you can try replacing it with a more flexible preference. Chapters 1, 2, and 3 discuss in greater detail how your thinking can influence how you feel and behave.

Being aware of your behaviour

Your emotions dictate your behaviour to a large extent. By acknowledging the ways you act when you're emotionally charged up, you can further determine the relative health of your feelings. Table 6-1 shows some of the typical behaviours that tend to go hand in hand with healthy and unhealthy emotions.

We also call behaviours *action tendencies* because you may feel like you want to act in a certain way but not actually do it.

Table 6-1	Action Tendencies of Healthy and Unhealthy Feelings		
Unhealthy Emotion	*Action Tendencies*	*Healthy Emotion*	*Action Tendencies*
Anger/rage	Shouting, being violent and abusive, putting the other person down. Insisting that you're right.	Annoyance/ anger	Asserting yourself in a respectful but firm manner. Not becoming abusive or violent. Being willing to consider the other person's point of view.
Anxiety	Avoiding threat. Seeking excessive reassurance.	Concern	Facing up to threats. Seeking a reasonable amount of reassurance.
Depression	Withdrawing from social reinforcements and meaningful or enjoyed activities. Self-isolating.	Sadness	After a period of mourning and reflection, reinvesting in the company of others. Carrying on with meaningful or enjoyed activities.
Acidic envy	Spoiling another's enjoyment of what you want but don't have. Sour grapes. Pretending you don't really want what they have.	Benign envy	Striving to gain what another has that you desire but don't have. Allowing others to enjoy what they have without trying to spoil it for them. Admitting that you want what they have.

Unhealthy Emotion	Action Tendencies	Healthy Emotion	Action Tendencies
Guilt	Begging forgiveness from or avoiding facing the person you have wronged. Taking too much responsibility for the wrongdoing.	Remorse	Asking for forgiveness and facing up to the person you have wronged. Taking the correct amount of responsibility for the wrongdoing.
Hurt	Sulking. Trying to hint at what the other person has done wrong so they have to make the first move.	Disappointment	Voicing your feelings. Giving the other person a chance to explain or apologise. Being willing to make the first move.
Acidic jealousy	Spying or checking up on another person. Questioning them and setting tests for them. Being suspicious.	Benign jealousy	Asking honest and straightforward questions. Being open minded.
Shame	Avoiding the gaze of others. Hiding away and withdrawing.	Regret	Maintaining eye contact with others. Holding you head up and keeping in contact with others.

Bear in mind that you can use any word you like to describe your actual emotion. You needn't use the labels in Table 6-1. Just make sure that you use a different term for your healthy emotion and the unhealthy alternative. Samantha, for example, may use the term *rage* to describe her unhealthy emotion and the term *hacked off* to describe her healthy emotion.

Using the terms from Table 6-1, you can now do a quick Behaviour Test to see what type of emotion you are experiencing. We use the example of Samantha again in Worksheet 6-10 to show you how it's done.

Worksheet 6-10	Samantha's Behaviour Test
Event:	Husband criticised the meal I prepared for us.
What did I actually do?	I shouted at him for being so ungrateful.
	I called him a lot of bad names.
	I stormed around the kitchen and broke several bits of china.
	I refused to speak to him for the rest of the evening.
What did I feel like doing?	I really wanted to hit or punch him when he said the sauce was insipid.
	I was sorely tempted to kick him out of the house and demand a divorce.

(continued)

Does my behaviour fit with a healthy emotion?	No.
My emotional label:	Unhealthy rage

Based on her Behaviour Test, Samantha can see that she was in the grip of an unhealthy emotion from dinnertime onwards.

Now it's your turn again, you lucky thing! Recall a recent event in your life when you think you experienced an unhealthy emotion and use the information in Table 6-1 and the space in Worksheet 6-11 to help you determine if your emotion was the troublesome sort.

Worksheet 6-11	My Behaviour Test
Event:	
What did I actually do?	
What did I feel like doing?	
Does my behaviour fit with a healthy emotion?	
My emotional label:	

Finding out what you focus on

Another way of really pinning down whether you're engulfed by the turbulent seas of an unhealthy emotional reaction or surfing the cresting waves of a healthy alternative is by noticing where your attention is focused. This tactic involves analysing the direction your thoughts take, what you're picking up within your environment, which memories you may dredge up, or how you are viewing your future.

Your emotions really do have an effect on your focus. For example, when you're depressed, you tend to focus on other painful losses in the past and view the future as bleak. If you're angry with someone, your attention is likely to hone in on additional reasons to be angry with them. When you're hurt, you may well find your thoughts tuning into ways that others and the world have done you wrong. Table 6-2 outlines common areas of focus for both healthy and unhealthy negative emotions.

Table 6-2	Attention Focus of Healthy and Unhealthy Feelings		
Unhealthy Emotion	*Attention Focus*	*Healthy Emotion*	*Attention Focus*
Anger/rage	You focus on any evidence of malicious intent from others. You focus on additional reasons to be angry with people.	Annoyance/anger	You don't look for malicious intent in the actions of others unnecessarily. Nor do you focus on additional reasons to support your anger.
Anxiety	You overestimate the degree of risk or threat. You underestimate your personal ability to cope with the risk or threat.	Concern	You view the degree of risk or threat realistically, fully acknowledging your ability to cope with or overcome the risk or threat.
Depression	You focus on past loss or failure. You see the future as hopeless or painful.	Sadness	You're able to imagine yourself feeling happier in the future. You don't dwell on past losses or failures.
Acidic envy	You focus on reasons to put down the desired possession or situation of another that you lack. You think about how to deprive the other person of the desired possession.	Benign envy	You focus on how you might reasonably obtain the desired possession or situation of another that you lack. You're able to focus on being pleased for the other person.
Guilt	You blame yourself entirely for the wrongdoing. You expect and look for punishment. You look for evidence that others are blaming you for the wrongdoing.	Remorse	You take appropriate responsibility for the wrongdoing and take into account other factors. You don't expect to be punished but rather are willing to make amends. You're able to recognise forgiveness from others and to accept their forgiveness.
Hurt	You focus on how badly you have been treated and on how undeserving you are of such treatment. You dredge up past hurts. You look for proof that the other person is uncaring and indifferent.	Disappointment	You're able to see the event in perspective without dwelling on past hurts. You don't focus on how unjustly you have been treated. You're able to see evidence that the other person does care.

(continued)

Acidic jealousy	You focus on threats to your relationship where they may not actually exist.	Benign jealousy	You're able to see the difference between a real and present danger to your relationship and mere hunches or suspicions.
Shame	You see disapproval from others where it doesn't exist. You overestimate the unacceptability of what has happened or been revealed about you.	Regret	You're able to respond to attempts from others to accept you. You view yourself with some compassion.

Take the Attention Focus Test as yet another way of determining the type of emotion you're experiencing in response to a negative event. Worksheet 6-12 is an example of how Samantha did it.

Worksheet 6-12	Samantha's Attention Focus Test
Event:	Husband criticised the meal I prepared for us.
What direction did my attention take?	I focused on how wrong he was to say what he did about the sauce and on how ungrateful he was.
	I assumed that he was being deliberately mean-spirited and unkind.
	I remembered lots of little incidents over the last few weeks when he has been uncomplimentary.
Does my attention focus fit with a healthy emotion?	No.
My emotional label:	Unhealthy rage

Guess what? Yes, it's your turn again. Does the fun *never* stop?

Use Table 6-2 and Worksheet 6-13 to do your own Attention Focus Test.

Worksheet 6-13	My Attention Focus Test
Event:	

What direction did my attention take?	
Does my attention focus fit with a healthy emotion?	
My emotional label	

Congratulations! You are now well equipped to take any emotion you experience and put it through these tests to see whether it's healthy or unhealthy.

Avoiding being fooled by physical feelings

Many (most) emotions, both healthy and unhealthy, are accompanied by physical sensations or *symptoms*. As a general rule, the symptoms you have when you're feeling healthy distress aren't as uncomfortable or debilitating as those associated with unhealthy disturbance. Physical symptoms of healthy distress also tend to reduce or disappear more quickly.

We use the word *distressed* to refer to healthy negative emotions and the word *disturbed* to describe unhealthy ones.

You can measure your physical feelings or symptoms in terms of intensity and duration.

Simon has a big presentation to give before the board at work. Simon usually puts a lot of pressure on himself to achieve highly and to not make mistakes. As a result he feels very anxious before giving a presentation. Happily for Simon, he has used this workbook and paid close attention to Chapters 1, 2, 3, and 6. He now can think more flexibly about the possibility of making a mistake and of not reaching his personal standard of achievement. So Simon can now feel healthily concerned before any future presentations.

Have a look at Simon's Symptom Synopsis in Worksheets 6-14 and 6-15.

Worksheet 6-14	Simon's Disturbed Symptom Synopsis
Unhealthy emotion:	Anxiety
Symptom description:	Sleep disturbance
	Sweating
	Shaking
	Churning feeling in stomach
Intensity:	9, on a scale where 1 is mild and 10 is severe

(continued)

Duration:	My sleep is disturbed for about four nights prior to the presentation. I wake up and worry about messing it up. That churning feeling in my stomach is there almost constantly from about a week before the presentation. My hands shake and I sweat throughout the entire presentation, although I do my best to hide it.

Worksheet 6-15	Simon's Distressed Symptom Synopsis
Healthy emotion:	Concern
Symptom description:	Minor sleep disturbance. Some sweating. Trembling in hands. Churning feeling in stomach.
Intensity:	4, on a scale where 1 is mild and 10 is severe.
Duration:	My sleep is a bit disturbed the night before the presentation, but I worry only slightly about messing it up. The churning feeling in my stomach only happens fleetingly when I'm reminded about the upcoming presentation and it goes away almost instantly. My hands tremble and I sweat more at the start of the presentation but that stops once I get into it.

You can probably see from the example of Simon that his physical symptoms are similar for both anxiety and concern but that in the latter case they are less intense and don't go on as long. You can use the same method to compare the intensity and duration of any physical feelings you have in conjunction with your emotion using Worksheets 6-16 and 6-17.

Worksheet 6-16	My Disturbed Symptom Synopsis
Unhealthy emotion:	

Symptom description:	
Intensity (on a scale where 1 is mild and 10 is severe):	
Duration:	

Worksheet 6-17	**My Distressed Symptom Synopsis**
Healthy emotion:	
Symptom description:	
Intensity (on a scale where 1 is mild and 10 is severe):	
Duration:	

The intensity and duration of any physical sensations that go along with your emotional experience can indicate which type of emotion you are feeling. But a degree of overlap exists in this area with both types of emotions.

Many of the physical reactions and sensations that you experience are similar for both types of emotions. For example, you may be tearful and lose your appetite whether you are sad or depressed. Sticking to using your thoughts, behaviours, and attention focus as reliable indicators of what type of emotion you are dealing with is therefore best.

Charting Your Problem Emotions

Once you're able to identify your emotions as either healthy or unhealthy, your next step is to decide which unhealthy emotions you want to target for change. These are probably the emotions you experience the most often or those that interfere most significantly with the smooth running of your life. You can use Tables 6-1 and 6-2 from earlier in this chapter to help you list your problem emotions in Worksheet 6-18.

Worksheet 6-18	My Problem Emotions

Identifying themes and triggers

Although your behaviour, thinking style, and attention focus are different for healthy and unhealthy negative emotions, the theme is the *same*. By *theme* we mean the key aspects of a broad situation that give rise to a particular emotion. Getting familiar with the themes that accompany different emotional experiences can help you to accurately pinpoint the nature of your feelings. You're then in a better position to work out whether your emotion is healthy or unhealthy.

Table 6-3 lists the themes attached to each emotional pairing.

Table 6-3	Feeling Themes
Unhealthy/Healthy Emotion	*Theme*
Anxiety/concern	Perceived threat, risk, or danger
Depression/sadness	Loss or failure
Acidic envy/benign envy	Another possesses something desirable that you lack
Guilt/remorse	Broken moral code by doing something wrong or by failing to do something (sin of commission or omission)
Hurt/disappointment	You are treated badly and are undeserving
Acidic jealousy/benign jealousy	Threat to your relationship
Rage/annoyance	Personal rule is broken and/or self-esteem is threatened
Shame/regret	Undesirable or unacceptable personal information has been publicly revealed by yourself or others

By noting any recurrent themes in your life you can begin to notice triggers or specific events that start you off on an unhealthily emotional rollercoaster.

Note how Samantha used the Theme and Trigger Tracker to identify her problem emotions more specifically in Worksheet 6-19.

Worksheet 6-19	Samantha's Theme and Trigger Tracker
Theme:	Personal rule is broken and/or self-esteem is threatened
Unhealthy emotion:	Rage
Triggers:	Husband criticises my cooking
	Boss unhappy with a report
	Someone nicks my parking space
	Friend turns up an hour late for a date

You just *know* that it's your turn now, so get to work on Worksheet 6-20.

Worksheet 6-20	My Theme and Trigger Tracker
Theme:	
Unhealthy emotion:	
Triggers:	

You may have more than one problem emotion and hence more than one theme and a throng of potential triggers. So feel free to use Worksheet 6-20 again – once for each problem emotion.

Making a problem statement

Okay. So here's the good news. Having possibly realised that you are littered with unhealthy negative emotional responses to life events and such, you can do something about it! Oh, yes. But first you need to make a problem statement. Have a look at Samantha's in Worksheet 6-21.

Worksheet 6-21	Samantha's Problem Statement
Feeling <u>rage</u> about my husband's <u>critical remarks</u>, leading me to <u>call him names, break plates, and give him the cold shoulder</u>.	
Goal: To be hacked off instead of raging.	

Samantha's Problem Statement includes her unhealthy emotion, the trigger, and her unhealthy behaviour. This statement provides a lot of information about where she can intervene to change her rage to healthy anger or annoyance, or as she calls it being *hacked off*.

Go on then. Fill in the blanks in Worksheet 6-22.

Worksheet 6-22	My Problem Statement

Feeling _____ about _____ leading me to _____ .

Goal:

You can do as many problem statements as you need to depending on how many problem emotions you have. Several chapters in this book can help you to overcome your emotional problems now that you're so good at identifying them. And if you do your utmost to *behave* in accordance with your healthy emotional goal, turn your *attention* to the things that fit with a healthy negative emotion, and, above all, strive to *think* in a flexible/preference-based way, then you're on the road to emotional well-being!

Chapter 7

Targeting Troublesome Tactics

. . . .

In This Chapter

▶ Recognising when your solution becomes the problem

▶ Tolerating short-term pain for long-term gain

▶ Visualising a vicious flower

. . . .

*I*f you feel emotionally disturbed, doing whatever reduces your emotional discomfort seems sensible. You may be doing what you think is best to help you cope with your psychological problems. Unfortunately some of the strategies you're using to make yourself feel temporarily better may well be maintaining your problem in the long run. You probably aren't aware of perpetuating your problems with some of your coping behaviours. Most people don't know exactly how to best help themselves overcome problems such as depression or anxiety. In this chapter we deal with some common self-defeating coping strategies.

Identifying Self-Defeating Strategies

The first step in identifying self-defeating strategies is recognising which of your tactics are actually maintaining your problems or even making them worse. Following are some examples of what we mean by *problematic strategies*:

✔ Avoiding situations that you fear or that provoke anxiety

✔ Taking drugs or using alcohol to block out uncomfortable emotions

✔ Hiding aspects of yourself that you feel ashamed about

✔ Putting off dealing with practical problems and tasks that you find unpleasant

✔ Withdrawing from your usual routine

✔ Isolating yourself from friends and family

✔ Worrying. Many people think that by worrying about potential negative events they will either prevent bad things from happening or prepare themselves to deal with such events. Although worrying may *seem* like a way of solving or preventing future problems, it actually becomes a problem itself because it promotes anxiety.

✔ Performing rituals. People who suffer with anxiety disorders like obsessive-compulsive disorder (see Chapter 13 for more on this condition) often insist that they perform everyday tasks like dressing or cleaning themselves in a very rigid, ordered pattern. They often worry that if they fail to execute tasks in a precise way that something bad will happen to themselves or others as a result. If the pattern is interrupted, these people become very anxious and often make themselves begin the ritual all over again, and may spend hours trying to get their rituals done exactly right.

✔ Checking things over and over. It's normal to check that you've locked the door or that you've got your keys in your bag once or twice. But people with anxiety problems often check things like this so many times that they find it very difficult to leave the house and arrive at work or appointments on time.

Obviously, you may be using many more possible troublesome tactics in addition to the ones listed here. The type of coping strategies you choose depends on what type of problem you're experiencing. We cover anxiety, depression, and obsessive-compulsive disorder (OCD) in more detail in Chapters 9, 12, and 13, respectively.

The old adage that sometimes you have to feel worse before you feel better is often true. In CBT we encourage you to drop your troublesome coping tactics in favour of healthier behaviours that ultimately help you overcome your problems. This approach can mean doing things that cause you short-term anxiety or discomfort in the spirit of getting well.

Demanding control and insisting on certainty

If you suffer from an anxiety problem such as post-traumatic stress, obsessive-compulsive disorder, or panic attacks, you probably like to be in control. No doubt you also try to be as certain as possible about situations before you enter them. You may have the same demands for control and certainty if you have an anger or jealousy problem.

The trouble is that if you're trying hard to control things that are beyond your control, such as other people's thoughts, certain physical sensations, or even your own thoughts, it can be pretty disheartening. The same goes for certainty. Many things exist in life that you simply can't be 100 per cent certain about, no matter how hard you try.

If you continue to try (in vain) to be in a state of absolute control and utter certainty at all times, you're likely to become even more anxious, angry, jealous, or depressed. Learning to accept limitations to your personal power and to live with uncertainty can really make a positive difference to how you feel.

Trying to control how others behave and what they think about you is common. But it's a fruitless endeavor because other people are outside your sphere of control; You can't control what other people do or think most of the time. You may be able to *influence* or *request* others to behave and think in desired ways, but it's ultimately up to them to decide on their own thoughts and actions. Try giving other people permission to make their own decisions and form their own opinions.

Also keep in mind that you can't and don't *need* to control your physical sensations, such as blushing, breathing, swallowing, or your heart beating. Try letting your body get on with physical symptoms of anxiety (Chapter 9 has a figure that shows some common physical sensations) and allow them to subside on their own. Trying to control a physical side effect of anxiety usually leads to further anxiety or panic. Also allow your body to get on with the business of operating without your guidance or intervention. Breathing is so automatic that you can do when asleep or even in a coma! Try trusting your body to do its job – even when you're feeling anxious.

They same goes for life events. Life is often unpredictable, uncertain and even unfair. If you insist that you need certainty about what life is about to deal you at all times, then you're very likely to have a lot of anxiety. No one can control random live events and trying too hard to do so will only generate worry and anxiety. Often people assume that because something negative happened to them once they're more vulnerable to the same sort of bad event happening to them again. Although this is rarely the case, people may go to great lengths to try to get a guarantee that nothing bad happens in their lives. This is understandable but ultimately problematic. Instead, try to have some faith in your ability to cope with adverse events if and when they occur. Also work on accepting the idea that life is uncertain and always has been. Living with uncertainty is part of being human and therefore something you do every day although you may not realise it.

The following worksheets help you clearly identify specific situations in which you may be trying too hard to gain control or certainty. They also help you to understand how your attempts to be *totally* in control and certain are maintaining problems like anxiety and depression.

Connie was involved in a serious road traffic accident 18 months ago. She recovered from her physical injuries but is still suffering psychologically. Connie was riding in the back seat of the car that crashed. Since the accident she avoids driving on the motorway and will only go in a vehicle if she can drive. If she begins to feel anxious when driving she tries very hard to control her breathing. She monitors how fast she is breathing and tries to make her breathing deep and regular. This unfortunately means that Connie becomes *over* aware of her breathing. Since breathing is an automatic bodily function, Connie doesn't need to focus on her breath. If she leaves it alone, her breathing will take care of itself. Connie also reads the weather reports before she travels in order to be certain that the conditions are favourable for driving. If anyone else is in the car with Connie, she insists that they do not speak to her or distract her in any way.

Connie is trying to be absolutely certain that she will not be involved in another accident. She used Worksheet 7-1 to help understand her demands for certainty and control and to monitor their effects.

Worksheet 7-1	Connie's Control and Certainty Check-Up
What is my main emotional problem?	Anxiety (post-traumatic stress disorder).
In what ways am I demanding control?	Trying to control my breathing when I feel anxious. Refusing to be a passenger so that I can be in control of the car. Telling others how to behave when I'm driving. Controlling where I drive and avoiding motorways.
In what ways am I insisting on certainty?	Checking the weather forecast so I can be certain that it won't rain or be stormy when I'm in the car. Telling people to be quiet in the car so that I can be certain I won't be distracted. Planning all journeys so that I can be certain to avoid the motorway.

(continued)

How are my control demands affecting my main emotional problem?	Demanding control keeps me feeling on edge when driving.
	Trying to control my breathing and anxiety symptoms doesn't work, it just makes me panicky.
	I then think of myself as weak for having a panic episode.
	I think of the accident a lot when I'm trying to control things related to driving.
	I feel more anxious and unsafe because of my control demands.
How is my insistence on certainty affecting my main emotional problem?	Going to such lengths to try to make certain that I stay safe and don't have an accident means that I'm always expecting something bad to happen when I'm in the car.
	I feel anxious just at the thought of car travel because of my certainty demands.
	The more I try to control my thoughts/images about the accident, the more distressing I find them.

Use Worksheet 7-2 to help you work out when to relinquish control and accept uncertainty.

Worksheet 7-2	My Control and Certainty Check-Up
What is my main emotional problem?	
In what ways am I demanding control?	
In what ways am I insisting on certainty?	
How are my control demands affecting my main emotional problem?	

How is my insistence on certainty affecting my main emotional problem?	

Adding up avoidance and getting yourself down

Avoidance is a very common unhelpful coping strategy. If you're afraid of something or feel anxious in certain situations, you're best off avoiding these things, right? Wrong. The more you avoid whatever frightens you and provokes your anxiety, the more you reinforce the idea that a real threat exists. Continued avoidance keeps you anxious and can diminish your overall functioning. Likewise, putting off tasks that you find distasteful or don't feel like doing can lead to practical problems and worsen depression. Sometimes, facing your fears and doing things you don't want to do is well worthwhile. Grinning and bearing it is often in your best interest.

In Chapter 9 you'll find more worksheets devised to help you construct exposure exercises for confronting avoidance and overcoming fears, and Chapter 12 has useful information and worksheets to help you schedule daily activities and re-engage with previously enjoyed practices. But here, we offer a few pointers to help you avoid avoidance and get on with neglected activities *now*:

1. **Make a list of the situations you're currently avoiding or neglecting due to your emotional problems of anxiety or depression.**

2. **Rank these situations in order of least frightening to most frightening or least anxiety producing to most anxiety producing.**

    Basically, rank the situations as to how badly you want to avoid them.

3. **Put yourself into your *least* feared situation regularly.**

    Try your hardest to push yourself into your anxiety provoking situations. Doing so helps you adjust to the situation and begin to take it in your stride.

    Also give yourself credit for being able to cope with uncomfortable feelings in these situations.

4. **Steadily work your way up your list.**

If you're depressed and don't find pleasure in activities you once enjoyed or feel like hiding away from people because of your low mood, urge yourself to do the opposite! Doing the things you like to do and being around other people may lift your mood, provide you with understanding and support, or even just help you to feel more like you again. Self isolation is a big feature of depression and reinforces loneliness. It's often worth going out with others just for the sake of it, whether you really enjoy it or not. You may not have the great time that you used to have, but being with others is very likely to stop you feeling worse.

Mark has been depressed for a few months. He was under a lot of pressure at work and at one stage worried that he would lose his job if he didn't work late to meet deadlines. His depression may have been partly triggered by protracted stress. Mark feels demotivated at work and has often called in sick. He's also stopped going to the gym because he just feels too tired. His friends invite him out, but he doesn't enjoy socialising as much as he used to and so he often declines. Mark spends much of the day in bed watching TV or dozing. The post is mounting up but Mark can't face opening it and so bills are going unpaid. Mark knows that he should visit his doctor to talk about his depression, but he feels hopeless.

Mark listed the activities his depression led him to avoid, his reasons for avoiding them, and the results of his avoidance in Worksheet 7-3.

Worksheet 7-3	Mark's Avoidance List	
My primary emotional problem:		
Things I'm Avoiding	**Reason for Avoidance**	**Effects of Avoidance**
Opening post	Can't face it.	Bills mounting up.
Going to work	Too stressful and overwhelming.	Boss keeps ringing. I worry about sick days mounting up. I get anxious and filled with dread at the thought of going back to work.
Talking to my boss about reducing my workload	He won't understand and will think I'm incompetent.	Stress remains and I don't get a chance to assert myself or find out what my boss would actually suggest.
Going to doctor	It's hopeless; he can't help.	I don't have a medical certificate. I'm not getting advice or help. I'm not on medication.

Worksheet 7-4 provides you with space to list the things you avoid, why you avoid them, and the price you pay for ignoring them.

Worksheet 7-4	My Avoidance List	
My primary emotional problem:		
Things I'm Avoiding	**Reason for Avoidance**	**Effects of Avoidance**

In Worksheet 7-5 Mark noted how his behaviour was reinforcing his depression.

Worksheet 7-5	Mark's Unhelpful Behaviours	
Unhelpful Behaviours	*Reason for Behaviour*	*Effect of Behaviour*
Staying in bed all day.	Feel unable to face the world.	More depression and fear. Sleep disturbance.
Not socialising.	I don't want to see anyone or let on how messed up I am.	I'm isolated from my friends, feel very alone, and think too much.
Not going to the gym.	I'm too tired and weak.	My fitness is diminishing and I feel less healthy and strong generally. I have no social interaction and more depressed thoughts.

Whether you're feeling depressed, anxious, unhealthily angry, or jealous (to name but a few, see Chapter 6 for more) now is the opportunity for you to underline whatever you may be doing to try and cope with and alleviate your emotional problem.

What helps you feel better in the immediate present often keeps your problem going into the future. Avoiding things like work, talking to others, and answering the telephone are typical examples of unhelpful avoidance. Also consider the things you may be doing to dull your unpleasant feelings – things like drinking too much, using drugs, shopping, eating or watching telly to distract yourself. Reversing these types of behaviours is often a key first step to overcoming your emotional problems. Use Worksheet 7-6 to list your unhelpful behaviours.

Worksheet 7-6	My Unhelpful Behaviours	
Unhelpful Behaviours	*Reason for Behaviour*	*Effect of Behaviour*

Very often doing the exact opposite of what your mood dictates, or encourages you to do, is the best thing for you in the long run. So if you feel like avoiding work or socialising, often you'll do yourself a world of good by thrusting yourself into social situations and confronting work issues head-on. Likewise, if immersing yourself in drugs and alcohol or mindless telly watching helps take your mind off your feelings in the present, resisting these behaviours may well aid you in confronting your problems and give you the chance to come up with possible solutions for them.

By allocating a time slot to constructive action, you make it more probable that you will carry it out. It's very easy to have good intentions but to let them slide because you've not given yourself a definite time slot to carry them out. Get good at giving yourself time frames for doing things that are in your best interest, whatever they may be. Cleaning the house, speaking to your boss, taking exercise, socialising, paying bills, returning phone calls and so on are all examples of tasks that you can allocate specific times to completing.

Mark used Worksheet 7-7 to record healthier ways of dealing with his symptoms of depression and to allocate specific times to perform neglected duties.

Worksheet 7-7	Mark's Alternative Behaviours	
Healthy Alternative Coping Strategies	*Potential Benefits of Healthy Coping Strategies*	*Allocated Timeslot*
Doing the opposite of what my depression dictates!	If I act against my depressed thoughts and actions then I may stop my mood from getting even worse.	
Sticking to a daily schedule and forcing myself to get up at the same time every day. Avoiding naps	If I get up at the same time every day and don't nap I may get my sleep routine back on track.	Get out of bed at 8am every morning
Going back to the gym	Going to the gym may give me a much needed endorphin rush.	Monday, Wednesday, and Friday at 3pm
Opening the post and paying the bills	I'll feel more on top of things and less hopeless if I pay the bills.	10am each morning
Contacting work about my illness	If I inform work of my depression at least they'll know what's going on. I won't need to hide under the duvet from the ringing phone.	Monday at 9am

Visiting the doctor	My doctor may be able to refer me to a therapist or give me some antidepressants, or both. A certificate for work will help secure my job.	Tuesday at 1pm
Keeping in touch with friends and family	Seeing friends and family may help me feel more 'normal' again. They might even be supportive and understanding. The more time I spend with others, the less isolated I'll be. Keeping busy gives me less time to focus on my depressed thoughts and lack of energy.	Thursday evenings and weekends

Chapter 12 looks at depression and how to use an activity schedule. Scheduling your activities (both leisure and labour) can really help you in getting on with things despite low energy and motivation.

Use Worksheet 7-8 to identify more healthy behaviours and assign a set time to carry out the tasks you've been putting off.

Worksheet 7-8	**My Alternative Behaviours**	
Healthy Alternative Coping Strategies	*Potential Benefits of Healthy Coping Strategies*	*Allocated Timeslot*

Some tasks seem far more off-putting when you just think about them than when you actually get stuck in. Doing tasks in the absence of energy and motivation can serve to increase both. If you're depressed, you may not get the same level of enjoyment from pleasurable activities in the first instance. But be assured that doing something is better than doing nothing. Feelings of achievement, satisfaction, and enjoyment will return in time. Be patient with yourself.

Worrying yourself sick

A bit of worry is entirely normal. Note we said 'a bit'. It's normal for problems or responsibilities to enter your mind and for you to try to think of how best to sort them out. But many people make worrying a full-time occupation. Excessive worrying is a non-productive bad habit. If you're someone who worries all the time about the tiniest everyday things, you no doubt find it exhausting.

The most fervent worriers frequently worry about events that haven't yet happened, may never happen, or over which they have no control. It's like trying to solve an unsolvable problem. The two main reasons you may be trapped in a cycle of excessive and undue worry are:

- ✔ You may believe that worrying somehow protects you from negative life events – as though worrying somehow better equips you to deal with bad things.

- ✔ You may also believe that worrying will magically prevent bad things from happening to you – as though worrying will somehow provide clues and insight into a bad thing before it happens.

You may think that the best way to deal with your practical or psychological problems is to worry them out. Not so. Life just isn't governable like that. You can worry until the cows literally come back home to be milked, and you still won't be able to control random events. Worry is *not* the same as problem-solving thought and action and is more a recipe for further anxiety and feelings of helplessness.

See your worry as a bad habit or a problematic process that needs to be interrupted. Don't let yourself dwell on the *content* of your worries; instead recognise that worry *itself* is your main problem. Chapter 5 offers some helpful hints on learning to accept and ignore your thoughts.

Worry is a moveable feast. So if you're one of those people who believes that if only you can work through *every* conceivable worry you'll be able to relax and enjoy life – lots of luck. It'll never happen. You'll always find another thing to worry about and you'll never learn to give your brain a break. You may even end up worrying that worrying so much is harmful. Actually, it isn't – but it is fruitless and very uncomfortable.

Worksheet 7-9 provides you with an opportunity to interrupt your worry process.

Worksheet 7-9   **My Worry Work-Out**

---

1. Am I currently worrying about something that hasn't yet happened?
(Answer Yes or No only) _____

---

2. Is this current worry a real-life problem that I can work on resolving?
(Answer Yes or No only) _____

> If Yes, what do I need to put into action to solve the problem? List specific actions you can take:

> If No, what can I do to interrupt the worry process? List specific activities that will absorb your attention:

3. Am I worrying in an attempt to prevent this negative thing from happening? (Answer Yes or No only) _____

4. Am I worrying in an attempt to protect myself from this negative event should it happen? (Answer Yes or No only) _____

5. Being as objective as possible, is this current worry just another example of my overall worry problem? (Answer Yes or No only) _____

> If Yes (as it probably will be!), revisit your 'If No' answer under Step 2 and turn your attention to more interesting and productive things! List them here:

When you first begin to resist the worry process you'll feel very uncomfortable and even unsafe or irresponsible. These feelings are simply because you're going against the grain of your tendency – you are worrying about not worrying! Expect to feel odd and drawn back to niggling worries as you begin the quest for a worry-free life. Stick with your resistance and over time you'll retrain your brain to let worries pass and to focus on more productive aspects of your life. Good luck!

When Feeling Better Stops You from Getting Better

Oh, but we all do like to take the edge off our uncomfortable feelings, which is very understandable but not always helpful in the long run. Often attempts to make yourself feel better only bring about the kind of results you most want to avoid. So if you desperately try not to be socially awkward, you may well end up being so self-conscious that you say something odd or behave in an aloof manner. That scenario is just one example of how trying to feel better in the 'here and now' can actually make you worse in the 'there and later'. We expand on this concept a bit more in the following sections.

Cease self-medicating your mood

Perhaps a little drink will take the sting out of your guilt, anxiety, or depression. Hmmm. Maybe a little extra dose of a sleeping tablet might quiet your anxious mind, stop the flashbacks, or quell intrusive images. Yep, can't argue with that. Drugs and alcohol are pretty effective mood-altering substances – in the short term. But be warned, these immediate interventions have long-term ramifications. So you may end up addicted to sleeping medication or dependent on alcohol. Or you may just feel more depressed and anxious the next day when you wake up with a hangover. Not fun.

Self-medicating habits can extend to normally innocuous activities such as shopping and watching television. Basically, anything you do to distract yourself or deal indirectly with a core problem is termed *self-medicating* in psychotherapy.

Verity has a problem with low self-worth. She feels very depressed and hates herself if she fails to achieve highly at work or falters in her personal life as a mother and partner. Verity often sees *total* failure in very minor things, such as being late to work or not having dinner on the table at a certain time. She drinks wine in the evenings to calm her anxiety and relieve her sense of guilt. At the weekends, Verity takes her kids out and buys them toys that the family can't afford to try to make up for her perceived shortcomings as a mother.

Verity used Worksheet 7-10 to highlight her self-medicating behaviours and to see how they're becoming problems themselves.

Worksheet 7-10	Verity's Mood Self-Medication Morass
My problematic unhealthy emotions: Depression and guilt	
How do I self-medicate my mood?	By drinking wine in the evenings (sometimes quite a lot) and by shopping for treats for the kids and sometimes for myself.
How does this affect my mood in the short term?	When I'm actually drinking the wine I get a feeling of relief and happiness. I feel great after I've bought something for the kids and I get a real buzz out of buying something for myself.
How does this affect my mood in the long term?	If I've drunk a lot the night before I feel ill, tired, and guilty the next morning when I wake up. I feel like a bad mother and a useless employee and this feeling can last for several hours or sometimes days. When I make myself feel better through shopping I often get a real mood crash after the initial euphoria wears off. This can happen an hour or a day after the spree. I then get credit card bills and feel overwhelmed and guilty about spending money so freely.

What other effects does self-medicating have on my life?	I'm getting into debt.
	I often drink too much when out and feel that I've been a bit inappropriate, which I then berate myself over.
	I think that I'm becoming dependant on alcohol to make myself feel okay and to feel I can cope with social situations and everyday life.

Self-medicating behaviours can include anything that you do for immediate relief or gratification. Usually anything that you're doing too much of can be classed as such a behaviour. Shopping, drinking, eating, sleeping, watching TV, or even innocuous activities such as sex and reading can become problematic solutions if done too much or in lieu of other more productive behaviours. So check out your motivation for whatever you're doing – as honestly as possible.

Use Worksheet 7-11 to assess your self-medicating behaviours and their short- and long-term effects.

Worksheet 7-11	My Mood Self-Medication Morass
My problematic unhealthy emotions:	
How do I self-medicate my mood?	
How does this affect my mood in the short term?	
How does this affect my mood in the long term?	
What other effects does self-medicating have on my life?	

Requesting reassurance and seeking safety

Looking for ways to secure your safety and asking others to reassure you that the worst won't happen are two other common self-defeating strategies for dealing with problems. People who suffer anxiety or jealousy problems often employ these tactics.

Why don't these strategies work? Well, the reality is that your problem is insecurity – not a real danger or threat to your relationship. Thus, if your partner reassures you that he or she isn't about to leave you, you'll feel better but only for a very short time because you can't be reassured. If you're told that the plane won't crash or your job is safe, you'll believe it for about ten minutes before you start obsessing and worrying again. Nothing sinks in for terribly long. You can't be convinced that you're safe. The more you look for reassurance and seek safety, the more anxious and unsafe you'll feel in the long term.

The answer to this conundrum is to accept the possibility that your partner could one day leave you (even if that situation isn't terribly likely) or that your safety will be compromised and you will either survive or not. Stop seeking safety and reassurance from others who can't actually give you any guarantees! Instead, start stopping your tongue and letting your fears subside on their own. They will, if you only let them!

Listing the people that you most often approach for reassurance helps you recognise your self defeating habits. As a rule, you tend to wrestle reassurance from the people you're most comfortable with like partners, close friends, and family. Resisting this helps you to learn to give yourself reasonable reassurance and may improve your relationships with those close to you. Try re-focusing your attention onto how the people you care about most are feeling and what's going on in their lives rather than using them solely to quell your fears and anxieties.

Use Worksheet 7-12 to help you to desist with pointless reassurance seeking and self-defeating safety seeking.

Worksheet 7-12   My Reassurance and Safety Seeking Checklist

My primary emotional/psychological problem:

Who do I go to for bouts of reassurance? List names of specific people:	
Does this reassurance last for more than a few hours or days? (Answer Yes or No only)	
How do I try to safeguard my safety? List specific actions:	
Who do I ask to try and guarantee my safety? List names of specific people:	
Do I then feel safe for more than a few minutes or hours? (Answer Yes or No only)	

Do I end up going through the same safety and reassurance processes over and over again? (Answer Yes or No only)	
What does this tell me about my attempts to make myself feel safe and reassured in the long term?	
Is it a long-term solution? (Answer Yes or No only)	
How might resisting the urge to seek safety and ask for reassurance benefit me in the long term?	

Putting Petals on Your Vicious Flower

You've heard of a vicious circle? We now give you the vicious flower. This flower involves all the principles embodied in the worksheets throughout this chapter and provides a more visual image of how you may be perpetuating your own problems without even realising that you're doing so! Some people respond better to visual aids than to written ones. Or maybe you want to use both, which is also fine.

Use these steps for filling out your vicious flower:

1. **In the trigger box, record an event that leads you to feel an unhealthy emotion such as guilt, depression, anxiety, or shame.**

   See Chapter 6 for more about healthy and unhealthy emotions.

2. **In the middle circle, write down any thoughts or meanings you give to the trigger.**

3. **In the top petal, record what aspects of the experience you focus on most when you're triggered off.**

4. **In the corresponding petals, record your emotions, behaviours, and physical sensations in response to the trigger event.**

Jon has panic attacks. When in the grip of an attack, he feels that he's about to collapse. He tries to sit down or to hold onto something solid such as a lamppost. Jon thinks that drinking water will stop the panic. He also tries to stop or abate physical sensations such as dizziness, heart racing, and sweating. He thinks that others will mock him about his attacks and behaviour. Worksheet 7-13 shows how Jon filled in the petals on his vicious flower.

Worksheet 7- 13	Jon's Vicious Flower

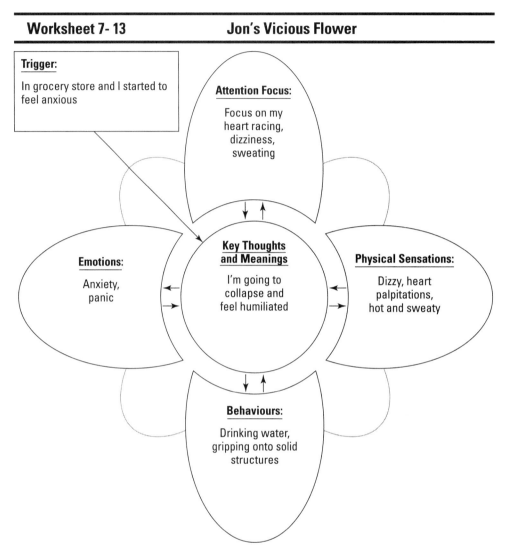

Trigger:

In grocery store and I started to feel anxious

Attention Focus:

Focus on my heart racing, dizziness, sweating

Key Thoughts and Meanings

I'm going to collapse and feel humiliated

Emotions:

Anxiety, panic

Physical Sensations:

Dizzy, heart palpitations, hot and sweaty

Behaviours:

Drinking water, gripping onto solid structures

Now think about your own psychological or emotional problem and fill in the vicious flower in Worksheet 7-14 for a visual view of your self-defeating coping strategies.

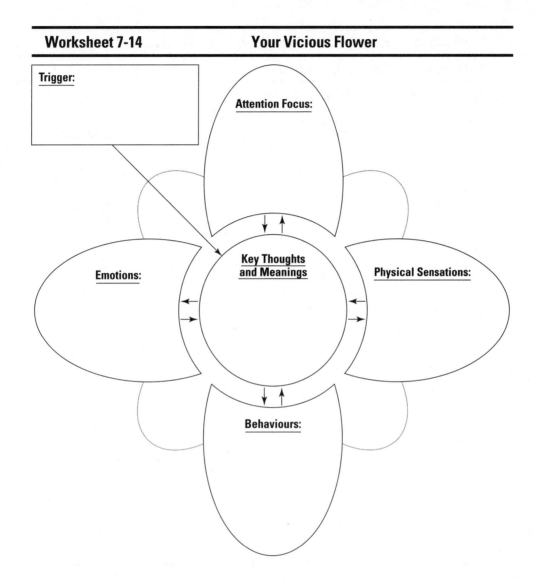

Worksheet 7-14 **Your Vicious Flower**

Trigger:

Attention Focus:

Key Thoughts and Meanings

Emotions:

Physical Sensations:

Behaviours:

Uprooting your vicious flower

Now you need to tear out the roots of your vicious, flaming, fretful, and ferocious flower! And doing so is pretty straightforward in theory, if sometimes not in practice. Hopefully, filling in the fearsome flower will bring to light how you're keeping the nasty thing growing.

Poor sweet Jon, as shown in Worksheet 7-13, tries to stop his panic symptoms by telling himself that he ought to be able to control his wobbly legs, racing heart, and sweating by sitting down or grabbing onto any available solid structure. But in actual fact, he only ends up increasing his feelings of anxiety and panic. Jon used Worksheet 7-15 to uproot his poisonous petunia.

Worksheet 7-15	Jon's Uprooting the Vicious Flower Format
My primary problem: Panic attacks	
My key thoughts and unhelpful attitudes about my primary problem:	I'll collapse if I don't stop my dizzy sensations! My legs are already wobbly and will give way from under me. This will be so humiliating; everyone will laugh at me and ridicule me!
Helpful attitudes about my primary problem:	If I collapse, so be it. Even if people laugh at me, I can take it. Chances are that someone will try to help me rather than ridicule me. I can still respect myself as a whole person in view of my panic attacks.
Physical sensations I can accept and not try to stop or control (even though I hate them!):	Dizziness Wobbly legs Racing heart
Behaviours I can try to resist in the face of my trigger situation:	Don't sit down Ride out the panic until it subsides Stop carrying a bottle of water with me everywhere Stop grabbing on to objects that may provide physical support

Now have a go at uprooting your own vicious flower in Worksheet 7-16.

Worksheet 7-16	My Uprooting the Vicious Flower Format
My primary problem:	
My key thoughts and unhelpful attitudes about my primary problem:	
Helpful attitudes about my primary problem:	

Physical sensations I can accept and *not* try to stop or control (even though I *hate* them!):	
Behaviours I can try to resist in the face of my trigger situation:	

Flaying that flower until it's dead

Now that you've seen how the vicious flower works in the preceding sections, you're in a good place to demolish it! Try putting yourself into situations you normally avoid with a view to strengthening your belief in your ability to cope.

Worksheet 7-17 can help you identify activities that challenge your self-defeating beliefs.

The more you confront feared situations, the more likely you are to extinguish your fear and increase your conviction in your ability to negotiate such situations successfully. If you use strategies to help you deal with fear or other unwelcome feelings in specific situations, you're best off dropping these all together. Dropping these safety behaviors (see Chapter 9 for more on safety behaviours) probably means that you'll feel worse in the short term, but you will benefit in the long run. You'll see that you can withstand the feelings of anxiety or general discomfort and self-consciousness you may feel by doing *nothing at all to stop or abate them*. Basically the message is that anxiety, embarrassment, social awkwardness, and self-consciousness are distinctly unpleasant but they won't – under any circumstances – kill you dead.

Worksheet 7-17	**Your Flower Flaying Fact File**
My primary emotional/ psychological problem:	
Situations I avoid to stop my problem being triggered:	
If I face these situations, how will it ultimately benefit me?	
Which safety seeking behaviours can I strive to drop?	

(continued)

How might dropping these safety behaviours help me to overcome my primary problem?	
What ultimate beneficial effect might flaying my flower have on my primary problem?	

Some of the exercises in this chapter may seem a bit repetitive. In our defence, we say to you, repetition is *essential!* Keep on flaying that individual psychological or emotional flower until it's very dead indeed.

Chapter 8

Getting Goal-Directed

. . . .

In This Chapter

▶ Using SPORT to score goals

▶ Increasing your motivation to change

▶ Making a goal statement

▶ Paying attention to your progress

. . . .

*U*nless you know where you're going, getting somewhere is difficult. Sometimes you may know that you're unhappy, emotionally distraught, or caught up in a cycle of self-destructive behaviours. What you may be less clear on is how exactly you want things to be different. Many people have difficulty breaking out of destructive patterns and over-coming emotional problems because they are too vague about their goals. Often we hear people say 'I just want to feel better' or 'I want my life to improve'. Whilst we're sure that these are sincere desires, they aren't specific enough to act on. In order to get the most out of any self-help, CBT, or other therapeutic treatment, you need to be clear about what your problems are and what your goals are in relation to these problems. This chapter helps you make clear problem statements and establish specific goals.

Giving Goals a SPORTing Chance

The acronym *SPORT* stands for *specific, positive, observable, realistic,* and *timed.* We'd like you to carefully consider these five aspects of your goals:

✔ **Specific:** Be precise about when, where, and with whom you want to feel and/or behave more constructively.

✔ **Positive:** State your goals in positive and pro-active terms. What do what to achieve or work towards? What do you want to strive to gain in your personal life?

✔ **Observable:** Consider how an objective individual could note that you've changed. What positive changes might you notice in your own thinking and actions?

✔ **Realistic:** Make your goals clear, concrete, and within your scope of achievement. Focus on goals which involve changing your personal reactions to life events rather than on changing others or life events over which you have very little power.

✔ **Timed:** Setting a time frame to help you keep your goals in sight. Think about setting yourself clear times to carry out identified tasks. Doing a task list with spotlighted times to do each task can help you to actually get on with what you need to do.

Feeling different

Choosing appropriate healthy negative emotions as goals in response to a negative life event is very important. You may be tempted to choose a goal of indifference. Denying real-ity may work for a short time but eventually your true feelings will catch up with you. For example, if you're going through a divorce, may want to not care about the divorce and to have no real feelings about it at all. This attitude is understandable but highly unrealistic.

If you really care about something happening to you then it is only normal and right that you should feel negatively about that situation. In order to not care about a divorce, you'd have to not care about your spouse or your marriage and this is clearly not the case. Going for a goal of indifference requires that you to lie to himself about your feelings. So you're wise to choose healthy sadness and healthy anger as emotional goals.

We strenuously recommend that you review Chapter 6 before doing the next two worksheets. Doing so will help you to choose the right emotional and behavioural goals for your situation.

The idea is not to avoid feeling any negative emotions but rather to experience healthy emotional distress instead of unhealthy emotional disturbance.

Give some serious thought to the situation/problem about which you're setting goals. Consider how you're currently feeling about the situation and what would be an appropriate and healthy emotion to feel instead. Then complete Worksheet 8-1.

Worksheet 8-1	My Emotional Goal
What is my problem situation?	
What is my unhealthy negative emotion?	
How is this emotion causing me further problems?	
What healthy negative emotion would I like to feel instead?	
How will I need to change my thinking in order to achieve this emotional goal?	
How will achieving my emotional goal be helpful to me?	

Acting different

The way you feel has great bearing on the way you act. Clear distinctions exist between behaviours associated with healthy and unhealthy negative emotions.

Healthy negative emotions allow you to adapt to circumstances and behave in constructive ways to better your situation where possible. Unhealthy negative emotions generally impede adaptation and potential problem solving (see Chapter 6). So when setting your emotional goals, including behavioural goals can be very helpful.

Completing Worksheet 8-2 can help you to clarify your goals further.

Worksheet 8-2	My Behavioural Goals
What is my problem situation?	
What is my healthy negative emotional goal?	
What sorts of actions are typical of this healthy negative emotion?	
What *specific* actions can I adopt that fit with my emotional goal?	
How will carrying out these actions be helpful to me?	

Structuring your goal statements

Your goal statement puts together the results from your completed worksheets and includes:

- ✔ Your problem situation or *trigger*
- ✔ Your emotional goal
- ✔ Your behavioural goal

Tom is currently going through a divorce. After two years of marriage his wife decided that she was no longer in love with him and initiated divorce proceedings. Tom is very angry with his wife. He finds it difficult to remain civil when they're discussing the sale of their house and other financial arrangements. Tom has not given his wife access to their home so that she can collect her belongings. The whole thing is getting rather messy and, because solicitors are involved, costly. Tom's performance at work is suffering because he is drinking to calm his enraged feelings and is often hung over or absent from work. He has stopped going out socially and spends most evenings at home brooding on how unfairly his wife has treated him. When he does speak to friends or family about the impending divorce, he either runs his wife down viciously or talks about how he might be able to get revenge. Tom knows that he's not handling this negative event very well and decides to set some goals to deal with it more constructively. His goal statement is shown in Worksheet 8-3.

Worksheet 8-3	Tom's Goal Statement

My goal is to feel _____healthy anger and sadness_____ (emotional goal)

about _____my wife divorcing me_____ (problem or situation)

and to act _____with civility toward my wife_____ (behavioural goal)

Make your own goal statement using the same template in Worksheet 8-4.

Worksheet 8-4	My Goal Statement

My goal is to feel _____ (emotional goal)

about _____ (problem or situation)

and to act _____ (behavioural goal)

Being a complete SPORT

Now you're ready to make a concise problem and goal statement. Take your work from these sections to your CBT therapist if you're seeing one. If not, keep your work and review your goals regularly to help keep you on track. Try not to lose sight of the carrot!

Worksheet 8-5 shows how Tom created his SPORT page and serves as an example of how to ask yourself the right kind of questions in order to set good goals.

Worksheet 8-5	Tom's SPORT Page
Specific: Where, when, and with whom do I want to feel/act differently?	
Where?	At work and at home.
When?	When I'm at work I want to be clear headed. I want to attend work regularly. I want to act differently when dealing with the divorce.
With whom?	My boss and work colleagues. My soon-to-be-ex wife.
How do I want to feel?	I want to feel healthy anger rather than rage.
How do I want to behave?	I want to behave in a civil and controlled manner with my wife. I want to be responsible and focused at work.
Positive: How can I state my goal in a positive form?	
What do I want to work toward feeling?	Healthy anger/annoyance.
What do I want to work toward doing?	Sorting out the divorce with a minimum of cost and disruption.

Observable: What changes will I notice when I am getting closer to my goal?	
How will I feel differently?	I'll feel sad about the end of my relationship and angry about my wife's decision but without the desire for revenge.
What will I be doing differently?	I won't drink to numb my feelings of outrage. I'll go to work regularly and without a hangover. I'll stop snapping at my colleagues and boss. I'll be able to talk to my wife calmly and coolly about arrangements for selling the house. I'll be paying less to the solicitors because my wife and I will be able to agree on details of the divorce without excessive legal mediation.
What changes might other people in my life notice?	People will see that I am at work and properly prepared to do my job. I'll be less volatile with others. My wife may notice that I'm calmer and no longer hurling abuse at her every time we speak. I'll go out more socially and make conversation other than solely discussing ways to take vengeance on my wife. I'll agree a time with my wife for her to collect her belongings.
Realistic: Is my goal concrete and within my reach?	
How hard will I need to work to achieve my goal?	Very hard at first but with practice and time I'll come to accept her decision even if I don't like it.
Do I have the necessary skills and resources to reach my goal?	Yes. I'm not usually aggressive and I'm capable of keeping a level head in other types of highly emotional situations.
Can I visualise/imagine myself reaching my goal?	Yes. I can imagine completing the divorce and moving on with my life in time.
Timed: What is a reasonable timeframe to set for achieving my goal?	
When can I get started with goal-directed behaviour?	I can start changing my angry behaviour today. The divorce should be complete within six months. I'll give myself until the actual divorce comes through to accept my wife's decision.
What days and times can I devote to carrying out goal-related tasks?	I can practise thinking in a healthy way about the divorce every day. I can also practise healthy anger tomorrow when I speak to the solicitor. I will try to be cool and controlled when I speak to my wife on Friday about the house and I'll let her come and get her stuff. I'll only drink at the weekend and abstain on week nights.
When and how often will I review my progress?	I will sit down and review my progress every Sunday evening at around 8 p.m., prior to dinner.

You can see that Tom keeps his goals to things that are within his sphere of control. Although he can't make his wife love him again, Tom can choose how to feel about and respond to the upcoming divorce.

Use the SPORT page in Worksheet 8-6 to help you really hone in on how you feel, act, and think differently.

Worksheet 8-6   My SPORT Page

Specific: Where, when, and with whom do I want to feel/act differently?

Where?	
When?	
With whom?	
How do I want to feel?	
How do I want to behave?	

Positive: How can I state my goal in a positive form?

What do I want to work toward feeling?	
What do I want to work toward doing?	

Observable: What changes will I notice when I am getting closer to my goal?

How will I feel differently?	
What will I be doing differently?	
What changes might other people in my life notice?	

Realistic: Is my goal concrete and within my reach?

How hard will I need to work to achieve my goal?	
Do I have the necessary skills and resources to reach my goal?	
Can I visualise/imagine myself reaching my goal?	

Timed: What is a reasonable timeframe to set for achieving my goal?

When can I get started with goal-directed behaviour?	
What days and times can I devote to carrying out goal-related tasks?	
When and how often will I review my progress?	

Aside from not setting SPORTing goals, another common error that people make with regard to goal setting is reaching too far and expecting too much, too soon. Your goals need to be realistic and achievable; if you set your sights too high, you may get discouraged.

Some disorders and problems can take longer than others to overcome, so try to be flexible about the time you allow yourself to reach your given goals. Avoid making your goals overly easy to achieve, though. You may decide that your goals are trivial and that reaching them isn't helping you if you fail to make them sufficiently challenging. Ideally, strike a balance between too easy and too hard.

Manufacturing More Motivation

Sometimes you may be very motivated to pursue your goals and other times you may be less enthusiastic or downright apathetic. Don't make the mistake of waiting too long for motivation to come before you get started on goal-directed action. Motivation isn't to be waited for, it's to be gone after with a club. After all, change requires effort and involves discomfort, so why would you expect to always feel utterly gung-ho about going for your goals?

You're not the only person on the planet who finds making positive change difficult and daunting at times – quite the opposite, in fact. Luckily you can use the techniques we offer in these sections to maximise your existing motivation and to get moving in the absence of motivation.

Writing up reasons for change

Inspiration and *benefit* are two watchwords here. Who or what inspires you to change your wicked (we jest, incidentally) ways and why? What are the short-, medium-, and long-term benefits of change? Thinking of sources of inspiration and recounting the benefits of carrying on with your goal pursuit can be really helpful.

Use Worksheet 8-7 to ignite your inspiration!

Worksheet 8-7	My Sources of Inspiration
Who are some role models who display characteristics I would like to adopt? (Include people you know personally or famous people and/or fictional characters)	
What characteristics do these people display that I'd like to adopt?	
How do these characteristics relate to my defined goals? (Include both emotional and behavioural goals)	
What are some inspirational stories I have heard that I can draw on?	
What lessons can I take from these stories about people overcoming adversity?	
How can I apply these lessons to my own life and my goal pursuit?	
What images or metaphors help me to visualise myself reaching my goals?	
What proverbs, quotes, song lyrics, or icons inspire me to carry on with goal-directed action?	

Carrying out a cost-benefit analysis

You can use the Cost-Benefit Analysis form (a CBA form for short) to review the benefits and the costs of your emotional and behavioural goals. Costs are inherent to giving up an unhealthy emotion or behaviour, although they very often are outweighed by the benefits of reaching your healthy emotional and behavioural goals. For example, one of the costs of giving up the unhealthy rage that Tom identifies is not impressing upon his wife and friends how badly he thinks he's been treated. Although this situation may be a short-term cost, in the long term it is small change in comparison to getting on with his life. Doing a cost-benefit analysis can help you to evaluate accurately what going for your goals *costs* you and what it ultimately *pays* you.

Short-term refers to benefits that you may feel immediately like pain relief, reassurance, fleeting anxiety/fear relief or reduced anger and/or jealousy. Short-term benefits for others may mean that you stop badgering your loved ones for specific answers or that you engage in family life rather than testing everyone.

Long-term costs and benefits relate to how you feel tomorrow, the next day or in the weeks that follow. They also include how others close to you may be affected by your behaviour in the long term. Think about whether your actions are making your relationships more secure and positive or less secure and potentially negative.

Don't forget to factor in the costs and benefits to your loved ones – close friends and family – as well as work associates who are affected by your destructive behaviour.

The more reasons you can come up with that support the benefit of positive change and emphasise the downside of staying the same, the more motivation you'll garner.

Complete the CBA form in Worksheet 8-8 to see if you can identify any costs of striving for your goals and also to highlight the benefits of doing so. Ideally, the benefits will by far outshine the costs, but remember to think *both* short and long term. Sometimes short-term pain is really a necessary step toward long-term gain!

Worksheet 8-8	**My CBA Form**

My emotional/behavioural goal: _____

Costs of obtaining my goal in the short term:

For myself:

For others:

Benefits of obtaining my goal in the short term:

For myself:

For others:

(continued)

Costs of obtaining my goal in the long term:

For myself:

For others:

Benefits of obtaining my goal in the long term:

For myself:

For others:

Do the benefits of obtaining my emotional and behavioural goals ultimately outweigh the costs in the long term?

For myself:

For others:

Why and how will I benefit most from obtaining my goals?

Tracking Your Progress

Keeping a watchful eye on your progress toward achieving your identified goals can really help to bolster motivation. Ignoring or overlooking your achievements, especially small ones, is all too easy. Even inching toward your goals is better than standing still. So take some time to review your progress, give yourself credit for effort, and note positive effects regularly.

Worksheet 8-9 provides some helpful questions to aid you in checking out your progress toward your goals. Use this report on a weekly or bi-weekly basis to help you both recognise changes and inspire you if you're flagging.

Be self-compassionate! Change is extremely hard work. So if you've not made as much headway as you'd like, be encouraging to yourself rather than being abusive or punishing. Kicking yourself when you're down is totally pointless. Instead, pick yourself up, shake yourself down, and give yourself an encouraging pat along.

Worksheet 8-9	My Progress Report
What problem/situation have I been tackling?	
What is my emotional goal?	
What is my behavioural goal?	
How long have I been working toward this goal? (Be specific about days, weeks, or months.)	
How intense is my emotional problem now? (Use a scale of 0–10 where 0 = no problem at all, 5 = Bad but I can deal with it, and 10 = The worst imaginable and impossible to cope with.)	
How intense are my behavioural problems now? (Use a scale of 0–10 where 0= no problem at all, 5= Bad but I can deal with it, and 10= The worst imaginable and impossible to cope with.)	
Has the intensity of these two problems reduced since I began working toward my identified goals?	
What changes (however small) have I made for the better?	
Is there anything that I could be doing to further my progress toward my goals?	

(continued)

Is there anything I can be thinking to further my progress toward my goals?	
How close am I to reaching my emotional and behavioural goals? (Use a scale of 1–10, where 1 = no progress at all and 10 = your goal is achieved.)	

Change is often not predictable or linear. So by all means use Worksheet 8-9 to track your progress but also be aware that you may sometimes relapse into unhealthy ways of feeling and acting. *Doing so is not a disaster.* Relapsing is very normal. Try to keep yourself on the straight and narrow, but also give yourself permission to stumble along the way. Taking two steps forward and one backward on the road to permanent change is only to be expected. Checking your progress weekly or bi-weekly (but not more often!) can help you to see that you *can* recover and move forward from a difficult week. Good luck going for your own personal gold!

Part III
Putting CBT into Practice

The 5th Wave — By Rich Tennant

"Dora's anxiety has always manifested itself in the 'flight response.'"

In this part . . .

 ow to get hands-on. The chapters in this part are all about putting CBT into practice on specific problems like anxiety, depression, addictions, poor body image, and low self opinion.

We also show you how to deal with Obsessive Compulsive Disorder and improve interpersonal relationships.

Chapter 9

Taking an Axe To Anxiety

· ·

In This Chapter

▶ Tolerating and accepting unpleasant physical effects of anxiety

▶ Facing your fears and defeating them

▶ Forming fear-defusing philosophies

▶ Working out what to do if you're a worrier

· ·

Anxiety is an emotion that leads to many uncomfortable physical sensations (see Figure 9-1 for a visual representation). Basically, *anxiety* is what you feel in response to a threatening situation. You may experience anxiety as extreme fear in the case of phobias, overwhelming physical feelings in the case of panic disorder, or as a relatively constant feeling of unease and agitation. Anxiety comes in many different forms and can affect just about anyone from any walk of life. Anxiety is not fun at all. It can be extremely unpleasant and uncomfortable. Severe anxiety can really interfere with your ability to live a satisfying life. At its worst, you may find that your anxiety restricts your socialising, prevents you from doing your job, or stops you from leaving your house.

Some people become anxious following a specific identifiable traumatic event. More often, however, anxiety slowly builds up without you being able to put your finger on a definite cause. In this chapter we show you how to confront anxiety and overcome it. No matter what form your anxiety takes, the techniques in this chapter are very likely to be useful to you.

Your doctor or psychiatrist may have diagnosed you with an anxiety disorder or you may recognise symptoms within yourself. It can be helpful to have a clear diagnosis of your particular type of anxiety problem, however, you can use this chapter to overcome your anxiety whether you've been given a formal diagnosis or not. Common anxiety disorders include:

- ✔ **Generalised anxiety disorder (GAD)** is a condition of feeling anxious to varying degrees almost all of the time. People with GAD often worry incessantly about the possibility of bad things happening to them or to their loved ones.

- ✔ **Obsessive-compulsive disorder (OCD)** can take a lot of different forms (see Chapter 13 for a comprehensive definition) but is characterised by unwelcome intrusive thoughts and a compulsion to carry out elaborate rituals in an unrealistic effort to prevent feared events from happening.

- ✔ **Panic attacks** often lead people to believe that they're having a heart attack, about to pass out, or even die because the physical sensations are so strong. Panic attacks may occur in specific situations or they can just seem to come out of the blue.

- ✔ **Phobias** are specific fears of everyday things or situations. Phobias are called irrational fears because the degree of fear experienced is out of proportion to the actual threat involved. People can develop phobias of nearly anything but more common ones include agoraphobia, a phobia of crowded places and/or being away from familiar areas where you feel safe; claustrophobia, fear of being in a confined space, needle and injection phobia, vomit phobia, animal phobias and fear of heights.

> ✔ **Post-traumatic stress disorder (PTSD)** is a state of anxiety resulting from a traumatic event which was either life threatening or significantly threatened a person's physical integrity. People can develop PTSD from witnessing an event that leads them to feel extreme fear and horror. Possible examples of traumatic events leading to PTSD may include traffic accidents, robberies, natural disasters, assault, and war events.

Philosophies that Fend Off Fear

Anxiety is pretty unpleasant, to say the least. We in no way wish to invalidate your physical symptoms, disturbing thoughts, or personal experiences, but we do want to encourage you to take on board some anti-anxiety attitudes. Think of your anxious feelings as a bully trying to convince you that he's bigger, tougher, and more dangerous than he actually is. More bark than bite, all talk and no trousers, full of hot air – you're probably getting the picture. You need to put an end to the intimidation!

Anxiety typically involves these ways of thinking:

✔ Overestimating the probability of a threat/negative event occurring.

✔ Overestimating how bad it would be if the threat/negative event did occur.

✔ Underestimating your ability to cope with or surmount the threat/negative event.

Axe your anxiety by using the following ways of thinking as weapons:

✔ Be realistic about the probability of the threat/negative event occurring: 'It could happen but it's not as likely as I imagine'.

✔ Put the badness of the threat/negative event into perspective. We call this tactic *anti-awfulising:* 'It's bad but not terrible, unfortunate but not awful, difficult but not disastrous, hard but not horrid'.

✔ Give yourself some credit for your coping abilities. Hold a high-tolerance philosophy: 'It's uncomfortable but I can stand it', 'it's difficult to cope with but I can cope', 'it's hard to bear but it's still bearable'.

The following sections give you opportunities to put these fear-defusing philosophies into practice with your specific anxiety problems and symptoms.

Surfing bodily sensations

Anxiety comes with a host of physical and mental sensations. These sensations can be intense and frightening. If you suffer from panic attacks, you're probably no stranger to many of the symptoms shown in Figure 9-1.

Misinterpreting your physical sensations as dangerous or as serious signs of ill health can be all too easy. If you don't recognise your bodily and mental sensations as part and parcel of anxiety, you may mistakenly think that you're going crazy, unable to breathe, about to pass out, having a heart attack, or even dying.

The types of symptoms shown in Figure 9-1 are very common. Though they can be deeply uncomfortable, they're not dangerous.

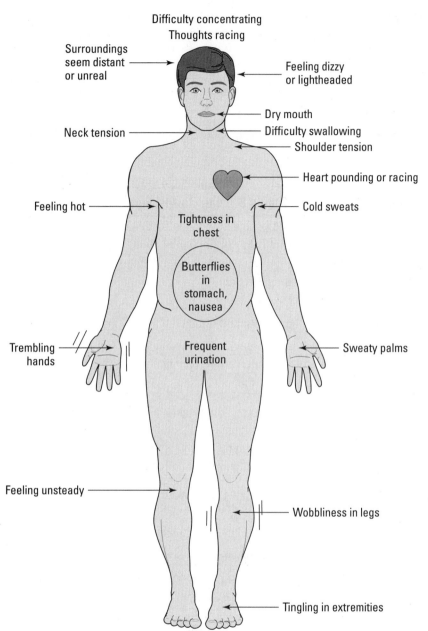

Difficulty concentrating
Thoughts racing

Surroundings
seem distant
or unreal

Feeling dizzy
or lightheaded

Dry mouth

Neck tension
Difficulty swallowing
Shoulder tension

Heart pounding or racing

Feeling hot
Cold sweats

Tightness in
chest

Butterflies
in
stomach,
nausea

Trembling
hands
Sweaty palms

Frequent
urination

Feeling unsteady

Wobbliness in legs

Tingling in extremities

Figure 9-1:
Common
physical
sensations
of anxiety.

It's understandable that you may wish to stop your symptoms and to control them. Unfortunately, these attempts to fight against the physical feelings of anxiety almost always have a paradoxical effect. You actually end up panicking about your anxious feelings and by trying to eliminate or control them, you actually worsen and perpetuate them. Your attempts to avoid, stop, or reduce physical sensations are also known as *safety behaviours*.

See your doctor if you have real health concerns worthy of medical investigation. Getting a clean bill of health prior to launching yourself into exposure exercises (more about these in the following sections and in Chapter 4) may help you to normalise your uncomfortable physical symptoms of anxiety. If you suffer from health anxiety, however (and worry that you may have a serious disease or illness despite evidence to the contrary), *resisting* seeing the doctor for frequent reassurance that you're not in ill health is probably in your best interest.

Stan suffers agoraphobia and panic attacks. He finds it almost impossible to imagine going further than a few streets from his house. If Stan can avoid public places such as shops or public transport, he does. He often gets a panic attack when he finds himself in unfamiliar surroundings or in the midst of a crowd. Usually Stan notices a hot feeling in his limbs first and then his chest tightens and he feels as though he's fighting to get enough air in his lungs. Stan tries desperately to stop the warm feeling in his arms and legs; he also frantically gasps for air.

Stan used Worksheet 9-1 to accept his physical symptoms and allow them to subside on their own.

Worksheet 9-1	Stan's Surfing Bodily Sensations Sheet
What are the main bodily sensations I experience when I'm anxious? (Refer to Figure 9-1)	Hot tingling feelings in my arms and legs Tightening in my chest Dizziness I feel like I can't breathe normally or get enough oxygen My jaw clenches and I grit my teeth
What 'awfulising' and 'I can't stand it' type thoughts do I typically have about my physical symptoms of anxiety?	As soon as I notice a physical anxiety symptom (such as heat in my limbs) I tend to think: 'Oh no, here comes another panic attack! Panic attacks are the most horrible thing in the world and I can't cope with having them anymore.' Before I knew what a panic attack was I used to think: 'Oh no, what's happening to me? I'm going to suffocate!' I also often have thoughts such as: 'I've got to prevent another panic attack' and 'I can't stand these feeling in my limbs and chest.'
What do I usually do to try and stop or control my physical symptoms of anxiety?	I try to cool myself down by sipping water or fanning myself and loosening my clothing. If I'm out in public I'll flee the situation as soon as possible and return home to safety. I try to do breathing exercises and get as much air into my lungs as possible. I grab onto something or sit down if possible. I look for places I can 'hide away' in case other people notice my behaviour and think I'm odd.

What effects do my attempts to stop or control symptoms tend to have?	I used to think that gasping for air prevented me from suffocating but it actually just makes normal breathing harder.
	Every time I flee a situation it reinforces my belief that I can't go out without panicking.
	By trying to stop my anxiety symptoms I actually focus on them more and end up making them worse.
	My attempts to sit down or hide from others reinforces my belief that panic attacks make me 'weird' and that other people will ridicule me rather than try to help me.
	Because I try so hard to stop a panic attack from happening, I deprive myself of the opportunity to see that I can actually survive them.
	All my attempts to control my anxiety symptoms lead me to panic about having a panic attack!
What are some helpful 'high tolerance'/'anti-awfulising' beliefs I can hold to help me allow these unpleasant symptoms to subside naturally?	As uncomfortable as these symptoms are, they're a natural result of anxiety and aren't dangerous.
	Having these symptoms may be extremely unpleasant but I can tolerate and cope with them.
	Panic attacks are bad but there are worse things that could happen.
	If I just let these physical sensations happen and carry on with my task, they will eventually pass by themselves.
	Anxiety doesn't make me a 'weird' or 'odd' person. I'm just a normal person who happens to have a problem with panic attacks. Other people may be more concerned about me and compassionate toward me than I imagine.

Now that you've seen how Stan used the bodily sensations sheet, you can use Worksheet 9-2 yourself.

Worksheet 9-2	My Surfing Bodily Sensations Sheet
What are the main bodily sensations I experience when anxious? (Refer to Figure 9-1)	
What 'awfulising' and 'I can't stand it' type thoughts do I typically have about my physical symptoms of anxiety?	
What do I usually do to try to stop or control my physical symptoms of anxiety?	
What effects do my attempts to stop or control symptoms tend to have?	
What are some helpful 'high toler-ance'/ 'anti-awfulising' beliefs I can hold to help me allow these unpleas-ant symptoms to subside naturally?	

After you adopt a few of your own fear-defusing philosophies and demonstrate to yourself the negative effects of working too hard to quell your anxiety symptoms, do your best to just leave them alone! Instead of fighting against the waves of anxiety, surf them. Imagine your unpleasant physical or mental sensations as a rough, choppy sea. Just let yourself ride with the waves until the storm is past. Chapter 5 offers techniques for dealing with troublesome thoughts, which can also be used to help you accept and tolerate unpleasant physical sensations.

Being realistic about the probability of bad events

When you have an anxiety problem, you fear bad things happening *and* tend to assume that they're very likely to happen. Whether you worry about becoming ill, harm coming to yourself or loved ones, being socially rejected, or having a panic attack, you overestimate the likelihood of these bad things happening.

Anxiety can influence how you think to a significant degree. You may find it useful to complete the next two worksheets *during* a bout of anxiety and again when you're *not* anxious. Doing so can help illustrate how greatly your emotional state can impede your ability to think rationally and problem solve.

Stan expects that if he walks to the town centre (about 3 miles from his home) he'll have a severe panic attack. He assumes that he'll be completely incapacitated and unable to get home again. Stan also thinks that anyone who notices his anguish will refuse to help him. He imagines being stranded far from home, with no one coming to his aid, and finally being found by the police. Stan used Worksheet 9-3 to readjust his ideas about the probability of bad things happening.

Worksheet 9-3   **Stan's Probability Page**

What is the bad event I'm imagining or predicting will happen?	*Being totally incapacitated by panic in the town centre. I'm unable to move and people look at me like I'm a freak. Hours later, the police pick me up.*

In reality, how likely is it that this bad event will happen?

0   1   2   ③   4   5   6   7   8   9   10

No probability at all	Highly unlikely to happen	Equal probability that it will or will not happen	Very likely to happen	Almost certain to happen

---

Of course, absolutely guaranteeing that the events you're imagining won't happen isn't feasible – many things are possible. But where anxiety is concerned, most of the events you predict will happen are extremely improbable.

Try being more realistic about the likelihood of your feared event occurring by using in Worksheet 9-4.

Worksheet 9-4   **My Probability Page**

What is the bad event I'm imagining or predicting will happen?	

In reality, how likely is it that this bad event will happen?

0   1   2   3   4   5   6   7   8   9   10

No probability at all	Highly unlikely to happen	Equal probability that it will or will not happen	Very likely to happen	Almost certain to happen

---

Bringing bad events back into perspective

Anxiety frequently leads you to make a feared event more terrible in your own mind than it actually is in real life. When riddled with anxiety you tend to inflate bad/negative events out of proportion and decide that they're awful, world ending, and unbearable. Happily, events rarely are this bad. Most of the time you'd cope with your feared event no matter how uncomfortable and difficult it may be.

Anti-anxiety ways of thinking involve increasing your belief in your ability to cope with unpleasant sensations and events. Try telling yourself that you can and will cope with your anxiety – even though it's not easy to do so. Remind yourself that you've come through episodes of fear and panic before, and despite finding it intensely uncomfortable, you've survived. You can also try to develop healthier attitudes about the possibility of other people judging you negatively. Attaching too much importance to what others may be thinking of you will cause you to feel even more anxious. Instead take the attitude that 'it's unfortunate if others think badly of me but it's not terrible or unbearable'. Bear in mind that however embarrassing you find your symptoms of anxiety, other people may be more compassionate and understanding than you expect.

Let's take Stan's fear of having a panic attack in the town centre and see how he used Worksheet 9-5 to put his panic predictions back into perspective. Stan tried to think rationally and objectively about his ability to cope with his panic sensations and other people's possible reactions to him.

Worksheet 9-5	Stan's Perspective Page
What is the bad event I'm imagining or predicting will happen?	Being totally incapacitated by panic in the town centre. I'm unable to move and people look at me like I'm a freak. Hours later the police pick me up.

In reality, how bad would it be if this event actually happened?

0	1	2	3	4	5	6	⑦	8	9	10

| Not bad at all | | Minimally bad but fairly easy to cope with | | | Moderately bad but many worse things could happen. I'd still manage to cope | | Very bad and extremely difficult to cope with | Worst possible thing ever | |

What thoughts/beliefs would help me to successfully cope with this bad event if it actually happened?	I'm having symptoms of anxiety and they will pass in time. I can tolerate these intensely unpleasant feelings and they will diminish of their own accord. If people think I'm a freak, they're wrong. I'm just having a panic attack!
What practical action could I take to resolve or adjust to the event if it actually happened?	I could try to redirect my attention away from my physical symptoms and onto a task such as shopping. I could allow my symptoms to subside and then make my way back home on foot as planned. I could ask for help if I really needed to. If I really was stranded, I could call a friend to pick me up.

Now try to really give yourself some credit for your coping skills as you fill in Worksheet 9-6.

Worksheet 9-6	My Perspective Page
What is the bad event I'm imagining or predicting will happen?	

In reality, how bad would it be if this event actually happened?

0	1	2	3	4	5	6	7	8	9	10

| Not bad at all | | Minimally bad but fairly easy to cope with | | | Moderately bad but many worse things could happen. I'd still manage to cope | | | Very bad and extremely difficult to cope with | Worst possible thing ever | |

What thoughts/beliefs would help me to successfully cope with this bad event if it actually happened?	
What practical action could I take to resolve or adjust to the event if it actually happened?	

Exposing Yourself

Exposure exercises involve identifying your fears and making plans to face up to them. Facing your fears in a planned and deliberate way is the best way we know to overcome anxiety problems. While facing your fears isn't fun, it is effective. Think about how fed up you are with your anxiety problem. Have you had enough of living your life through a veil of fear? Do you think the short-term pain of doing exposure work is worth it for the long-term gain of beating anxiety? We hope so. Following is a list of points for executing effective exposures:

✔ Make your exposures challenging enough to be pretty uncomfortable but not so overwhelming that you're unlikely to stick with the technique.

✔ Keep exposing yourself to feared situations regularly and make them progressively more challenging each time.

Once is not enough. As a rule you need to keep exposing yourself to your fears regularly until you become habituated or desensitised to them.

✔ Make your exposure sessions long enough for them to work. Stay in the situation until your anxious feelings reduce by about 50 per cent.

✔ Take note of things you do to try to avoid or control aspects of your anxiety. We call these actions *safety behaviours*. During exposure sessions make every effort to resist any safety behaviours.

✔ Remind yourself that FEAR in CBT terminology stands for: Face Everything And Recover!

✔ Hold the belief that you can accept, tolerate, and withstand the discomfort of anxiety. You don't have to *like* it but you can *survive* it.

✔ Keep a record of your exposure work so that you can track your progress.

In the following sections we include worksheets to enable you to put these points into practice.

Challenging yourself to a duel

The idea is not to fight your symptoms of anxiety but rather to fight the avoidance and safety seeking behaviours that fuel your anxiety.

The next worksheet involves two simple steps:

1. **In the first column, make a list of 5 to 10 situations in which you typically experience anxiety.**

2. **In the second column, give each situation a rating from 0 to 10, where 0 = No anxiety at all, 5 = moderate anxiety, and 10 = extreme anxiety, as bad as it gets based on the degree of anxiety you anticipate experiencing.**

Worksheet 9-7 shows panic-attack prone Stan's list.

Worksheet 9-7	Stan's List of Challenges
Anxiety-provoking Situation	*Anticipated Degree of Anxiety*
1. Going to the corner shop	3
2. Phoning work about my sick leave	9
3. Walking to the town centre	10
4. Going shopping for groceries	8
5. Going to the local pub	6
6. Going back to work	10
7. Taking the bus	7
8. Sitting in my garden	1
9. Answering the phone	2
10. Going to my friend's house	5

Now make your own list of challenges using Worksheet 9-8. You don't need to list them in order of difficulty at this stage. Just record them as they come to your mind and then give them an anxiety rating from 0 to 10.

Worksheet 9-8	Your List of Challenges
Anxiety-provoking Situation	*Anticipated Degree of Anxiety*
1.	
2.	
3.	
4.	
5.	
6.	
7.	
8.	
9.	
10.	

Include situations that you've been avoiding due to your anxious feelings. If you've been anxious and avoidant for a long time, you may forget to include activities that you once did. Really thoroughly investigate aspects of your life that have been neglected due to anxiety.

This is the easy bit. Simply refer to Worksheet 9-8 and the ratings you allocated to feared situations. Next list your rated situations from mildest (minimal anxiety) to most severe (major anxiety) in Worksheet 9-9. The final column of the worksheet can be used to rate how high your anxiety actually was when you confronted a specific situation. Often times this rating will be lower than your anticipated rating. This is because the anticipation of doing something you fear is often worse than the actual doing of it. The idea is to fill in this column *after* your exposure work.

Worksheet 9-9	My Graded Hierarchy	
Anxiety-provoking Situation	*Anticipated Anxiety Level (on a scale of 0–10)*	*Actual Anxiety Level (on a scale of 0–10)*

And there you have it, your fear-facing heirarchy. Now you can plan when and where to face your anxiety provoking situations starting from baby steps to giant steps. Your hierarchy gives you a sensible order of anxieties to confront and overcome and the next section help you devise a plant to do that.

Preparing your exposure plan

Now you need to transform intention into action. Most people are unlikely to get started with exposures unless they allocate the time to do so. Frankly, exposing yourself to your fears isn't a barrel of laughs and so putting it off is easier than getting on with it. But putting off exposure work in the present means putting up with anxiety in the future. Chapter 8 shows you how to conduct a cost–benefit analysis that can help elicit personal commitment to a goal. You may want to do a CBA form from that chapter if your commitment to exposure work is waning.

Exposing yourself often isn't as bad as you think it will be. The more often you do exposure work, the more quickly you'll overcome your anxiety problem.

Using your results from Worksheet 9-9, list your least anxiety provoking situations and the anxiety rating you gave to each. Stan, for example, recorded sitting in his garden, answering the phone, and going to the corner shop as his first three exposure activities. These become your first targets of specific exposure activities to confront. Now decide exactly which day and at what time you will do your first exposure session. Committing yourself to a definite time helps you to actually do it. Also allocate times to repeat the *same* exposure since repetition is the key to overcoming your anxieties. Don't leave more than a day between repetitions if at all possible. The more often you do exposure work the better. Stan decided to sit in his garden for half an hour three times a day for the whole week. He also decided to answer his phone every time it rang and to go to the corner shop once on Monday, twice on Tuesday, and three times on Wednesday.

The time you need to spend in any exposure situation will vary but the rule of thumb is to remain in the situation until your anxiety has significantly diminished (ideally by about 50 per cent). After you've done a few exposure sessions for each of your identified anxiety-provoking activities you can review hierarchy gradings and see how much your anxiety has decreased.

Use Worksheet 9-10 to help you prepare your exposure plan.

Worksheet 9-10		My Exposure Plan	
Specific Exposure Activity	*Hierarchy Grading*	*Day and Time Allocated to First Exposure Session*	*Days and Times Allocated to Repeat Exposures*

Progressing through your graded hierarchy ensures that you challenge yourself without overwhelming yourself. However, don't go too slow! Think about whether you'd be able to manage going up the tiers of your hierarchy two at a time. Jump in at the deep end if you think you can manage it.

Keeping good accounts

A record of your efforts helps you to see the progress you've made. Maintaining a record also helps you to see whether or not you're staying in the situation long enough for your anxiety to come down *naturally.* The length of time you need to stick with an exposure session in order for it to be effective varies. Sometimes 20 minutes may be long enough, but in other situations you may need to tough out your discomfort for an hour or even longer. So rating your anxiety at the beginning, middle, and end of an exposure session can be a useful tool.

Use Worksheet 9-11 to record your exposure work. Again 0= no anxiety at all, 5 = moderate anxiety, and 10 = severe anxiety

Worksheet 9-11	My Exposure Activity Account			
Description of Exposure Activity	*Total Length of Exposure Session*	*Initial Anxiety Rating 0–10*	*Middle Anxiety Rating 0–10*	*End Anxiety Rating 0–10*

Searching Out Your Safety Behaviours

Chapter 7 is all about solutions that are ultimately self-defeating. In other words, these so-called solutions may give you some short-term relief but they end up keeping your problems going or even making them worse. Sometimes your anxiety may remain high during an exposure. If this situation occurs, you may be using a safety behaviour without realising it. Searching out all your safety behaviours and to making a note of them is crucial for just this reason. Doing so gives you a much better chance of dropping them.

A *safety behaviour* is anything you do to try to minimise your anxious feelings, prevent others from noticing your anxiety, or keep yourself safe from imagined events like collapsing during a panic attack. The list of possible safety behaviours is pretty much endless but Stan provides an example of some of the more common safety behaviours people use to deal with panic.

To uncover your own safety behaviours take careful note of what you do in anxiety provoking situations, however minor, because you think it will help you to cope.

Stan realised that he was using a lot of different behaviours because he thought they'd either stave off panic or curtail his panic sensations. Stan recorded his self-sabotaging strategies for dealing with his panic attacks and agoraphobia on Worksheet 9-12. Have a look at a few examples.

Worksheet 9-12	Stan's Safety Behaviours
Feared Situation	**Typical Safety Behaviours**
Going on the bus	Sitting by the door
	Listening to my iPod
	Avoiding eye contact with others
	Monitoring my breathing
Going to the corner shop	Going when it's quiet
	Having the correct change in advance
	Paying quickly and rushing home
Going to the local pub	Facing away from others
	Dressing in light clothes to stop feeling hot
	Planning when I can leave and go home
	Avoiding alcohol in case I get dizzy
	Fiddling with my keys and phone to hide my shaking hands
	Monitoring myself for symptoms of panic

Now look at your graded hierarchy in Worksheet 9-9 and really think about anything you do in those situations to try to stop, minimise, or control your anxious feelings and physical sensations. List them on Worksheet 9-13.

Worksheet 9-13	My Safety Behaviours
Feared Situation	*Typical Safety Behaviours*

Ways Out Of Wearisome Worry

If you have an anxiety problem of one kind or another, chances are that you worry. Sure everyone worries from time to time. In order to avoid worry all together you'd have to not care about anything. But there's a big difference between healthy concern and unhealthy anxiety. The latter involves unproductive worry. (Refer to Chapter 6 for further information about the differences between healthy and unhealthy negative emotions.) Worry takes up a lot of time and energy, is unproductive, and feeds anxiety.

You can use Worksheet 9-14 to figure out whether or not you're a full-blown worrier.

Worksheet 9-14	My Worrier Worksheet

What are my top 3 current worries?

1.

2.

3.

Do my worries have common themes? Do I tend to worry about the same types of things over and over? Record themes below:

Theme 1:

Theme 2:

Theme 3:

Is worrying disrupting my sleep, dampening my enjoyment of life, damaging my relationships, or impairing my ability to concentrate/function? List specific examples of how your worry is problematic:

Do you believe that you're able to effectively cope with your identified worry themes?

❑	❑	❑	❑
Definitely yes	Possibly not	Probably not	Definitely not

Once you resolve one worry, do you soon afterward find yourself focusing on a new worry?

❑	❑	❑	❑
Almost never	Sometimes	Often	Almost always

Do you think that if only you could resolve all your worries that you'd finally be able to relax?

❑	❑	❑	❑
Almost never	Sometimes	Often	Almost always

Do you frequently worry about possible negative events that haven't even happened?

❑	❑	❑	❑
Almost never	Sometimes	Often	Almost always

Do you try to solve every potential problem before it happens?

❑	❑	❑	❑
Almost never	Sometimes	Often	Almost always

Do you believe that worrying will either prepare you for bad events or prevent bad things from happening?

❑	❑	❑	❑
Almost never	Sometimes	Often	Almost always

If you notice that your current most pressing worries tend to recur time and again albeit in slightly different forms, then you have some definite worry themes. This means that you probably tend to worry about these areas of your life too much, even when nothing is going wrong. Common worry themes often include finances, health, relationships and other people's opinions of you. This worksheet is devised to help you understand that you may have a worry problem more than you have actual problems. In other words the process of worrying is what's causing you the most trouble.

If you ticked lots of 'definitely' and 'always' boxes in Worksheet 9-14, you probably worry to an unhealthy degree.

If you've been worrying for a long time, you may not understand that you can train yourself to let go of worrying thoughts. Worrying is like a bad habit and with persistence you can break it. Doing so takes a lot of hard work but the result is soooo worth it. You may feel strange and even vulnerable when you first start resisting your worry habit. With time you'll get used to the sweet relief of no longer being a constant worrier.

Don't give yourself too much time to worry. Absorb yourself in activities and become skilled at redirecting your attention away from worrying thoughts. Chapter 5 has more advice on how to redirect your thoughts. (You may find some of the exercises in Chapters 12, 13, and 18 useful too.) Choose activities that require concentration, like solving puzzles, doing accounts, or listening to others. Exercise is also good for you in so many ways and can really help you to 'sweat out' your worries.

When worry takes hold, try using Worksheet 9-15 to break its grip.

Worksheet 9-15	My Worry Whacker Worksheet
My current worry:	
Is this worry an actual problem that I can work to solve today?	
If yes, what practical actions can I take to solve the problem?	
Step 1:	
Step 2:	
Step 3:	
Step 4:	
Step 5:	
If not, what activities can I turn my attention to instead of focusing on my worrying thoughts?	
1.	
2.	
3.	
4.	
5.	

Worry is a stubborn customer. Don't be fooled by niggling feelings that you should be worrying about something. Remind yourself that worrying does nothing to prevent or solve problems. You can negotiate life just fine minus the worry habit.

Chapter 10

Attacking Addictive Behaviours and Attitudes

*E*xcessive use of alcohol and illicit or illegal 'recreational' drugs has become increasingly commonplace over the past five years or more. With the advent and continued sophistication of the Internet, online gambling, pornography and shopping have become available to virtually everyone. It is even possible to order prescription drugs via the Internet, though this is a very dangerous practice since you have no medical supervision and no way of verifying the quality of the drugs you receive.

As a result of the stigma attached to the label 'addiction' or 'addict' many people are reluctant to confront their problem. Sometimes the term 'dependency' is more palatable. Whichever term you feel most comfortable using, the strategies offered in this chapter are likely to be of help to you. Throughout this chapter we refer to your drug of choice as your 'DOC' for the sake of ease. DOC means any substance you put into your body or any compulsive behaviour you consistently rely upon to function daily and/or facilitate stress relief. We also use the term 'use' to refer to engaging in or partaking of your DOC.

Giving up an addiction (or dependency) on drugs, alcohol, gambling, Internet porn and so on is far from easy. However, much as you may understand the negative impact of your addiction on your life, it may also be difficult to imagine life without it. You may be one of the many people in the world who doubts your ability to cope with life stress without falling back on your DOC as a crutch. Despite how difficult it may seem to deprive yourself of the immediate comfort of using a substance or activity – you can do it. But doing so does require some stubbornness and commitment on your part. This chapter offers some guidance for determining how serious your dependency actually is, tips on getting on the road to recovery and plenty of worksheets to keep you on the path toward a healthier and happier lifestyle.

Keep calm and carry on!

Defining Dependency

If you are reading this chapter then you are probably aware that you do, in fact, have a DOC and that using it is causing some degree of disruption to your work life, social life, relationships, study or general day-to-day productivity and enjoyment. It is slightly tricky to isolate the point at which 'use' and 'misuse' (of a substance or activity) cross over. When use of substances, or engagement in activities like gambling for example, begin to have a discernible negative impact on the quality of your relationships, your work performance or your financial, security, your DOC use has very probably got out of hand. And you may well have crossed the threshold from 'use' to 'misuse'. You may be 'addicted' or 'dependent'. Both terms are much the same in terms of definition, though you may feel more comfortable applying one or the other to yourself.

Dependency (or addiction) usually refers to a habitual reliance on a substance (drugs or alcohol) or a compulsive behaviour (shopping, gambling or porn use). Reliance means typically that you have difficulty doing without your DOC either most days, during stressful times or find yourself using it in a 'binge' fashion. This means going 'dry' for days or even weeks and then having a real blowout.

Worksheet 10-1 can help you to decide whether or not you have a dependency and how severe it may be. Check the boxes that apply to you and your DOC, whatever it may be.

This is a personal exercise for your own benefit. You can decide with whom to share it – if, when and where. In the first instance, it is most important that you be honest with yourself and that you answer the questions as openly as possible. You have nothing to lose by being frank with yourself; but you do stand to gain valuable insight into the reality of your DOC use, and hence a chance to turn things around in your life!

Worksheet 10-1	Determining Dependency Checklist

During the past three weeks, have I:

- ❏ Lost time at work as a result of DOC use?
- ❏ Used my DOC on a given day, despite resolving to resist?
- ❏ Used my DOC at times of day that others would consider inappropriate or socially unacceptable?
- ❏ Found it very difficult to go for a day or more without using my DOC?
- ❏ Made efforts to minimise or hide my DOC use from others?
- ❏ Tried to normalise or justify my DOC use (using arguments such as 'I really need it right now' and 'everyone else does something like this, too')?
- ❏ Felt irritable or down when deprived of my DOC?
- ❏ Neglected daily tasks or previously enjoyed activities as a result of DOC use and/or effects of using?
- ❏ Allowed work/family/social commitments to suffer as a result of hangovers, come-downs, actual using or preoccupation with my DOC?
- ❏ Suffered an accident, injury or financial mishap as a result of DOC use?
- ❏ Been confronted (directly or indirectly) by friends/family members/employers/ co-workers/my doctor about the effects of my DOC use?

If you have answered 'yes' to even one of the items in this checklist, you may have a dependency worthy of attention. Answering 'yes' to three or more items may mean that you need to take serious steps toward addressing your addiction. These steps may include seeking external support from medical professionals and addiction recovery groups. The remainder of this chapter will steer you toward further addressing your DOC use and point you toward a recovery plan. So please don't be tempted to slam the book shut – read on and give yourself a fair chance to make positive changes.

Trying to 'talk yourself out of' facing up to addictive behaviours isn't uncommon. One morning you may be determined to quit and by the afternoon you've convinced yourself that you can handle moderate use and you don't actually need to go cold turkey. The lure of a DOC is very deceptive, manipulative and compelling. Don't let your addictive urges talk you out of a recovery plan.

Acknowledging Addiction Antecedents

Addictions serve a purpose. Though ultimately damaging in the long term, they usually start out as providing instantaneous or short-term relief from emotional, physical or mental pain – and sometimes all three. One of the first steps in overcoming your addiction is to fully recognise the function it serves in your life. In order to 'give it up', you need to replace your DOC with other, healthier, substitute behaviours, so really examining the reasons you rely upon it makes sense.

You can use Worksheet 10-2 in one of three ways. You can consider when you most recently used your DOC, or when you typically use your DOC, or the circumstances around your using behaviour over the past one to two weeks. Looking closely at when you are most likely to use gives you a good indication of why you do so. Worksheet 10-2 provides some questions to guide your exploration.

Kit smokes marijuana every day. Sometimes she waits until the evening to have her first joint but on her days off and at weekends she tends to start smoking as soon as she wakes up. As a result of this behaviour, Kit has stopped doing activities that she used to enjoy. Some of her friends have told her that they are concerned about how much she smokes. Here's how Kit completed Worksheet 10-2.

Worksheet 10-2	Figuring out the Function of my DOC Use
What day/time of day was it?	Thursday. About 6:30pm.
What type of mood was I in?	I was fed-up and mentally tired from work.
Who was I with?	I'd just got in from work and was alone.
What thoughts were going through my mind?	I was thinking about how dull my job is and wondering if I should look for something different.
What emotions was I experiencing?	I was a bit low and kind of fed-up.
Did I justify my using to others or myself?	I thought I deserved to get high on account of having been at work all day.
What had been going on earlier that day?	I'd been at work slaving away in front of a computer screen, as usual.

Was I trying to avoid an unpleasant task by using?	Not on this occasion.
What might I have done instead of using?	Gone out for a walk with the dog, had a bath, maybe called a friend to de-brief about work.
When (at what stage) did I make the decision to use?	Probably around lunchtime.

From her answers to Worksheet 10-2 Kit can see that she smoked (on this occasion) largely as a means to 'de-stress' from work, which she finds dull. She also made the decision to smoke much earlier in the day than she realised. Chances are Kit uses her DOC for different reasons at different times. Filling out Worksheet 10-2 on a regular basis can help her to understand when she is at most risk of using and/or relapse.

Now follow Kit's example and use Worksheet 10-3 to better understand the function of your own addiction.

Worksheet 10-3   Figuring out the Function of my DOC Use

What day/time of day was it?	
What type of mood was I in?	
Who was I with?	
What thoughts were going through my mind?	
What emotions was I experiencing?	
Did I justify my using to others or myself?	
What had been going on earlier that day?	

Was I trying to avoid an unpleasant task by using?	
What might I have done instead of using?	
When (at what stage) did I make the decision to use?	

Give a good deal of thought to the answers you provide in Worksheet 10-3. The more you understand about the reasons you use your DOC, the better armed you are for anticipating high-risk situations (times when you are most inclined to use) and recognising the point at which you decide to use (affording you a chance to revoke your decision).

Targeting Triggers

The use of substances such as alcohol and illicit drugs (or engaging in compulsive behaviours like gambling, excessive shopping and porn use) is sometimes referred to as 'self-medicating'. Mental health professionals often use this term because it reflects the addicted individual's misguided attempt to manage emotional pain and mental discomfort. If you're suffering from an anxiety or a depressive disorder, for example, you may resort to alcohol as a means of getting some temporary relief. The problem is that using a DOC for immediate relief from discomfort leads to worsened symptoms in the long run (and additional practical problems), for example:

✔ Alcohol is a depressant. Excessive drinking often does have the immediate effect of reducing feelings of stress and alleviating depressive rumination (recursive bleak thoughts). However it can also heighten existing mood states, leading you to lash out in anger when drunk or become very tearful and maudlin. Hangovers typically magnify depressed feelings (and sometimes suicidal thoughts) and can also produce anxiety symptoms and feelings of paranoia. Quite a high price to pay for very short-lived pain relief.

Steering clear of DOCs

Not everyone with a history of addiction needs to remain abstinent from their DOC forever. However, most people do, certainly in early recovery. Many recovered addicts say that not starting (drinking, gambling, surfing porn or getting high) at all is easier than trying to stop once started. For example, you may put your recovery at tremendous risk by trying to become a 'social' drinker or smoker when moderate use has never been your strong suit. Be wary of hoodwinking yourself into believing that you can use in moderation after a few weeks or months of abstinence. Err on the side of caution and give your DOC a wide berth. Otherwise you may just have to go through the pain and effort of giving up all over again.

✔ Illicit and illegal drugs such as cocaine, marijuana and heroin (to name a few of the more common ones) also can promote relaxation, energy and a sense of well-being whilst actually active in your system. But what goes up must come down – and in the case of a drug high, the comedown can be a tremendous thud.

✔ Compulsive activities like gambling, pornography use and 'shopoholic' sprees also provide immediate distraction from mental/emotional anguish. Afterwards, however, you may be plagued by anxiety about money spent, guilt, shame and self-reproach.

In addition to the psychological pitfalls of DOC use that we've just outlined,, it also very commonly results in serious practical problems that can be difficult to rectify, such as:

✔ Debt, financial crisis, inability to get credit, loss of savings or loss of home.

✔ Driving bans, trouble with the police and the law.

✔ Work problems such as damage to professional reputation, disciplinary action (resulting from failure to meet targets or repeated absence) and even job loss.

✔ Damage to social and familial relationships sometimes resulting in divorce, separation, loss of contact with children and alienation from peer group.

✔ Health problems resulting from the long-term effects of DOC use and injuries incurred whilst under the influence.

Are the minimal immediate benefits of using your DOC really worth the maximum price you pay in the longer term?

Having investigated the function of your DOC on specific occasions (in Worksheet 10-3), you're now ready to get really specific about your using triggers.

Have a look at Worksheet 10-4 and tick off the items you recognise as triggers for your DOC use.

Worksheet 10-4	Typical Triggers Checklist
❏	Hurt. These are often a result of interpersonal conflict and ructions in significant relationships, both in the home and workplace. DOC use may help to take the sting out of criticism or rejection – temporarily. Ultimately, though, your DOC use is very likely to cause further interpersonal difficulties of its own. (Chapter 15 covers relationship difficulties.)
❏	Anger. Being angry with a person or situation can lead to DOC use to 'take the edge off' your feelings. Everyday hassles like queues, rude shop assistants and traffic jams can provoke frustration. Addiction, however, can make you irritable (as a result of hangovers, comedowns or financial crisis) and more susceptible to provocation in the first place. (Chapter 15 has tips for controlling anger.)
❏	Boredom. Feeling 'at a loose end' or 'fed up' are often triggers to DOC use. You may no longer remember healthy activities that you once used to relieve boredom because your DOC has become your default solution. Try to unearth alternative activities long buried beneath your DOC and reintroduce them into your daily life. (Have a look at Chapter 18 for extra hints and tips.)

❑   Depression and disappointment. These emotions can be very painful and leave you feeling hopeless and helpless; you then resort to using a DOC. Talking to friends or professionals can really help you to find solutions to practical problems and help assuage painful feelings. (Chapter 12 looks more closely at depression and how to deal with it.)

❑   Guilt and/or shame. These feelings can become a vicious circle. You may feel fundamentally guilty and ashamed about your DOC use and then use it even more to block out these feelings. Accept yourself as a fallible, worthwhile human being with a dependency/addiction. Don't let yourself off the hook – the responsibility for your recovery from addiction lies with you – but be compassionate and encouraging with yourself during recovery. (See Chapters 14 and 23 for more tips on how to befriend yourself in your time of need.)

❑   Grief. Loss of a loved one through death, relocation or relationship breakdown is a unique kind of pain. It's common for people to try to anaesthetise the pain of grief with alcohol or drugs. However, doing so can impede the grieving process, making it longer and ultimately more painful. You need to adjust to loss and come to terms with life without your loved one. Let others give you support and understanding. Using a DOC merely prevents you from feeling appropriately sad and confronting the painful reality of loss.

❑   Reward. An ice-cold beer after a long day working in the office may seem perfectly deserved and reasonable. However, using your DOC as a means of self-reward is often just a convenient justification. Every small task can become an 'I deserve it' opportunity to use. Other, healthier, ways of rewarding yourself for hard work exist – you just need to think creatively.

❑   Loneliness and isolation. If you're feeling alone and apart from others, your DOC can seem like an accessible, undemanding companion. Unfortunately, your DOC doesn't just want to be your friend – it wants to be your only friend. Increased using inevitably leads to further isolation and loneliness. Re-engage with friends and put yourself back into the social sphere by joining clubs, a dating agency or taking a class. (Also consider getting a pet! We always suggest finding a furry friend.)

❑   Anxiety and stress. Sometimes just the thought of (or initial decision/plan to use) your DOC can provide instant stress relief. Such is the psychological power of addiction. Drugs and alcohol do alter your mood state and can reduce feelings of anxiety and stress in the short term. However, they do little to solve the root of the problem. Lifestyle change or professional treatment to reduce your stress and anxiety are far more permanent and sustainable solutions. (Chapters 6 and 9 cover anxiety and stress.)

❑   Self-pity. 'Woe is me', 'why me?', 'poor me', 'helpless me' and so on – okay, we get it. You suffer. Whilst that is unfortunate, suffering is also part of the human condition and you are not alone in feeling pain. Having a good old moan from time to time is one way of venting your woes. Or you can seek external help (professional or otherwise) with problems. Using your DOC is really just a cop-out. Train yourself to deliberately focus on positive things in your present and future life, rather than stewing in your own negativity-infused juice. (Have a glance at Chapter 18 for more on self-pity.)

❑   Physical pain/discomfort. Many medical conditions involve chronic pain and/or discomfort. You may no longer be physically capable of executing certain tasks or enjoyable activities as a result of your condition. This situation can be enormously disheartening and you may feel that you really need your DOC just to get by day-to-day. Alternatively, a good medical practitioner should sympathise with your situation and be able to prescribe legitimate pain relief medication. Chronic pain clinics also exist dedicated to helping people manage pain with psychological (often CBT-based) techniques. Talk to your GP or specialist about the possibilities. (See Chapter 21 for more about working with professionals.)

(continued)

❏ Difficulty sleeping. DOC use often means not so much 'falling asleep' as 'passing out'. You may think you're getting restorative sleep, but many people report feeling tired all the time, despite using alcohol or drugs to aid sleep. Natural sleep is the best sleep. Even a few hours of non-drug induced sleep is generally more restorative than a longer comatose state. Try using basic sleep hygiene rules (see Chapter 22 for more on these), and be patient. Getting back into a normal sleep cycle after a long spell of reliance on chemical assistance can take time.

❏ Emotional honesty. Perhaps you doubt your ability to effectively convey to others how you are feeling in actual words. You may need a belly-, lung- or vein-full of your DOC before you can begin to contemplate talking about your feelings, needs, troubles and experiences. Perhaps by gambling, using porn or shopping yourself into frightening debt, you imagine others will intuitively divine your distress. Communicating your feelings gets easier with practice; you may be amazed by your own communication skills if you give yourself a chance to use them. (Chapter 6 has some useful tips on emotional honesty.)

❏ Procrastination. We all have a tendency to put off unpleasant, tedious or difficult tasks and duties. DOC use can provide distraction and an excuse for not getting on with the jobs you most wish to avoid. However, failing to pay the bills, discuss arrears with your mortgage provider or even open the post can result in much bigger (sometimes irreversible) problems later on. Facing these mundane and daunting tasks head on, and dealing with them before they evolve into something even larger and more frightening, can boost your confidence and sense of overall security. Setting goals can help you to get going (as Chapter 8 highlights).

❏ Peer/social pressure. Children and young people aren't the only ones to experience peer pressure. People of any age can be unduly influenced by others. Many work environments cultivate a culture of heavy drinking and drug use. Reckless behaviour around substances, and risky amusements such as gambling, are sometimes seen as part and parcel of a 'high-powered life style'. Somewhat perversely, refusal to partake may be viewed with suspicion and leave the abstainer ostracised. If this is true of your situation, you may need to consider a job move or even a career change in the interest of your long-term recovery.

❏ Thrill-seeking. Excitement can come from many sources other than those involving your DOC. Again, you need to think creatively and create opportunities for healthy adventure. Even a portion of the money (and time!) your DOC has consumed over the years is probably enough to furnish you with new sports equipment or fund other types of hobbies and interests.

❏ Inhibitions/self-consciousness in social settings. Worry about what others may think of you is very common and plagues many people when in social situations. Using drugs and alcohol as social lubricants, however, may lead you to act in ways that you regret the next day. If you experience social anxiety you are very probably focusing too much of your attention on your 'performance'. Focusing on the conversation and on your environment instead can greatly reduce self-consciousness and allow you to react more spontaneously. (Refer to Chapter 5 for tips on taking control of your attention.)

Acquiring Alternative Activities

Once you've dumped your DOC you'll be left with time on your hands. Finding substitute behaviours to help you deal with stress and negative emotions is very important. You also need something absorbing or relaxing to do when you're accosted by cravings, beset by boredom or requiring a reward. Categorising activities according to the primary function they serve can help you to remember to actually use them instead of falling off the proverbial wagon.

Worksheet 10-5 lists some of the activities Kit identified to fill the gap left by her DOC.

Worksheet 10-5   **Kit's Alternative Activities Action Plan**

Activities that help me to de-stress:

❏   Taking the dog out for a walk after work

❏   Taking a luxurious bath and listening to classical music on the radio

❏   Burning scented candles

❏   Sitting outside in the garden

Activities that help lift my mood:

❏   Going to the gym and having a good workout

❏   Spending time with my close friends

❏   Having a good telephone chat with mum

❏   Getting an early night

❏   Watching one of my favourite comedy shows or YouTube clips

❏   Window shopping or trawling through charity shops for a bargain

Activities that help to alleviate my boredom:

❏   Reading a gripping novel

❏   Doing something creative like drawing or rearranging my furniture

❏   Socialising

❏   Getting on with household chores

❏   Taking the dog out for a walk in a new place

❏   Surfing the Internet for holiday destinations

❏   Exercise in general

❏   Grocery shopping

Activities that I can use as a reward:

❏   Making myself a nice meal

❏   Baking some cakes

❏   Buying myself a treat

❏   Going to the cinema and having a big bucket of popcorn

Activities that help me to resist cravings:

❏   Doing crosswords

❏   Singing along loudly to music

❏   Going for a long drive in the countryside

❏   Knitting

❏   Chewing gum or nibbling on raw carrots and celery

❏   Seeing friends or talking to them on the telephone

❏   Watching television

Put some real thought into your answers to Worksheet 10-6. This alternative activities action plan is more important than it may seem. You need healthy substitute activities to be in place to help you avoid relapse. Otherwise, you're doing the equivalent of crossing your fingers and leaving your recovery to chance.

Worksheet 10-6   My Alternative Activities Action Plan

Activities that help me to de-stress:

_____

_____

_____

Activities that help lift my mood:

_____

_____

_____

Activities that help to alleviate my boredom:

_____

_____

_____

Activities that I can use as a reward:

_____

_____

_____

Activities that help me to resist cravings:

_____

_____

_____

When you're trying to beat addiction and lay down new, healthy, habits, enrolling yourself in some groups or classes that interest you can be helpful. Try out things you've never done before and look for activities or subjects that really grab your attention. When you're able to lose yourself in an absorbing pursuit surmounting cravings is much easier.

Using more than one substance (or activity) in a problematic and addictive manner is not uncommon. Many gamblers also drink; many drinkers also use drugs, and so on. Often, dropping one DOC (say, alcohol) can lead to increased use and reliance on a second DOC (like marijuana). Beware of the multi-headed Hydra that addiction can become. Don't let yourself fall into the trap of substituting one addictive behaviour for another – and kidding yourself that you're on the road to recovery. Instead, use Worksheet 10-6 to identify some genuinely harmless alternatives.

Setting a Date to Divorce Your DOC

Why choose to recover and abstain in a meaningful way? Most people get serious about recovery when they hit some form of rock bottom. Their business is at risk, their partner has left them (or threatened to), the doctor has told them that they are at risk of liver damage or the bank has foreclosed on a loan. Or perhaps DOC-induced depression and anxiety have become so painful that the negative impact of addiction can no longer be ignored.

However bad things get, your intention to quit can unfortunately get put off and off and off. You may think 'once this period of work stress has passed, then I'll quit using'. Or maybe 'once I get into a relationship with someone, I'll be ready to kick the habit'. Getting clean won't be significantly easier if you choose one time over another – it's always a real battle. There's really no point in putting it off; decide on a date within the next five days at the most. Otherwise you increase your chances of going on a farewell mega-binge that may not end.

Kit used Worksheet 10-7 to commit herself to a DOC divorce date. She attached one to her fridge door, another to her bathroom mirror and one to the inside of her diary.

Worksheet 10-7   **Kit's DOC Divorce Date Document**

I, Kit Smith, pledge to myself that I will no longer smoke marijuana from 30 November 2011.

This idea may seem ridiculously simple – but putting your intentions in writing can really help you to stick to them. Every time you see your pledge displayed in places you can't miss, you'll be reminded not to use. Try it for yourself by filling out Worksheet 10-8.

Worksheet 10-8   **My DOC Divorce Date Document**

I, _____, pledge to myself that I will no longer _____ from _____.

Working Out Why Dropping Your DOC is Worth It

Your DOC has probably been your main (or only) coping strategy for life problems for some time. Like Kit in the earlier example, DOC use may have stealthily crept up on you, destroying healthier coping mechanisms in its wake. Deciding to quit therefore is rarely a decision that is made lightly. You stand to lose a lot in the pain relief department. Or do you?

Being honest with yourself about what you are losing by giving up your DOC is important. You are going to get cravings to use, and pretending that your DOC never gave you *anything* is pointless and untrue. But your DOC has been a false friend. It giveth with one hand and taketh away with the other. You need to make a balance sheet of what you stand to lose and what you stand to gain through abstinence. Doing so will help to bolster your motivation to stay off the stuff when the going gets tough.

Kit used Worksheet 10-9 to address the inevitable *losses* associated with abstinence from marijuana- and to weigh those up against what she stands to *gain* from abstinence in the near and more distant future.

Worksheet 10-9   Kit's Losses and Gains Balance Sheet

Losses incurred from divorcing my DOC:

1. I lose the chance to just shut off the day and veg out in front of the TV.

2. I lose the failsafe descent into sleep I get when I'm sufficiently stoned.

3. I lose the whole ritual of building a spliff and marking the end of the day.

4. I lose the pleasant relaxing and tranquil state of being stoned.

5. I lose something to look forward to at the end of the working day.

Gains derived from divorcing my DOC:

1. I gain hours to do something creative and constructive in the evenings like reading a book or spending time outdoors with my dog, seeing friends or dealing with housework, bills and so on.

2. I gain the ability to have a natural sleep and wake up feeling properly refreshed in the morning.

3. I gain the chance to feel proud of having done something productive at the end of the day, rather than every night being the same as the last. I gain variety and a choice of activities to mark the end of the day.

4. I gain the feeling of being awake and involved in my own environment. I gain the chance to remember what I've seen on TV. I gain the opportunity to relax in ways that I feel good about, such as cooking a nice meal and having a long hot bath and a mug of cocoa.

5. I gain the chance to look forward to other enjoyable activities at the end of the day (and the energy and mental clarity to do them!).

Now it's your turn to use Worksheet 10-10 to record the losses and gains you feel you'll experience from dropping your DOC.

Worksheet 10-10	My Losses and Gains Balance Sheet

Losses incurred from divorcing my DOC:

1.
2.
3.
4.
5.

Gains derived from divorcing my DOC:

1.
2.
3.
4.
5.

You may have more than five items to record in each column and that's fine; just carry on. Try to get at least five on each side, however, to really give you solid reasons why embarking on recovery is worth the effort and discomfort involved.

You don't have to look very hard in the media to find examples of famous people whose lives have been damaged or even lost because of drug and alcohol addiction. The recent death of Amy Winehouse is one very tragic example. Though truly sad to read about, you can give yourself more motivation to ditch your own DOC by reviewing the damage others have sustained as a result of their DOC use.

Reducing the Risk of Relapse

Committing to abstinence is half of the battle; guarding against relapse is the other. You may need to think very creatively to fill out Worksheet 10-11. We include Kit's example to give you some ideas and to spur you on toward realistically reducing your own risk of relapse.

Worksheet 10-11	Kit's Relapse Reduction Reckoner

Places I need to avoid:

The local pub where I used to meet my dealer

Music festivals (at least for a summer or two)

Certain house parties where I know a lot of people will be smoking dope

Certain holiday destinations, such as Amsterdam or Ibiza

People I need to avoid:

My dealer

My friend Stuart, who smokes even more than I do

My sister-in-law Jan, who winds me up and always makes me want a smoke after I see her

Steps for cleaning out my house:

Get rid of all my smoking paraphernalia, including tobacco, rolling papers, lighters, my special drug tin and all ashtrays

Make sure I've got plenty of carrots, celery and chewing gum in stock

Move my favourite smoking chair into the spare room and sit on the sofa instead

Stock up on crosswords, good books, DVDs, knitting patterns and wool, and so on

Rearrange all the furniture to give the whole flat a new look

Freshen up the place with a thorough clean and burn incense to remove all residual smoking smells

Positive obstacles I can put in place:

Never have more than £10 cash on me at any time

Make plans to walk my dog with a friend in the evenings

Tell Stuart and my other smoking friends that I'm quitting

Delete my dealer's number from my phone

Attend a Narcotics Anonymous meeting at least twice each week

Positive ways to use up my energy:

Join a pottery class

Renew my gym membership

Put my profile on a dating site

Save up the money I'd normally burn up in smoke toward a beach holiday (with a non-smoking companion)

Volunteer at the local dog rescue centre for a few hours every weekend

Visit my mum more often

Read all those novels that I'm interested in

Take my dog out for a ramble every morning and evening

Look for a new job, sign up with some recruitment agencies

Warning signs of relapse:

Getting really stressed out with work and starting to feel sorry for myself

Not returning phone calls and emails to 'clean' friends and family

Thinking fondly about smoking marijuana and only focusing on the 'good times'

Starting to smoke cigarettes

Toying with the idea that I can smoke in moderation

Feeling lonely and depressed

People I can turn to for support when relapse bells are ringing:

Mum

Friends from Narcotics Anonymous (including my sponsor)

My friend Tabitha, who is never judgemental but also never lets me off the hook

My doctor

Scooby (my dog) who deserves a clear-headed mistress

Use Worksheet 10-12 to draw up your own relapse reduction reckoner.

Worksheet 10-12   **My Relapse Reduction Reckoner**

Places I need to avoid:

People I need to avoid:

Steps for cleaning out my house:

Positive obstacles I can put in place:

Positive ways to use up my energy:

Warning signs of relapse:

People I can turn to for support when relapse bells are ringing:

TIP

Keep Worksheet 10-12 close to hand in early recovery and even when you feel confident that you've conquered your DOC demons. Relapse can be avoided by facing up to the risks and deliberately putting steps in place that make 'accidental' DOC resumption less likely. Give yourself the best chance possible of recovery success by keeping a close eye on relapse risks.

Getting your support team together

Support and encouragement from others is very useful in recovery; in fact, it is pretty essential. Friends and family members can be a great support, but they may also be the people who've suffered most from your DOC use. As a result, they may find it difficult to be objective and unbiased when you're in early recovery. You may need to seek extra support from addiction recovery groups such as Alcoholics Anonymous (AA) or try other recovery group formats. You can research such groups in your local area via the Internet or by GP referral. Ensure that you choose only well-recognised groups with a proven track record of success. Lots of CBT-informed recovery programmes are now on offer. If your addiction is severe (refer to Worksheet 10-1), inpatient treatment may be your first port of call. Perhaps you've tried to give up on your own several times but never been able to sustain abstinence for more than a few days or weeks. Talk to your doctor about the options. Most residential treatment centres require you to be an inpatient for a minimum of 28 days. This prospect may seem daunting but it could be the supportive boost you need to adopt skills and strategies for staying clean on your own.

Chapter 11

Being Better Friends with Your Body

*B*eing concerned about or interested in the way you look is very normal. Most of us take a degree of pride in our personal appearance and tend to the basics, such as keeping clean and well-groomed, making the most of our best features, dressing in clothing we like and that suits our shape and size, wearing perfume or aftershave and accessorising with jewellery, handbags, briefcases, scarves and so on. All pretty normal stuff. It's also pretty normal to prefer certain aspects of your physical appearance over others. You may have a lovely head of hair, for example, but wish your skin were clearer. Or you may like being tall and thin but hanker after a bit more curve as well. You may wish you were more, or less, muscular. Again, having some degree of dissatisfaction with aspects of your appearance is pretty run-of-the-mill – most of us do. Although caring for (and about) your appearance is normal and healthy, placing undue importance on the role your attractiveness plays in your overall enjoyment of life can be problematic.

Body image problems afflict both men and women alike. It is no longer true that insecurity about physical attractiveness is exclusively a female problem – if, in fact, it ever was. Men are every bit as capable of agonising over their looks as women, so the stuff in this chapter applies to both sexes regardless of age, education, occupation, sexual orientation, social-economic standing or even culture.

The severity of body image problems varies widely, from mild discomfiture to really debilitating emotions like depression. This chapter focuses mainly on mild to moderate levels of body image problems. We do, however, offer some information about more severe problems associated with body image and direct you toward appropriate help if this applies to you.

Getting to Grips with Poor Body Image

The term 'body image', as defined by psychologists, refers to your internalised sense of what you look like – both to yourself and to others. Body image essentially means how you assess your looks and assume others assess them: mostly good, mostly bad, mixed or neutral. Body image also refers to your attitude and beliefs about how important physical appearance is in the grand scheme of things.

If you have a good or 'healthy' body image, you may not think your looks will stop traffic, but you accept the way you look and can get on with life largely unhindered by worries about your attractiveness. You're also able to appreciate your most attractive features and not dwell on the less impressive ones. You can believe that someone else may be attracted to you (or even find you irresistible) and accept that as their honest opinion. You understand that your actual physical appearance is only a part of what makes you attractive to others.

On the other hand, if you have a poor or 'unhealthy' body image, none of the above holds true. Instead, you may desire to look radically different from how you do, be preoccupied by dissatisfactions with your appearance (and particular aspects thereof), dismiss the possibility that anyone could find you physically attractive, become depressed about and even ashamed of your perceived 'ugliness' and/or assume that you can never be happy unless you somehow become more attractive. You fail to understand that physical appearance is not the sole factor in attraction. It's not a recipe for feeling good or living life to the full.

The next section helps you to pinpoint your relationship with your appearance as a preliminary step to improving it.

Finding out how you feel about your appearance

Perhaps you suspect that you're not exactly best friends with the mirror. Maybe you have a few 'fat' or 'ugly' days each month, and these negatively impact on your mood when they hit.

But you may not be sure whether or not you've got a real problem with the way you look. Sometimes you can become so accustomed to thinking negatively about your looks and attractiveness that you view them as 'unfixable' and 'just the way you are'. It is possible to live more happily with your looks but recognising your dissatisfaction, and the degree of your dissatisfaction, is the first step.

To determine if you have a body image problem and, if so, how severe it is, complete Worksheet 11-1.

Worksheet 11-1	**Do I Have a Body Image Problem?**
Read the following points and tick off those that apply to you.	
❑	Close friends, family members, romantic partners or medical professionals have told me that my concerns about my looks/an aspect of my looks are disproportionate and/or groundless.
❑	I continue to be very distressed about my looks/an aspect of my looks despite reassurances from those close to me.
❑	The amount of time I spend thinking and worrying about (and/or checking) my looks amounts to more than one hour each day.
❑	My dissatisfaction with my looks/an aspect of my looks often prevents me from going out socially.
❑	My dissatisfaction with my looks/an aspect of my looks stops me from forming intimate relationships.
❑	My physical appearance is more important to me than any other feature of my personhood.

☐   I assume that other people will judge me instantly and solely on the basis of how I look.

☐   I often compare myself negatively with others in terms of appearance.

☐   My preoccupation with my looks/an aspect of my looks has a serious negative impact on my mood (for example, feeling depressed or anxious).

☐   I have considered extreme solutions such as cosmetic surgery.

If you've ticked off any three of the points in the checklist, you do have a mild or moderate body image problem and the worksheets and techniques offered in this chapter can help you. Ticking off half or more than half of the points (and in particular points 1 and 3) indicates that your body image problem is more severe. This chapter will still be of benefit to you but you probably also need some face-to-face professional help.

If your concerns and negative feelings about your physical appearance lead you to feel so desperate and depressed that you're thinking about the possibility of ending it all (committing suicide), seek professional help immediately. Right now. The accident and emergency department at your local hospital is a good place to go at any time if you feel at risk of harming yourself. Your GP can also be a helpful first port of call; although you may be better off requesting referral for consultation with a psychiatrist who specialises in the treatment of eating disorders or BDD and associated body image problems. You have nothing to lose by seeking professional help and everything to gain (refer to Chapter 21 for tips on working with professionals).

Being aware of BDD and exploring eating disorders

Body dysmorphic disorder (BDD) is a psychological disorder that involves extreme preoccupation with one or more physical features, such as facial skin texture or quality, nose shape, overall facial shape, scars, hair thickness or texture, teeth, lip shape, amount of facial hair, bags or darkness under the eyes, wrinkles and so on. Usually the pinpointed imperfection or physical anomaly is on the upper half of the body, including the torso, but it's not uncommon to experience severe dissatisfaction with lower limbs and other areas of the body below the waist – including the genitals. The physical features that BDD sufferers consider abnormal and unacceptable are typically unnoticeable or only slightly observable to others. The degree of distress the sufferer experiences is, however, all too real. People with BDD spend an hour or more each day focusing on the area of dissatisfaction and go to great lengths to compensate for or draw attention away from it. This can include camouflaging with heavy make up, adopting certain hairstyles, wearing hats, scarves or glasses, or emphasising other parts of the body through dress, such as wearing very short skirts to distract others from focusing on their upper body and face. BDD becomes a full-time job in severe cases, and takes over all other aspects of the sufferer's life. Relationships, study, work and interests suffer; sometimes just going out of the house becomes a massive undertaking in itself.

Anorexia nervosa is an eating disorder characterised by a morbid fear or phobia of being overweight, gaining weight or even of being a normal weight. The focus of the anorexic is tightly welded to body shape and size. Anorexics resemble BDD sufferers in their degree of preoccupation, emotional distress and desperate attempts to control how they appear. The salient difference is that the anorexic's singular goal is to maintain an unhealthily low body weight through strict restriction of food intake. Like BDD, anorexia takes over and leaves little room for normal living. It also can lead to long-term health problems arising from poor nutrition, such as osteoporosis, liver damage and, in some cases, infertility. Anorexia often includes self-induced vomiting and/or use of laxatives. This behaviour is called 'purging' and is a key feature of bulimia nervosa, another eating disorder similar in many respects to anorexia, although sufferers are usually not underweight.

BDD, bulimia and anorexia affect males and females alike. If you think you're suffering from one of these conditions, you are advised to seek out professional advice and support.

Dealing with Poor Body Image Ponderings and Practices

People who have a poor relationship with their bodies and faces tend to think about their looks in particular, unhelpful, ways. Some or many of the attitudes and beliefs listed in Worksheet 11-2 may be very familiar to you. If so, you need to alter your attitude in order to nurture a healthier body image (tips for changing your attitude are provided in later sections of this chapter – so fear not).

If you're pale and pasty, you also probably perpetuate your problem by engaging in practices like those listed in Worksheet 11-3. You may do these things without fully realising it – they're just part of your everyday regime. Even if you do know you do them, you may not be aware of the degree to which they perpetuate your body image problems.

Worksheet 11-2	Typical Toxic Thoughts about Appearance

	This list includes the kind of common beliefs and attitudes that underpin unhealthy body image. Tick off those that reflect your own thinking about your appearance.
❏	I couldn't stand it if someone thought I was plain/ugly/fat/short/dumpy/scrawny!
❏	If I am not physically attractive, I have no real worth whatsoever.
❏	Other people must not find any fault with my looks! Hiding myself away is better than facing that unbearable possibility!
❏	Other people are sure to judge me negatively, ridicule me and reject me on the basis of my looks.
❏	I absolutely should be better looking than I am.
❏	Good-looking people are happier, more interesting and more valuable than I am.
❏	Physical attractiveness is the most important aspect of a person.
❏	Only attractive people can expect to be successful in life.
❏	Other people value physical attractiveness as much as I do.
❏	Being unattractive (plain, ungainly, overweight or in poor shape and so on) is a sign of moral weakness and character deficiency.

Adopting More Accurate Body Image Attitudes

Now that you've identified problematic thinking that consolidates your negative feelings about how you look, you can make a concerted effort to replace it with more balanced beliefs and attitudes. Consider the following:

✔ Other people may not value physical appearance as highly as you do.

✔ Your looks are largely determined before you are even born; therefore, believing that being less attractive says something about your moral fibre or overall strength of character is ridiculous.

✔ Being overweight means that you probably eat too much and don't exercise enough – nothing else.

✔ It is possible that others will make snap judgements about you based on how you look, but that's life – you probably do it yourself. These initial judgements aren't wholly accurate in the majority of cases and are frequently altered and updated as people get to know one another better.

✔ Physical beauty is only one part of what makes an individual 'attractive' overall; personality, values, intelligence, sense of humour and interpersonal conduct are also integral to attractiveness.

✔ Plenty of physically downright unattractive or average-looking people have been happy and successful in life. By the same token, many physically beautiful people have been unhappy in their lives. (Think about both famous people and those whom you know personally.)

✔ Whilst being judged as ugly or unattractive by others is not pleasant or desirable, far worse fates are possible (use your imagination).

✔ You have much, much more to offer the world than just a pretty face or a muscular body, if you choose to recognise it.

✔ You have worth by virtue of being alive. What you do with your life – how you live it – is far more profound than how you look.

✔ Looks do make an impression on others (especially unusually good ones) but other considerations must also be at play, or most of the planet's population would be on the dust heap.

✔ Your happiness is dependent on your attitude and the choices you make, not on the cuteness of your face, butt or biceps.

✔ Being average-looking merely invites you to join the majority of the human race.

 Even if you find these ideas and attitudes hard to believe at first, the more you practise them, the more you'll come to feel that they're true. Your negative thoughts have no more evidential basis than those listed here (far less in actual fact). You've simply been accepting your negative beliefs uncritically for a number of years. Familiarity is what makes your negative appearance-based beliefs and attitudes feel true – nothing else.

Worksheet 11-3   Problematic Poor Body Image Practices

Alongside 'bad body image thinking' stride 'problematic practices'. Thinking and behaviour typically go hand-in-hand, reinforcing each other. Tick off the points in the following list that apply to you.

❑   Constantly comparing yourself negatively to others on the basis of physical attributes and overall appearance.

❑   Taking ages over your appearance before going out in public (dressing, putting on make-up, fixing your hair and so on).

❑   Being on a constant diet, frequently going on fad diets or fasting to lose weight (this may include purging via self-induced vomiting or using laxatives).

❑   Exercising excessively to lose weight, improve body shape or promote muscle growth. ('Excessive' means never being able to just exercise to feel good and enjoy it; you always have a driven need to improve yourself. Also, you may feel guilty and low if you can't exercise according to your routine for some reason.)

❑   Wearing lots of make-up (to mask imperfections, improve your appearance or draw attention away from other parts of your body).

(continued)

❏	Saving up for corrective cosmetic surgery (hoping that physical improvements via surgery will enable you to increase your self-esteem and social confidence).
❏	Wearing certain styles or items of clothing to mask (real or imagined) imperfections.
❏	Avoiding conversation about weight or looks in general (even with close friends and family) and/or verbally criticising your own appearance on a regular basis.
❏	Calling yourself ugly names in your head (especially when looking in the mirror).
❏	Avoiding looking at yourself in the mirror or in reflective surfaces as much as possible.
❏	Excessively checking your appearance in the mirror to see if an imperfection is exposed or has worsened, or to assess how 'bad' you look overall.
❏	Rejecting and dismissing compliments about your appearance.
❏	Avoiding spending time with people who you think are 'out of your league' in terms of attractiveness (in order to save yourself from looking worse by comparison).
❏	Choosing only to spend time with people you think are more attractive than yourself in the hope that your own looks will either be overlooked or more favourably assessed by association.
❏	Attempting to hide away from potential scrutiny (even from close friends and lovers).
❏	Seeking reassurance about your appearance from select parties (then discounting it soon after!).
❏	Avoiding clothes shopping, haircuts and other forms of self-care (because you believe that you can't make a silk purse out of a pig's ear).

By engaging in these kinds of behaviours regularly, your negative beliefs about your appearance (and the importance of looks in general) become more entrenched. You can get caught in a mutually reinforcing vicious cycle of negative thoughts and unhelpful actions.

Promoting Positive Body Image Practices

New thinking and new action are what's needed to break the cycle of poor body image. Whilst stubbornly reminding yourself to adopt the healthier and more accurate attitudes offered above, hit your body image problem from both angles by also trying some of these practical suggestions:

- **Observe others (and appreciate the way they look if you wish) but without forming comparative judgements about yourself.** Make a strict rule that you're not allowed to visually seek pretty people out in order to make yourself feel bad by comparison.

- **Use the mirror sensibly.** Use it to fix your hair and so on but don't allow yourself to home in on your areas of dissatisfaction. If you typically spend a lot of time scrutinising yourself in the mirror (and magnifying your imperfections), only allow yourself an average of three mirror sessions per day and put a strict time limit on how long you're allowed to spend in front of the mirror (roughly one minute is usually enough).

✔ **Put a limit on time spent preparing to go out.** Stick to one outfit rather than changing clothing frantically in an effort to find something that you think you look okay wearing. Otherwise you'll probably just feel stressed and defeated. Put on appropriate clothing, have a quick look in the mirror and get out the door.

✔ **Think twice or even thrice about cosmetic surgery.** It's expensive and can be an unnecessary risk. You may find that, once you've worked on accepting yourself within the context of your appearance, you no longer consider surgery the solution.

✔ **If someone compliments any aspect of your appearance, say 'thank you', then shut up.** Other people have every right to like things about your appearance even if you find that hard to believe.

✔ **Don't bother asking for reassurance that you look acceptable (or, perish the thought, nice) if you're just going to dismiss what others tell you.**

✔ **Outlaw bad language.** You're only allowed to say nice or neutral things about your appearance. Calling yourself names in your head like 'fat pig' or 'ugly cow' is, unsurprisingly, very detrimental to your overall self-esteem. Don't let yourself verbally disparage your looks either, not even in apparent jest.

✔ **Spend time with people you like.** Leave appearances out of the equation.

✔ **Stop trying to mask yourself through clothing choices or loads of make-up.** All that effort probably does little to improve your actual appearance and only makes you feel more self-conscious. Reverse the tendency to mask physical imperfections by highlighting your preferred features instead.

✔ **Take care of yourself.** You deserve a nice haircut or to wear clothing and accessories that you both like and perhaps reflect your individual style choices. No rule says that only 'beautiful' people are entitled to enjoy fashion.

You may find putting the preceding ideas into regular practice difficult and uncomfortable, but you'll get better at it with time and consistent application.

Having a Look at the Whole Package

There's more to who you are than just your outward physical appearance. Looks are just the packaging for your personality. You body is just the vehicle you have been given to experience life. So, whilst appearance may seem to be very important, it is not the whole deal. You probably realise the truth of those last three sentences on some level, but you may forget or dismiss their validity when you're in the clutches of an ugly duckling moment. If your goal is to improve your relationship with your body and your looks in general, you really need to start giving equal appreciation and value to other components of yourself.

Harnessing a holistic outlook

Taking a truly holistic look at yourself can be difficult to do if you've been focusing almost entirely on one aspect, like physical looks, for a long time. The process isn't just about rediscovering (or discovering for the first time) things that are 'good' and 'attractive' about yourself – it's about really getting to know yourself as a whole person.

No harm exists in scraping the bottom of the barrel. Little things matter. Really think about the things you know and like about yourself that have nothing to do with your appearance; however minor they may seem, they carry significance.

Gwynne is an athletic 29-year-old woman, who's about 5 feet 5 inches tall. She's a member of a running club, which she greatly enjoys. Despite being obviously fit, Gwynne worries about her weight. She thinks that she should be taller and leaner like some of the long-distance runners she trains alongside. In particular, Gwynne focuses on her thighs. She thinks they're fat and 'too big', although she knows that they're really just very muscular. Gwynne also worries that her breasts are too small and that her top half is grossly out of proportion with her bottom half. She also frets that her hair is too thin. Gwynne can trace her dissatisfaction with her overall looks back to her early teenage years.

Here's how Gwynne filled out Worksheet 11-4.

Worksheet 11-4	Gwynne's Healthy Holistic Overview
1. What are my personal values and philosophies for living?	Treat others as you would like to be treated.
	Hard work pays big dividends.
	A smile costs nothing and gives much.
	I believe in forgiveness, generosity and the sharing of good fortune.
	I value self-education and a thirst for knowledge.
	I value trying new things and embracing experiences others have to offer.
	I believe in charity and contributing to the kind of society I want to live in.
2. What are my hobbies and interests?	I love outdoor activities like walking and camping.
	I love animals, horse-riding, going to city farms or zoos and bird watching.
	I love reading sci-fi novels and watching crime thrillers.
	I love running.
	I'm interested in politics and world economics.
	I like baking.

3. What are my idio-syncratic talents, skills and abilities?	I'm a good runner.
	I have a wide vocabulary.
	Most sports come easily to me.
	I can bake cakes and puddings very well.
	I have a way with animals and children that makes them comfortable around me.
	I can mimic accents well and imitate people accurately.
	I can juggle, ice-skate and horse-ride.
	I'm usually a good mediator between others when they're in conflict.
	I can change a tyre on my car.
4. What are my deco-rating tastes and personal fashion choices?	I like cosy interiors with lots of patterned fabrics, wooden floors and rich colours.
	I like decorating with objects collected from my travels or inherited from my family.
	I like candles and low light emitting from interesting lamps and light fixtures in my sitting room and bedroom.
	I like to dress in smart but comfortable clothing for work and socialising. At home I like to wear tracksuits and casual stuff like jeans and T-shirts.
	I like delicate and unusual designs of gold or gold plated jewelry.
	I prefer classic fashion styles rather than trendy stuff.
5. What personality traits do I possess?	I'm very reliable and punctual.
	I have a short fuse but I'm also quick to forgive.
	I have a dry sense of humour but I also enjoy slapstick.
	I'm pretty easy-going and friends tell me that I fit into most social situations readily.
	I care a lot about the welfare of others.
	I can keep a secret.
	I'm better at arts and humanities than sciences.
	I try to accept others without judgement.
	I am open-minded and not easily shocked.
	I don't hold a grudge.

(continued)

6. What is my cultural identity and what are my current spiritual beliefs?	My mother is Welsh and my father is Italian; I identify with both cultures. I was brought up as a Catholic but I'm drawn toward Buddhist philosophies.
7. What are my future plans and goals?	I want to run a marathon. I would like to live in the country one day and have my own horse. I'm going to college to study osteopathy in the autumn. I want to have children one day. I plan to do a first aid qualification in the next year or so.
8. What is my attitude toward social responsibility and the treatment of others?	I try to give others the benefit of the doubt. I believe that the majority of people are kind. I believe in the promotion of community cohesion, especially in larger cities. I do not litter or vandalise public property and think it is socially irresponsible to do so. I believe in making use of my right to vote.
9. What characteristics do I value most in the people close to me?	Warmth and humour. A lust for life. Honesty and loyalty. Kindness. Intelligence and critical thinking. Appreciation of other cultures and ideologies.
10. What sort of things really make me laugh?	My sister and her husband when they banter. Situational comedies. Animal antics (like my cat scaling the curtains).

By completing Worksheet 11-4, Gwynne came to realise that she's so much more than a pair of thighs. Complete Worksheet 11-5 to view yourself more holistically. Put real thought into the answers you provide. Give your body a backseat briefly, in the interest of learning to live more happily within it.

Worksheet 11-5	My Healthy Holistic Overview
1. What are my personal values and philosophies for living?	
2. What are my hobbies and interests?	
3. What are my idiosyncratic talents, skills and abilities?	
4. What are my decorating tastes and personal fashion choices?	
5. What personality traits do I possess?	
6. What is my cultural identity and what are my current spiritual beliefs?	
7. What are my future plans and goals?	
8. What is my attitude toward social responsibility and the treatment of others?	
9. What characteristics do I value most in the people close to me?	
10. What sort of things really make me laugh?	

Showing a little appreciation

Those thighs that Gwynne disparages for being 'big' also enable her to run, skip, jump and climb stairs. She'd certainly miss them if they ceased to function for some reason. Your body serves more than an aesthetic function. It enables you to engage with life: experience sensations through your five senses, do fun, interesting, tedious and essential activities, hug other people, shout at other people, see the great panorama of your environment, cry, laugh, listen and learn, walk and talk. You are not a static work of art to be appraised and assessed purely on what the eye can see. Rather, you are a complex, ever-changing, multi-faceted creature (profound, right?). Don't just take our word for it; think about it for yourself.

Giving your body a grain of gratitude

Instead of giving your dutiful body a hard time for being less than drop-dead gorgeous, try being thankful for all it does for you. Try taking better care of it simply because it's the only one you've got, and without it you'd definitely be missing out. Physical beauty is not an achievement; it's the luck of the draw. Sure it makes sense to make the most of what you've got in the looks department – people do look best when they're fit and healthy – but ultimately you need to accept yourself with the looks you were born with.

Your body and face do a lot of things for you that you may take for granted or shrink the importance of in your own mind. We urge you to step out of the 'appearance is all' trap and begin to honour your body for more than its presentation. Read Ray's story below.

Ray is a 22-year-old university student. He is 6 feet 1 inches tall, and very broad, or 'stocky'. Ray gains weight easily if he doesn't get a reasonable amount of exercise. During his final year of secondary school, he became slightly overweight because he prioritised studying for his A-levels over his active hobbies. From that time onwards, Ray became very self-conscious about being 'a fat lump', even though his friends and family didn't comment much on his weight gain. Ray also now thinks that his facial features are too broad and that he 'looks like a thug'. His new university mates refer to him good-naturedly as 'big Ray'. Ray often feels awkward, though he doesn't consider himself to be fat, as such. He feels too big and clumsy to be found attractive by anyone.

Ray completed Worksheet 11-6 to help him appreciate his body and change his negative perception of his physical appearance.

Worksheet 11-6	Ray's Fanfare for Physical Function Form
What my body enables me to do:	Conduct the basic tasks that are part and parcel of day-to-day living like brushing my teeth, walking around, seeing the world, and so on.
	Do my job and thus earn money to pay the bills and so on.
	Go walking through the countryside and take photos.
	Drive my car.
	Communicate with people on the phone, over the Internet and in person.
	Get to know other people, make friends and form relationships.
	Learn and develop in my career and personal life.

What my body enables me to feel:	All the emotions, both good and bad.
	The sunlight on my skin.
	The pleasure of a hot bath, massage, good food and fine wine, sex and so on.
	The pain of personal grief and empathy/compassion for others in strife.
	Excitement and hope.
	Love from others.
	Pain (physical and emotional) and relief when it stops
What my body enables me to express:	Love and care for others.
	My values, interests and opinions.
	My personal tastes, desires and goals.
	My emotions.

Ray's example is merely a generic taster to help you get started. Your own answers may be far more detailed and specific than Ray's. See his answers as a jumping off point. Get all deep and meaningful with yourself as you complete Worksheet 11-7.

Don't be reluctant to wax lyrical on this form. Get into the spirit of the exercise by letting your imagination go wild.

Worksheet 11-7	My Fanfare for Physical Function Form
What my body enables me to do:	
What my body enables me to feel:	
What my body enables me to express:	

Your body is really just the outward husk or vessel for your existence. Appreciate it, love it, enjoy it and care for it but – above all – accept it.

Implementing Healthy Home Improvements

If your body is your house, then keeping it in order is good for your physical and mental health. Good housekeeping involves all the standard stuff: eating sensibly, taking regular exercise, reducing stress, making time to relax and avoiding bad habits such as smoking or drinking too much alcohol.

Decorating and refurbishment (to extend the metaphor) are also considerations on the way to healthy body image. Part of accepting your looks is taking a modicum of pride in your dress and grooming. You don't need to live in a mansion to be house-proud. Care for your body, face and hair; pamper yourself a bit. You've every right to do so, even though you may not be a natural cover girl or boy.

If you've been riddled with body image doubts for a long while, you may have stopped buying clothes and accessories, wearing perfume and cologne or even thinking about style and fashion. Making an external change can help you break out of the bad body image psychological rut. Try wearing something that you've not worn for ages. Accessorise with different colours, buy a new pair of shoes, try a different hairstyle or treat yourself to a new suit. Like rearranging the furniture in a room or painting it a new colour, making changes to the way you dress can be refreshing and mood-lifting.

Embarking on exercise regimes, healthy eating plans and diets are utterly okay things to do. However, if your goal is to have a better relationship with your body for the long haul, then do these things for rational or 'righteous' reasons:

- ✔ To improve your energy and overall fitness.

- ✔ To achieve and maintain a healthy weight.

- ✔ To be able to play actively with your children, nieces and nephews or any other small, energetic people in your life (or your pets!).

- ✔ To improve flexibility and to combat pain (such as back or joint pain).

- ✔ To increase longevity.

- ✔ To rectify health problems like high blood pressure, high cholesterol, liver damage, back problems, sleep problems and so on.

- ✔ To combat/ neutralise the effects of life stressors.

- ✔ To better enjoy hobbies.

- ✔ To increase sexual appetite and confidence.

- ✔ To help defeat depression and/or anxiety disorders.

All of the reasons listed for eating well and taking exercise will also have the bonus effect of helping you really look your best. It is possible to have a healthy attitude towards your body, and about appearance generally, yet still make improvements where you can. The key principle to remember is that you're worthwhile regardless of how pretty or handsome you are. So be wary of making appearance-based improvements with the sole purpose of lifting your self-esteem. Instead, aim for improved physical confidence and an overall sense of well-being.

Ray used Worksheet 11-8 to identify things about his physical appearance and health that he wants to change and rational reasons for making improvements.

Worksheet 11-8	Ray's Building on my Bountiful Body Basics Worksheet
Areas targeted for improvement:	My weight. My abdomen muscles. My hair.
Specific improvements to go for:	Lose one stone. Build up muscle tone in my abdomen. Let my hair grow a bit.
How to attain these identified improvements:	Eat more fruit and veg. Only have one take-away meal each month. Start playing tennis. Join the gym and go 3 times a week. Stop drinking beer.
Reasons for doing so:	I'll feel less clumsy and more energised if I shed a stone. Improving my stomach muscles will help my lower back pain and improve my posture. Having more hair will soften my facial features and help me overcome the idea that I look like a thug.

Use Worksheet 11-9 to plan for your own physical adjustments and improvements.

Worksheet 11-9	My Building on my Bountiful Body Basics Worksheet
Areas targeted for improvement:	
Specific improvements to go for:	
How to attain these identified improvements:	
Reasons for doing so:	

Chapter 12

Dealing a Blow to Depression

. . . .

In This Chapter

▶ Checking for signs of depression

▶ Understanding how avoidance and blocking out maintain depression

▶ Realising the worst about ruminating

▶ Activating yourself for more rewarding living

. . . .

Depression is a painful and common emotional problem. It can range from feeling down for a few weeks and often improves of its own accord, to being severe enough to require hospital treatment. Fortunately, CBT is a scientifically proven treatment for depression supported by dozens of research trials. CBT can work with or without anti-depressant medication and is proven to reduce relapse rates.

Almost by definition, a depressed mind will say 'trying anything is pointless, nothing can be done to help me'. As we hope you'll discover, this belief is very far from the truth and is one of the vicious rumours depression will try to fill a person's mind with in order to keep them depressed.

This chapter focuses on the Behavioural in CBT and shows you that gradually facing up to things you're avoiding, increasingly engaging in activities you find rewarding, and constructively dealing with any difficulties you have can have a profound effect on your low mood. Alongside this we outline how '*ruminating*' (going over and over things in your mind) can sometimes appear to be a way of solving problems, but in fact may well be driving down your mood. Spotting and interrupting rumination is another powerful tool for overcoming depression.

Deciding whether You're Depressed

Identifying common symptoms of depression has a number of advantages. It can give you a clearer idea of whether you're suffering from 'ups and downs' or 'the blues' or whether you have symptoms of a recognised illness. Use Worksheet 12-1 to identify any symptoms of depression you experience. You can then choose to show this checklist to your doctor and discuss possible treatment options. You can also use the checklist as a reference point to come back to as you work to overcome your depression, to see how your symptoms are improving.

Worksheet 12-1	My Symptoms of Depression Checklist
1. ❏	I constantly feel sad, down, depressed, or empty.
2. ❏	I have a general lack of interest in what's going on around me.
3. ❏	I've noticed a big increase or decrease in my appetite and weight.
4. ❏	I have difficulty sleeping. I'm unable to get off to sleep and/or wake early and am unable to get back to sleep.
5. ❏	I feel slow and lacking in motivation.
6. ❏	I feel guilty or worthless.
7. ❏	I find concentrating and making decisions difficult.
8. ❏	I feel that I might be better off dead.

If you tick items 1 or 2 and four others and have felt that way for at least two weeks, there's a good chance that you're suffering from depression. The principles outlined in this book will probably help you but you may also consider seeking professional help from a doctor, counsellor, or therapist. See Chapter 21 for more on working with a healthcare professional.

Assessing Your Avoidance

As we point out in more depth in Chapter 7, the strategies human beings use to try to help themselves feel better often make emotional problems worse. Avoiding daily tasks and social interaction is part of depression. It can be very tempting to give in to your depressed feelings and hide away from other people and your responsibilities. However, such avoidance can often lead to a life that is less rewarding, leave you less in control of your life, lead to financial problems mounting up, reduce your ability to problem solve, and decrease the support you get from other people.

Consider what you might be avoiding doing (including pleasures and chores) and what you might be doing to try to block out painful thoughts and feelings. The effect of some activities varies according to what function they serve. Enjoying a favourite TV programme, for example, might be rewarding and be part of a mood-lifting plan, but watching endless hours of TV to block out the world will maintain your depression.

Blocking out behaviours tend to be things you do instead of getting on with tasks that are in your best interest to address. So watching TV instead of opening post or answering the phone may be an example of a blocking out behaviour and an avoidance behaviour. Often you'll engage in blocking out behaviours because your mood is so low that everything seems pointless and overwhelming. Unfortunately, the more you let things pile up the more depressed you're likely to feel.

Blocking out behaviours can also include things like using drugs, alcohol or food to help numb your depressed feelings. These things may work in the short term but they usually lead to worsened depression the next day.

Table 12-1 shows common types of avoidance and blocking out behaviours that feature in depression. Use the table to help you identify your own depression-maintaining behaviours. You can then target these for change and replace them with more constructive behaviours.

Table 12-1	Avoidance and Blocking-out Behaviours
Activities You Avoid	*Blocking-out Behaviours*
Seeing friends in social situations	Trying not to think about problems
Answering the phone/e-mail	Watching TV or films
Opening and dealing with the post	Drinking alcohol or using other substances to escape
Taking care of your home – paying bills, doing household chores	Staying in bed or going back to bed during the day
Taking care of yourself – washing yourself and your clothes, eating properly	Using sex or pornography excessively
Getting out of bed in the morning	Playing computer games
Speaking to people about your problems	Comfort eating
Communicating with people close to you	Surfing the Internet and using chatrooms
Taking part in your hobbies and interests	Exercising excessively

Rhashid has been feeling depressed since he missed a promotion at work. He lives alone, has been off work for six weeks, and has become quite isolated. He used Worksheet 12-2 to assess his avoidance and blocking-out behaviours.

Worksheet 12-2	Rhashid's Avoidance and Blocking-out Assessment
What are you avoiding?	Picking up the phone and responding to e-mails I keep making excuses so I don't have to see my friends I'm not really clearing up after myself
What are the undesirable or unhelpful effects of this avoidance?	I feel lonely much of the day and really stuck in a rut. The flat is becoming shamefully messy.
What are you doing to try to block out painful thoughts or feelings?	Watching TV and old DVDs most of the day. Drinking wine and eating junk food at night.
What are the undesirable or unhelpful effects of these strategies?	Feeling fat and unhealthy. I'm not really dealing with anything, so just end up feeling helpless.

Now, use Worksheet 12-3 to identify things you're avoiding and strategies you're using to try to block things out.

Worksheet 12-3	My Avoidance and Blocking-out Assessment
What are you avoiding?	
What is the undesirable or unhelpful effect of this avoidance?	
What are you doing to try to block out painful thoughts or feelings?	
What are the undesirable or unhelpful effects of these strategies?	

Use what you've learn from analysing your avoidance and blocking out to help guide your activity scheduling in the 'Actively Attacking Your Depression' section later in this chapter.

When you're depressed, focusing your attention on almost anything other than your internal thoughts is likely to lead you to feel at least a little better. Accepting the presence of distressing thoughts and images as part and parcel of depression but then choosing to turn your attention to other things will probably help your depression to stabilise rather than worsen.

Reckoning with Rumination

The word *rumination* has its origins with the way cows repeatedly chew over grass ('chewing the cud') as part of their digestive process. Humans also spend time ruminating, by going over things in their minds, but with more harmful results. Generally,, when they feel depressed, people ruminate over past events that cannot be changed or questions that cannot be answered, such as:

- ✔ What if . . . ?
- ✔ If only . . . (I'd done things differently).
- ✔ Why do I feel this way?
- ✔ Why didn't I do things differently/make different choices?

Identifying where and when you ruminate is half the battle, as this knowledge will help you avoid getting caught up in it. Recognising what you tend to ruminate about will also help you sidestep this toxic trap.

Rachael has been depressed since she separated from her husband. A feature of her depression is that she often ruminates about the way her relationship broke down. She used Worksheet 12-4 to identify her rumination patterns.

Worksheet 12-4	Rachael's Recognising Rumination Record
Which time(s) of day are you most likely to ruminate?	In the morning and at night if I wake up.
Where are you when you tend to ruminate?	Lying in bed, in my bedroom, or in the bathroom.
What kinds of activities are you doing when you ruminate?	Trying to get back to sleep or getting dressed and ready to go to work.
What do you commonly ruminate about?	I try to work out why things broke down with my husband. I try to figure out why I can't snap out of this depression.

Now carry out your own analysis of your rumination in Worksheet 12-5.

Worksheet 12-5	My Recognising Rumination Record
Which time(s) of day are you most likely to ruminate?	
Where are you when you tend to ruminate?	
What kinds of activities are you doing when you ruminate?	
What do you commonly ruminate about?	

Actively Attacking Your Depression

An activity schedule is one of the most (if not *the most*) effective psychological tools you can use to combat depression. This tool is often overlooked or under-used by both therapists and sufferers because it seems too simple, but research shows it works.

An *activity schedule* is a diary sheet for each day with times of the day clearly marked in two-hour blocks. Getting active again is a vital step to beating depression. Because depression saps motivation and promotes lethargy, your activity schedule can really help you to get on with daily tasks you may be avoiding. Research shows that the simple action of planning your daily activities and allocating specific times to specific tasks greatly increases the likelihood of carrying them out. Once you get started using an activity schedule your motivation to do the things you once enjoyed and found rewarding will begin to return.

You can use your activity schedule for a number of jobs:

- ✔ Recording a week's activity to provide a baseline to return to in future weeks to compare your progress against.

- ✔ Beginning to steadily face up to things you've been avoiding and becoming more activated

- ✔ Reducing blocking-out behaviours and replacing them with more rewarding or productive activities.

- ✔ Structuring your daily routines to give your appetite and sleeping patterns the best possible chance of returning to normal. By *normal* we mean eating regular meals three times a day and getting roughly eight hours of sleep each night.

- ✔ Planning your day or week to help get chores done, keep social engagements, and set aside time for hobbies and interests.

- ✔ Monitoring that you *gradually* increase your activities in a steady and realistic way rather than overloading yourself with all the things you think you should do.

Worksheet 12-6 is an example of an activity schedule:

Worksheet 12-6			**Activity Schedule**				
	Monday	**Tuesday**	**Wednesday**	**Thursday**	**Friday**	**Saturday**	**Sunday**
6–8 a.m.							
8–10							
10–12							
12–2							
2–4							
4–6							
6–8							
8–10 p.m.							

Now complete your own activity schedule to record your typical week for your baseline. Use subsequent forms to gradually increase your levels of activity. Use the assessment in Worksheet 12-3 to guide you in deliberately targeting for change those avoidance and blocking-out behaviours you identified as being part of the maintenance of your depression.

	Monday	Tuesday	Wednesday	Thursday	Friday	Saturday	Sunday
6–8 a.m.							
8–10							
10–12							
12–2							
2–4							
4–6							
6–8							
8–10 p.m.							

	Monday	Tuesday	Wednesday	Thursday	Friday	Saturday	Sunday
6–8 a.m.							
8–10							
10–12							
12–2							
2–4							
4–6							
6–8							
8–10 p.m.							

	Monday	Tuesday	Wednesday	Thursday	Friday	Saturday	Sunday
6–8 a.m.							
8–10							
10–12							
12–2							
2–4							
4–6							
6–8							
8–10 p.m.							

Chapter 13

Overcoming Obsessions and Cutting Out Compulsions

*O*bsessive-compulsive disorder (OCD), health anxiety, and body dysmorphic disorder (BDD) are examples of obsessional problems, which can be extremely distressing and interfere greatly in sufferers' lives. This chapter shows you how these problems are maintained and offers some key techniques for overcoming them. Fortunately, CBT has proven to be successful in helping people overcome each of the obsessional problems we discuss here.

Observing Obsessive Behaviour

Only a doctor can diagnose whether you're suffering from an obsessional problem. This section has checklists of common features of three of the most prevalent obsessional problems, which will give you a clue if you're suffering from this type of problem. As we show, understanding what your problem is is a critical step in ridding yourself of excessive and disabling anxiety, obsessions, and preoccupations.

If you can identify obsessions and/or compulsions in the lists in the following sections, and they cause you distress and/or interfere in your life, you may want to show the lists to your doctor and discuss possible diagnosis and treatment for OCD.

The way you cope with your obsessions may be part of maintaining them – in other words, your solution may be the problem. Understanding this concept is a really important part of recovering. Use Chapter 7 to help you build a profile of the strategies you are currently using that are fueling the problem.

Checking out OCD

Obsessive-compulsive disorder (OCD) is in the top ten most disabling illnesses, according to the United Nations' World Health Organisation. This illness is characterised by *obsessions,* which are distressing thoughts, images, impulses, or doubts, and compulsions, which are rituals and regimented behaviors that a person feels compelled to perform.

Work through Worksheet 13-1 to ascertain whether you have any of the features of OCD.

Worksheet 13-1	Obsessions Checklist

❑ Distressing unwanted religious, blasphemous, sacrilegious thoughts or images intrude into my mind.

❑ I am greatly troubled by intrusive thoughts or images of violent acts such as stabbing, pushing, hitting, and burning.

❑ Unacceptable or inappropriate sexual thoughts or images repeatedly enter my mind against my will and cause me distress.

❑ I frequently worry greatly about contamination from dirt, germs, bodily fluids, excrement, chemicals, sticky substances, or other material.

❑ I frequently worry greatly that I might lose something important or regret throwing something away.

❑ I often worry that I might be responsible for a bad event such as a fire, flood, car accident, or burglary through not being careful enough.

❑ My obsessions cause me significant levels of distress.

❑ My obsessions are on my mind for at least an hour each day.

❑ My obsessions interfere with my ability to function in important areas of my life such as my social life, work, family life, and relationships.

The first six items on Worksheet 13-1 can help you identify the type of obsessions that trouble you. These are very common types of OCD. Ticking even one is sufficient to indicate that you're suffering with OCD. Many people have more than one form of this disorder however, so don't be alarmed if you tick more than one of the first six items. The last three items on the worksheet help you determine how severe your problem is and how much it's disrupting your life. OCD is what is called a *spectrum disorder* which means that it can range in severity. People with mild OCD may find their obsessions irksome but are not bothered by them for more than an hour each day and their OCD doesn't stop them from living a normal life. If you have more severe OCD, you probably find your obsessions very distressing and distracting. Your obsessions are on your mind for at least an hour and possibly several hours every day. The more severe your OCD, the more it impedes your ability to function. Everyday tasks like locking doors, going to work, interacting with friends and family, getting dressed, and taking care of household chores can become extremely time consuming when you have moderate to severe OCD. Happily, however severe your OCD, CBT can help you to overcome it.

OCD is a broad topic. There are many different forms of OCD and to discuss each one in depth is unfortunately beyond the scope of this chapter. CBT treatment has been proven effective with all sorts of OCD problems and the principles outlined in this chapter (as well as the exercises in Chapters 4 and 9) can really help you. You may also wish to consult other books that deal exclusively with OCD. We recommend a book by Rob Willson and David Veale called *Overcoming Obsessive Compulsive Disorder* published by Robinson and Constable.

Discovering body dysmorphic disorder (BDD)

The American Psychiatric Association says BDD is characterised by a preoccupation with an imagined defect in appearance or markedly excessive attention to a minor physical defect. BDD is a profoundly distressing and disabling problem that goes far beyond imagined ugliness. Sufferers tend to be very preoccupied with their appearance and highly afraid of being humiliated because of what they perceive as their 'revolting' or 'freakish' looks.

Use Worksheet 13-2 to check out any symptoms of BDD.

Worksheet 13-2	BDD Symptoms Checklist
❑ I spend more than an hour each day worrying about my appearance.	
❑ I believe that I look ugly or unacceptable, despite being reassured by others that this is not the case.	
❑ I worry that I will be embarrassed or humiliated because of my appearance, especially if I don't conceal or camouflage my defect(s).	
❑ I tend to compare my appearance to that of other people, including people I encounter in my real life and those in magazines and on television.	
❑ I spend a lot of time thinking about how I might improve or camouflage my appearance through cosmetic or dermatological procedures, clothing, dietary supplements, exercise, make-up, and so on.	

If you tick three or more of items, you're probably suffering with BDD. The same sort of CBT techniques that work for OCD can help you overcome BDD. You can use the worksheets in this chapter to help you understand and beat BDD.

Highlighting health anxiety

Hypochondriasis is the old term for health anxiety, which has now been largely dropped by professionals as it suggests someone who is constantly suffering from different ailments and is a bit neurotic. In fact, real health anxiety can be severely distressing. It involves being preoccupied with constant worries about having or developing serious illnesses.

Use Worksheet 13-3 to help you recognise features of health anxiety.

Worksheet 13-3	Health Anxiety Checklist
❑ I spend at least an hour a day worried by a fear of being ill or an idea that I am ill with cancer, heart disease, Multiple Sclerosis, AIDS, or something similar despite having been given medical reassurance.	
❑ I have a strong sense that I am vulnerable to illness.	
❑ I worry that if I'm not vigilant for signs of illness I might miss something important.	
❑ I worry a lot that anxiety itself may cause harm.	

If you ticked the first item, that alone probably indicates that you have health anxiety. If you ticked the first item and one or more other items, the probability that you suffer from health anxiety increases.

Obsessive compulsive disorder, body dysmorphic disorder, and health anxiety all respond very well to CBT treatment. The same CBT exercises are effective in overcoming all three of these disorders, which is why we include them all in the same chapter. We urge you to read Chapters 4 and 9 for more techniques to help you defeat these disorders.

Checking out compulsive behaviours

Compulsions are actions that you feel compelled to carry out over and over again or in a precise and exact manner. Health anxiety, OCD, and BDD all involve compulsive actions and rituals. Rituals and compulsions are largely similar in that you feel duty-bound to complete them and feel very uncomfortable and anxious if you're somehow prevented from doing so. Rituals, however, are often more elaborate than straightforward compulsions. For example, you may feel compelled to get dressed in a precise order and go through a highly specific ritual for putting on items of clothing. Or you may have a ritual about how you brush your teeth. You may be very particular about how much toothpaste you use, how many times you brush each layer of teeth and so on. An example of a compulsion may be feeling like you need to check you've locked the door ten or more times.

The problem with compulsions and rituals is that the more you carry them out, the more you reinforce the idea that you need to keep on carrying them out. Worksheet 13-4 helps you to identify common rituals and compulsions associated with health anxiety, OCD and BDD.

Now use Worksheet 13-4 to go through the list of common compulsions. If you carry out any of the actions listed in the worksheet more than three times, you're doing them excessively and more than is considered necessary by most people without obsessional problems. Equally, if the time you devote to tasks listed in the worksheet means that you neglect other duties or are late for appointments, then you're doing them to excess.

Worksheet 13-4	Compulsions Checklist
❏	I frequently check things such as locks, water taps, gas taps, and electrical items more often than is necessary.
❏	I spend an excessive amount of time washing.
❏	I frequently seek reassurance from my partner, friends, or family. (Asking repeatedly for reassurance that nothing bad is about to happen, that you don't have a disease or that you look 'normal' or 'acceptable')
❏	I frequently repeat words and phrases in my mind, or re-play images.

❑ I spend an excessive amount of time putting things in order, tidying, or making things 'just so'.

❑ I have an excessive amount of clutter and hoarded items in my home.

❑ I try hard to push upsetting thoughts out of my mind.

❑ I become significantly distressed if I'm prevented from or am interrupted in carrying out my rituals.

❑ My compulsions interfere with my ability to function in important areas of my social life, work, family life, and relationships.

The kinds of excessive behaviour highlighted in this worksheet underpin and maintain your obsessional problem. Once you're aware of your individual rituals and compulsions you know what you need to be doing less of.

It can be useful to monitor and record just how many times you check things, repeat words or phrases, ask for reassurance, or engage in other rituals. You can also record exactly how much time you spend on certain tasks. Doing this can help you fully realise the degree to which compulsions are interfering with your life.

Carrying out compulsive and ritualistic actions is a symptom of the disorders mentioned previously. Bear in mind that reducing and stopping these actions is a major element in overcoming your obsessional problems

Assessing and Acting Against Obsessional Attitudes

Research has narrowed down the common underpinnings of obsessional problems. Intolerance of doubt and uncertainty, excessive responsibility, a need for control over your mind, health, or attractiveness are common characteristics of obsessive thinking. See if any of the following examples strike a chord:

- ✔ If a thought or image of harm happening to myself or others occurs to me, it means I am responsible for preventing that harm.
- ✔ I need to be certain that my fear will not come true.
- ✔ I should be able to control the thoughts, doubts, images, or sensations I have.
- ✔ Because an upsetting thought or image comes from my mind, it must say something about me – that I'm bad, evil, dangerous, or otherwise disturbed.
- ✔ If something bad happens and I have not taken all possible steps to prevent it, I am to blame for it happening.

The exercises in the following sections are aimed at helping you fight back against the attitudes that drive your obsessive behaviour.

Pitting Theory A against Theory B

If you've read any of the other chapters in this book before this one, you're familiar with the idea that the more extreme the meaning you give to an event, the more extreme your emotional response to it is likely to be.

Theory A is the negative, catastrophic definition you give to your problem. For example 'an intrusive thought about abusing a child means I must want to do it, and that proves I'm a paedophile', or 'an imperfection in my appearance means I'm hideous and will be totally humiliated if I approach someone I find attractive', or 'this lump on my skin means I have a cancer that hasn't been detected, I'll die in a few months, and my children will be devastated'.

Theory B is a more realistic and likely definition you choose to give to your problem. So, 'intrusive thoughts about abusing a child means I've got OCD and am worrying obsessively about being a paedophile', or 'an imperfection in my appearance is something I focus on too much because I have BDD' or 'I'm worried about this lump because I have health anxiety not cancer'.

Worksheet 13-6 gives you a structure for developing a less threatening and more accurate theory for your obsessional problem. Then it's up to you to adopt the theory that best fits the facts – Theory B! Next strive to behave as if you really believe that Theory B is correct. When you act according to Theory Authors, you engage in all sorts of rituals and compulsions like those described in Worksheet 13-4 which only makes your obsessions worse. Acting according to Theory A leads you to resist compulsions and rituals and re-engage in other activities that help you overcome your obsessions.

For many years Sharon had experienced obsessive thoughts about harming her daughter. She used Worksheet 13-5 to work out a theory to help her deal with her problem.

Worksheet 13-5	**Sharon's Constructing a Workable Theory Worksheet**

Intrusive thought, doubt, image, impulse, urge, bodily sensation, or area of concern:

Whenever I'm near an object that could potentially do someone harm, such as a knife or scissors, I have an image of hurting my child with that object.

Theory A (upsetting/negative theory)	*Theory B (alternative theory)*
This means I am an evil and dangerous person who should be locked up and never see her child again.	This means I am extremely worried about being dangerous to my child and am afraid of her coming to harm.

What can I try to do to treat my problem as if Theory B is correct?

I need to try to worry less about being dangerous and interpret intrusive images as reflecting what I quite naturally don't want to happen. This means training myself to become more comfortable with sharp/ potentially dangerous objects, like I used to be a few years ago and most people are. I also need to let my intrusive images and doubts pass through my mind without making them so significant and without fighting them or seeking reassurance.

Now consider a Theory A and a less disturbing Theory B for your own obsession, using Worksheet 13-6.

Worksheet 13-6   My Constructing a Workable Theory Worksheet

Intrusive thought, doubt, image, impulse, urge, bodily sensation, or area of concern:

Theory A (upsetting/negative theory)	*Theory B (alternative theory)*

What can I try to do to treat my problem as if Theory B is correct?

_____

_____

_____

_____

_____

_____

Realistically appraising responsibility

Excessive responsibility leads to excessive worry and guilt, and to trying excessively hard to prevent bad things that lie outside of your control from happening. It lies at the very heart of obsessional problems. Reducing your tendency to assume excessive responsibility for causing or preventing harm, monitoring your health, or being humiliated on the basis of your appearance is a big help in reducing your obsessions themselves.

Clive worries excessively about passing on toxic substances and bodily fluids to other people and them becoming ill or dying as a result. Worksheet 13-7 shows how he assigned responsibility for his problem.

Worksheet 13-7   **Clive's Realistic Responsibility Pie Chart**

Clive

Other people have responsibility for looking after their own health.

People and companies that use toxic chemicals are responsible for disposing of chemicals properly and safely.

The government is responsible for regulating toxic chemicals and informing the public of risks.

Chemical companies that produce toxic chemicals are responsible for safely handling and dispensing them.

To work out your responsibility pie chart, first fill in Worksheet 13-8. The first rating is important because it represents the amount of responsibility you take before you actually analyse other contributing factors. Generally you'll give yourself an unreasonable and inflated amount of personal responsibility for your feared event in the first instance. Also be sure to list all contributing factors before yourself and place yourself within the pie last. Otherwise you risk overlooking factors besides yourself and giving yourself an overly generous slice of the pie.

Worksheet 13-8	My Assigning Responsibility Worksheet
Define your feared event:	
Rate how much responsibility (0–100 per cent) you would give yourself if this feared event occurred:	
List all the factors you consider would contribute to your feared event, placing yourself last on the list.	
Now allocate a portion of responsibility to each of the factors you listed, putting yourself in last.	

Use the percentages from Worksheet 13-8 to fill in your own pie chart in Worksheet 13-9.

Worksheet 13-9	Your Realistic Responsibility Pie Chart

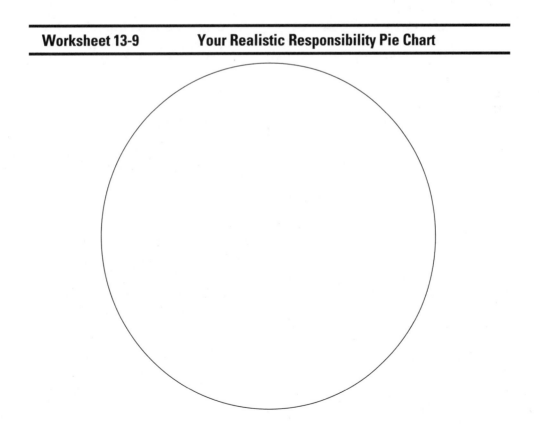

Steering in the right direction

'How can you know for sure?' is the question we get asked *a lot* by our clients with obsessional problems. 'How can you be sure I won't cause someone harm?' 'How can you be sure I'm not ill?' 'How can you be sure I won't get ill?' 'How can you know I won't be rejected and humiliated?' 'How can you be sure I'm not dangerous to children?' The answer, of course, is that we can't be sure of any of these things. But we can be pretty sure that if you keep searching for answers to these doubts and uncertainties you're likely to maintain your obsessional problem.

If you identified an obsessional problem in yourself and are worried about something, you can't be certain that your fear won't come true. However you can be fairly sure that you're likely to over-estimate the chances of disaster. This knowledge has a very important implication: Instead of worrying, you can choose to safely assume that things are okay and then act accordingly.

Think of your mind as a boat travelling along a wide river. As you sail, the left side of the river represents 'assuming the worst' and the right side 'assuming things will be okay'. Now, as you sail down the river that is navigating the world, you notice that wind (anxiety) and current (obsessions) move the boat towards the shore of assuming the worst. So to avoid colliding with the shore you need to steer your boat towards the shore of assuming things will be okay, at least until the current and wind subside.

Mike worries that he'll inadvertently cause harm to people. For example, if he's walking down the street he fears he might accidentally push someone into oncoming traffic. Worksheet 13-10 shows how he started to combat his bias.

Worksheet 13-10	Mike's Taking Control Worksheet
Trigger:	Passing a woman in the street.
What I tend to assume:	That I will hurt her.
How I act as a consequence:	I give people a wide berth as much as I can and repeatedly look backwards or re-trace my steps to check for signs of an accident.
The results of thinking and acting in this way:	It slows me down and I realise I'm acting quite strangely. It also only reassures me for this one moment, and I often worry that I might have hurt another person while I was distracted checking the original person.

Alternative (assuming things are okay) assumption:	That a doubt or image of knocking someone into oncoming traffic reflects my brain being overly alert to this kind of danger. I can afford to assume I haven't caused anyone harm.
How I can act as if I'm assuming things are okay:	Keep moving without excessive caution and without looking or listening for signs of an accident.

Now identify the kinds of unhelpful catastrophic assumptions you would benefit from steering away from using Worksheet 13-11.

Worksheet 13-11	My Taking Control Worksheet
Trigger:	
What I tend to assume:	
How I act as a consequence:	
The results of thinking and acting in this way:	

(continued)

Alternative (assuming things are okay) assumption:	
How I can act as if I'm assuming things are okay:	

Use this exercise sparingly to help set the course against your obsessional problem. Avoid using it if you sense that you're doing so to gain reassurance that you're definitely not going to act on your obsessions and are absolutely safe from doing so. Otherwise, you can end up making this worksheet another ritual! Instead, use it to recognize the benefits of acting according to your alternative assumption that things are okay.

People with obsessional problems like OCD, BDD, and health anxiety typically demand cast-iron guarantees that certain bad things won't happen. Demands for certainty can very rarely be met and therefore they produce anxiety. So when you're working to overcome obsessional problems, it's important to learn to tolerate doubt and uncertainty.

Reining in Rituals

Alongside deliberately confronting triggers for your fears, doubts, and intrusive thoughts, you need to reduce and stop the rituals and compulsions you use in response. This section offers some suggestions for controlling rituals. (For more advice on deliberately confronting your fears, see Chapter 9.)

Checking out and changing your termination criteria

One of the keys for cutting out rituals is to become aware of why you finish a session of washing, checking, seeking reassurance, or performing some other ritualistic behaviour. This reason is known as your *termination criteria*. People who wash their hands excessively, for example, tend to finish washing when they *feel right*, whereas the average person finishes washing when their hands look clean enough if they were visibly dirty, or just go on autopilot to do a convenient quick wash after using the toilet since they don't regard it as all that important. Table 13-1 lists helpful and problematic reasons for stopping a behaviour.

Table 13-1	Good and Not-so-good Reasons to Stop Compulsive Behaviour
Problematic reasons	*Ordinary, acceptable reasons*
It feels right	That's long enough; any more is too much hassle
I'm comfortable	It's convenient to do it this way
It's 'just so'	I can see that it's done and can live with a doubt that it's not
I feel sure	I've taken enough care, I don't have to be certain
	That's as much care as most people take
	Let's get on with the next task/appointment

Harold washes his hands at least 30 times a day for several minutes at a time, using very hot water and anti-bacterial soap. Worksheet 13-12 shows how changing his termination criteria helped him to cut down.

Worksheet 13-12	Harold's Changing Criteria Worksheet
The ritual or compulsion I want to reduce or stop:	My excessive handwashing.
The unhelpful criteria I tend to use to end this ritual or compulsion:	When I feel completely sure I've removed any trace of germs and get a sense of relief.
The alternative criteria I'm going to train myself to use to end my action:	To make handwashing quick and functional. To stop once I have briefly lathered my hands with soap and rinsed it off. I only need to wash for more than a few seconds if I can see dirt on my hands without carefully examining them.

Use Worksheet 13-13 to discover a point at which to stop your rituals.

Worksheet 13-13	My Changing Criteria Worksheet
The ritual or compulsion I want to reduce or stop:	
The unhelpful criteria I tend to use to end this ritual or compulsion:	
The alternative criteria I'm going to train myself to use to end my action:	

Recording and resisting rituals

Keeping a record of the rituals or compulsions you carry out is a simple yet surprisingly helpful step in cutting them down. A chart that records the frequency of your rituals helps you to:

✔ See just how often you use them and improve your awareness.

✔ Record your progress.

✔ Boost your motivation to resist!

Mark is troubled by a fear causing harm to people in the street through his negligence. This leads him to constantly check when he passes people to ensure that he hasn't hit them or tripped them. Mark is constantly looking over his shoulder to make sure people he's been near are unhurt. When he walks down the street he keeps his arms close to his sides and won't carry sharp objects or large bags in case he injures someone. When he gets home, Mark carefully checks all his clothing for any traces of blood which may mean that he's unknowingly caused another person injury. Worksheet 13-14 shows his ritual record sheet.

Worksheet 13-14	Mark's Ritual Record							
Ritual/Compulsion	SUN	SUN	MON	TUES	WED	THURS	FRI	SAT
Checking over my shoulder when I pass people in the street to be sure I haven't hit or tripped them.	5×	5×	3×	1×	0	11×	13×	2×
Checking my clothes for traces of blood when I return home.	2×	2×	2×	1×	0	6×	6×	2×
Pulling my arms tightly to my body and checking that they stay in that position.	10×	10×	12×	4×	0	6×	6×	2×

You might be carrying out rituals in your head as well as in your behaviour, so record mental rituals too.

Use Worksheet 13-15 to identify rituals you want to reduce. Stop your compulsions and start recording!

Worksheet 13-15	My Ritual Record							
Ritual/Compulsion	SUN	SUN	MON	TUES	WED	THURS	FRI	SAT

Chapter 14

Lifting Low Self-Esteem

Rating yourself as 'good' or 'bad', a 'success' or a 'failure', 'worthy' or 'worthless' on the basis of your achievements or circumstances is extremely common. Being common practice doesn't make it good practice, though. In fact, attaching your self opinion to external conditions is at the very root of self-esteem problems. Your opinion of yourself is vulnerable to plummeting if your existing state of affairs isn't maintained. Life is unpredictable and prone to change, hence your mood and view of yourself can shift wildly if you consistently anchor your value to your job, relationships, financial situation, and so on.

Even the term *self-esteem* is problematic as it implies that a person can be given an accurate overall rating or 'estimate' even if the person doing the rating is you! Assessing a piece of jewellery or a diamond and estimating its overall market value is easy. People however are living, changing creatures and far more complex than inanimate objects. An alternative to self-esteem is the concept of *self-acceptance*.

CBT encourages you to stop giving yourself overall or global ratings altogether. Rather, accept yourself as a fundamentally worthwhile person and only rate individual aspects of yourself, your lifestyle, behaviour, and so on. In this chapter we expand on the concept of self-acceptance and offer you some practical exercises for applying an accepting attitude toward yourself and others.

You can use most of the exercises in the chapter to increase your tolerance of other people, too. The sames rules for self-acceptance apply to other acceptance. Practising an attitude of other acceptance can help you put a stop to unhealthy anger, jealousy, and hurt.

Acquiring Self-Acceptance

All human beings are equal in worth. Stop for a moment and consider how much you agree with that statement. Isn't all human life sacred? Isn't that why murder is a crime regardless of who's killed? Essentially, most of us are taught that human beings have *intrinsic* value and worth (meaning we're valuable and worthy just because we exist). But we frequently behave as if some people are more worthy than others.

We commonly attach too much importance to (or over value) certain things prized in western society such as wealth and social status. You may mistakenly assume that people who possess these prized conditions or traits are superior to yourself or others who lack them. At the same time, you may attach too little importance (or under value) aspects of your personhood such as generosity, social responsibility, and kindness.

Comparing yourself to others on the basis of external conditions leads you to feel either superior or inferior, in turns. Both positions are unhealthy because you're either putting down yourself or others.

Acquiring self-acceptance (and acceptance of others as well) means that you're able to recognise that we're all equal in worth but unequal in specific aspects. So you may be an excellent cook and a poor driver while your neighbour may be the exact opposite. You're still both worthy individuals but have different strengths and limitations. One of the first steps toward self-acceptance is noting particular conditions to which you typically attach your self worth.

Worksheet 14-1 is a checklist of general areas or domains that people frequently judge their overall worth against. Check off the ones that resonate with you, then add a couple of your own not included in the list.

Worksheet 14-1	External Conditions Checklist
❑	Academic/educational qualifications
❑	Career or job success
❑	Creativity/artistic talents
❑	Ethnicity
❑	Fame/celebrity status
❑	Family background
❑	Intelligence
❑	Mental health
❑	Parenting skills
❑	Physical attractiveness/fitness
❑	Physical disabilities
❑	Physical health
❑	Quality of relationships
❑	Religious observance
❑	Social popularity/social ease
❑	Socio-economic status
❑	Wealth/material possessions
❑	_____
❑	_____

Now that you've pinpointed the areas that you tend to give yourself a global rating on, you can use this knowledge to help yourself overcome low self-esteem and to adopt self-acceptance instead. The techniques offered in the following sections can help you to do so.

Realising reasons not to rate yourself

Human beings are too complex to be given an overall rating. We're all a mixed bag of good, bad, and neutral traits. Sure, there are things about yourself or your life circumstances that you may wish to improve, but doing so doesn't up your worth. Making positive changes where possible may help you to enjoy life more but your human worth remains constant.

You probably have areas that you're dissatisfied with but that you're unable to improve or alter. For example, you may not be artistic or you may not be a social butterfly and that's just the way you are. Sometimes you're best off just accepting reality and focusing on other skills and talents that you do possess. Rating yourself negatively because of your limitations can lead to emotional problems such as anxiety, depression, and shame.

Your emotional problems aren't solved by rating yourself as 'bad' or 'worthless' for having them in the first place. Kicking yourself when you're down isn't the most effective way of getting yourself back on your feet. If you rate your entire worth based on just one aspect of yourself, you're making the 'part-whole' error: Judging (and probably condemning) your whole self on the basis of one or two parts of yourself. Don't do it. Judging yourself in this way is bad news.

As a human being you are always changing and growing from the day you are born until the day you die. You are also unique and individual – no one else on the planet is exactly the same as you. Your human complexity involves all your past, present, and future experiences, deeds, and adventures.

Use Worksheet 14-2 to list reasons *not* to give yourself a global rating.

Worksheet 14-2	**Reasons Not to Rate Myself**
Giving myself a global rating is inaccurate because I am ever-changing. These are some ways in which I'm a changing and developing human being:	
I'm too complex to be able to accurately rate or judge myself on the basis of one or more individual traits or actions. My complexities as a human being include:	
As a human being I am unique. Some of my unique traits, skills, limitations, likes, and dislikes include:	

Leaving behind loathsome labelling

In addition to unhelpfully giving yourself negative global ratings, you probably call yourself names, and nasty ones at that. You may call yourself nasty names silently in your own head or you may even say them out loud at times.

Even if you don't think that you always really *mean* the hateful things you call yourself, they can have a negative impact on your self opinion. So if you don't mean it, don't call yourself it! And even if you do mean it, stop it!

The names you call yourself can further erode your sense of worth plus reinforce negative core beliefs (see chapter 16 for more info on core beliefs and how to change negative ones). Another term for name calling is *labelling* (see Chapter 2 for more about labelling). Some typical examples of loathsome labelling include expressions such as:

I'm inadequate	I'm worthless
I'm weak	I'm no good
I'm a failure	I don't matter
I'm defective	I'm stupid
I'm unlovable	I'm pathetic
I'm useless	I'm a loser
I'm bad	I'm disgusting
I'm inferior	I'm crazy

The main method of losing loathsome labels from your life is to resist using them. It's like breaking a habit. Catch yourself in the act and refuse to call yourself horrid labels – either inside your head or out loud.

One of the tactics we sometimes use with patients is to have them put a 50 pence piece into a jar everytime they call themselves negative names. Doing this can help you to see just how often you resort to name calling and can help remind you to stop. You can then donate the money in your jar to your favorite charity or another worthwhile cause.

Instead of calling yourself globally negative labels like those just listed, try to label only your actions and be very specific about what aspect of your actions you're displeased with. So instead of saying 'I'm a total loser' specify what you've lost by saying something like ' I lost my job', 'I lost the golf match' or 'I lost the promotion'. Being specific helps you to accept that you're capable of losing sometimes but aknowledge that you're also capable of winning sometimes. Hence no one is ever a 'total loser'.

Also substitue more accurate names and labels for the globally negative ones you typically use. You don't need to veer into wildy positive self statements like 'I'm fantastic' or 'I love myself', and in fact we strongly discourage you from doing so for two reasons. Firstly, you're unlikely to truly believe such globally positive things about yourself , especially if you've been battling low self-esteem for some time. Secondly, these statements, although positive, are still unhealthy because they are global and unrealistic. No one is ever totally bad and therefore no one is ever totally good. Instead, try using alternative self statements that are balanced and realistic. Table 14-1 shows some appropriate alternatives.

Table 14-1	Healthy Alternatives to Labels
Loathsome Label	*Alternative Healthy Self-statement*
I'm inadequate	I have skills and talents
I'm worthless	I'm a worthwhile person
I'm weak	I have both strengths and weaknesses
I'm no good	I have many good qualities
I'm a failure	I'm a fallible human being capable of both success and failure
I don't matter	I have siginificance
I'm defective	I may have certain defects (like any person) but I'm not defective
I'm stupid	I can do stupid things sometimes but that doesn't mean I'm stupid

Loathsome Label	Alternative Healthy Self-statement
I'm unlovable	People can love me and I am worthy of being loved
I'm pathetic	I have capabilities
I'm useless	I do many useful things
I'm a loser	I'm a normal person who can both win and lose
I'm bad	I'm a person with both good and bad traits
I'm disgusting	I'm acceptable
I'm inferior	I have equal worth to others
I'm crazy	Even if I sometimes do crazy things, I'm not totally crazy

Rajesh anchors his self-worth to his career success and his social popularity. He often tells himself that he's inadequate and a total failure if he makes a blunder at work or embarrasses himself even slightly in a social setting. Often Rajesh feels anxious before going to social events and prior to work meetings. Because of his beliefs that he *must* succeed in his career and be popular, Rajesh often experiences unhealthy negative emotions such as shame and depression when his personal rules are not wholly met. He doesn't give himself much room for human error. Rajesh used Worksheet 14-3 to readjust his self-labelling and assess the effects of doing so.

Worksheet 14-3	Rajesh's Loathsome Labels and Alternatives List
Areas I commonly rate my whole self on the basis of:	My career and job success. My social success/popularity and social ease.
What negative labels do I most often use about myself?	I'm a failure. I'm useless. I'm unlikable.
What are three good reasons for losing these labels?	1. I feel really bad about myself and depressed when I call myself these things. 2. I tend to avoid social outings and work stuff when I'm thinking of myself in line with these labels. 3. I decide that I can't improve and give up trying to reach goals when I'm stuck in name-calling behaviour.
What are helpful self-accepting alternatives for these labels?	Everyone makes work errors and social gaffs from time to time, not just me. I'm a human being capable of success and failure just like any other person on the planet. Just because I make mistakes doesn't make me totally useless. I do plenty of things that are useful. Lots of people seem to enjoy my company, and I have several friends. Just because I may put my foot in my mouth sometimes or feel a bit awkward socially doesn't mean that I'm not likeable. No one can be everybody's ideal cup of tea.

After you generate some healthy alternative statements to replace your loathsome labels, you need to reinforce your belief in them. Practise saying your healthy alternatives to yourself several times every day – particularly in situations in which you would typically resort to loathsome self-labeling. Also act as if you truly believe your healthy alternative. For example, if you truly believe 'I'm worthwhile', then you look after your health, join in social activities, voice your views and opinion, and make eye contact with others. The more you act according to the new way you want to think of yourself the more you will come to believe in its truth.

In order to successfully change a habit, you need to stick with it for a minimum of three weeks. You'll notice changes after one week or even after a few days, but you need to keep on practicing alternative healthy ways of thinking about yourself for several weeks. In time, and with deliberate effort and practice, thinking in positive and balanced ways about yourself will become more automatic. In other words you'll have developed a new constructive thinking habit.

Worksheet 14-4 shows how Rajesh monitored his progress.

Worksheet 14-4	Rajesh's Three-week Progress Report
After 1 week:	It takes a lot of reminding and effort to resist calling myself nasty names. I obviously do it a lot more than I realised before following this exercise.
After 2 weeks:	I feel generally better about myself and am more able to stick with uncomfortable situations when I'm resisting calling myself names and labelling myself negatively.
After 3 weeks:	It's getting much easier to resist name calling. I find that I'm thinking in a more balanced and helpful way about work and social situations almost automatically. I feel less depressed and ashamed plus I like myself more than I did 3 weeks ago.

In Worksheets 14-5 and 14-6 list your own nasty name calling habits and record the results of refusing to call yourself names any longer!

Worksheet 14-5	Your Loathsome Labels and Alternatives List
Areas I commonly rate my whole self on the basis of:	
What negative labels do I most often use about myself?	
What are three good reasons for losing these labels?	
What are helpful self-accepting alternatives for these labels?	

Take notice of the positive changes, benefits, and overall effects you experience as you shed your loathsome labels in Worksheet 14-6.

Worksheet 14-6	Your Three-week Progress Report
After 1 week:	
After 2 weeks:	
After 3 weeks:	

Acting on Acceptance

Self-acceptance beliefs and attitudes have the following three characteristics:

- ✔ They make logical sense. For example, just because you *prefer* to not make mistakes doesn't mean that you *must* not make them.

- ✔ They are consistent with reality. For example, you're capable of making mistakes. Thus, giving yourself permission to screw up reflects the reality of your capacity to screw up now and then.

- ✔ They are helpful. For example, if you give yourself room for error, you won't be unduly depressed when you make a mistake. You'll be more able to make amends or solve problems if you're not absorbed in condemning yourself for your errors.

At the risk of repeating ourselves (but some points bear repeating), rRating your whole self on one component of your behaviour isn't helpful. Figure 14-1 gives you a more visual example of your human complexity. Plus it highlights the silliness of giving yourself a global label.

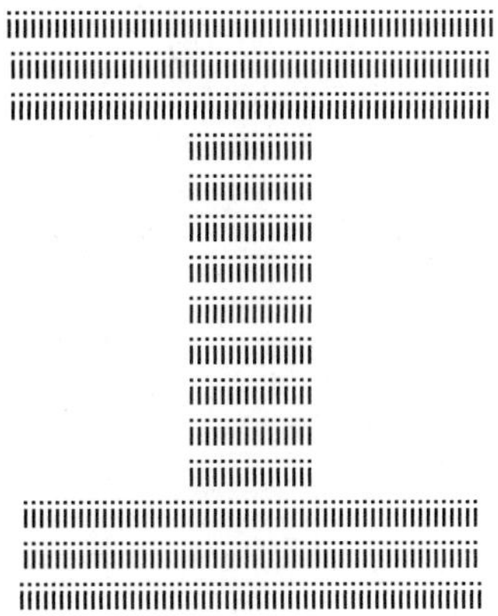

Figure 14-1: Which do you see first, the big 'I' or all the little ones?

The big *I* drawn in Figure 14-1 represents your *whole* self – past, present, and future; good, bad, and neutral. Absolutely every last little thing about you. The smaller *i*'s represent your various behaviours, traits, skills, attributes, talents, experiences, dreams, limitations, mistakes, upsets, and so on.

Adding up the Evidence

Self-acceptance may seem a pretty straightforward concept, but like many CBT principles, it's considerably harder to put into practice. Because it isn't easy, self-acceptance needs to be rehearsed, rehashed, and revisited time and again before you begin to feel the positive effects. The more proof or evidence that you can gather to support your attitude of self-acceptance the more you'll reinforce it as true.

Follow these steps to complete Worksheet 14-8:

1. **Describe a negative event or situation in which you called yourself nasty names.**

2. **Record the unhealthy label you gave yourself in your own words.**

3. **Record your alternative healthy self-statement.**

4. **Look for and record evidence in the situation that supports your healthy self-accepting attitude and contradicts your unhealthy negative label.**

Worksheet 14-7 provides an example of how Rajesh worked to reinforce his self-acceptance attitudes.

Worksheet 14-7	Rajesh's Evidence Epistle
Situation:	Spilling my drink and stumbling over my words when I arrived at an after-work social evening.
Negative label:	I'm a total loser and not likeable.
Self-accepting alternative attitude:	Okay, so I got a bit flustered. I'm not a loser but I am a fallible person, and I'm still likeable despite this minor social blip!
Evidence supporting my self-accepting attitude:	Everyone laughed and joked about me spilling the drink. A colleague instantly went to the bar and bought me another. Everyone chatted to me and asked me questions as though nothing serious had happened. My desk mate pulled me onto the dance floor. No one gave me funny looks or the cold shoulder because of my awkwardness.

Now reinforce your self-acceptance attitudes using Worksheet 14-8.

Worksheet 14-8	My Evidence Epistle
Situation:	
Negative label:	
Self-accepting alternative attitude:	
Evidence supporting my self-accepting attitude:	

Now check Worksheet 14-7 again and include any extra evidence that you may have overlooked or discounted the first time round.

Feeling fine about human fallibility

You're human and hence fallible – you make mistakes. Deal with it. Your fallibility is inevitable. Perfect people don't exist. So instead of putting yourself down, making yourself ashamed and depressed about mistakes, insisting that you *must* do better, or writing yourself off completely face up to your fundamental fallibility.

Worksheet 14-9 helps you to embrace your ability to make gaffs, slip-ups, minor errors, or major screw-ups and still think of yourself as a basically okay person. Give it a whirl.

Worksheet 14-9	My Feeling Fine about Fallibility Form
Recent events that I'm putting myself down for:	
How is putting myself down affecting my mood?	
How is putting myself down affecting my behaviour?	

(continued)

Review the event/events again. Did I do something bad or behave poorly?	
Did I make a mistake or fail at something?	
Considering my human fallibility, can I take a more compassionate or forgiving view of myself in light of these recent events?	
How might I make amends for poor or bad behaviour, if appropriate?	
How can I rectify a mistake or failure, if appropriate?	
In light of these events, are there conditions I can strive to improve/change?	
In light of these events, are there elements of them that I can strive to accept as they are?	
How will accepting myself as fallible motivate me to get on with solving my problems?	
How will accepting myself as fallible benefit my mood and self-opinion?	

Being very specific

An antidote to global rating is to be *very specific* when judging your actions, deeds, or intentions. So instead of telling yourself what an utter failure you are, ask yourself in what *specific* way you have failed on this occasion. Rather than labelling yourself as utterly incompetent, ask yourself in which *specific* area you've behaved incompetently. Own up to the nitty-gritty, fine details rather than just throw your whole self out of the window with the dirty bath water.

Worksheet 14-10 shows how Rajesh got specific.

Worksheet 14-10	Rajesh's Specific Synopsis Sheet
What exactly happened?	I was a bit nervous and foolish when I first arrived at an after-work social event.
What specific aspect of my/others' performance, behaviour, or emotional response am I displeased with?	I spilled my drink and spoke incoherently.
How can I put my displeasure into perspective given my understanding of myself/others as mistake-making human beings?	Okay, so I spilled my drink and stammered. Not the end of the world. The rest of the evening went well and even if it hadn't, it wouldn't mean that I'm useless or unlikeable. It would simply mean that I get anxious in social situations. Not a major crime but a personal inconvenience that I'm trying to surmount. My social anxiety has more negative impact on me than it does on those around me. So really I don't need to worry about what other people are thinking of me quite so much.

When you judge yourself harshly and are unforgiving, you're probably doing the same to others. Judging is a double-edged sword that can ultimately negatively affect your personal relationships. So use Worksheet 14-11 on both yourself and others! When using the worksheet on another person, remember to resist globally rating them on the basis of their actions. Be specifc about what they've done or failed to do that you're displeased with. Finally remind yourself that others are fallible too – just like you. Applying these basic principles of acceptance to others as well as to yourself can greatly reduce disharmony in relationships.

Worksheet 14-11	My Specific Synopsis Sheet
What exactly happened?	
What specific aspect of my/others' performance, behaviour, or emotional response am I displeased with?	
How can I put my displeasure into perspective given my understanding of myself/others as mistake-making human beings?	

Using the best friend technique

It's often easier to be understanding and compassionate with the people you love than yourself. You may find that you can forgive and overlook short comings in the people you care about but find it difficult to cut yourself the same slack. Learning to be more understanding and compassionate with yourself is an important part of self-acceptance and promotes good emotional health. Ever heard of double standards? One rule for you and another rule for me? Hmmm. Think of a recent event that you may be bludgeoning yourself about. Now imagine that your best friend or someone that you deeply care for came to you berating themselves about the same event. What would you say to your loved one? Use Worksheet 14-12 to highlight what you would say to your best friend if they were in your situation. Next make a real effort to apply the same advise to yourelf.

Worksheet 14-12	Your Best Friend Form
What exactly happened?	
What am I telling myself about what happened? What does it mean about me?	
Would I advise my best friend or loved one to hold this view of themselves about the event?	
If not, why not?	
What would I say to my best friend or loved one in the same circumstances?	
How can I apply the same advice I would give to a friend or loved one to myself?	

Accepting and Improving Yourself at the Same Time

Perhaps you think that accepting yourself means that you can surrender self-improvement and let yourself off the hook for any bad actions you may take or good actions you neglect to execute. We hope not, because that really isn't our message. On balance, if you accept yourself as fundamentally worthwhile in view of your shortcomings or bad behaviours, you're in a better place to work on them than if you condemn yourself. We suggest that you simultaneously give yourself room to be less than perfect and still strive to make personally important changes. Doing so really is a recipe for self-improvement success.

Selecting specific areas for self-improvement

If you want to make improvements to your personal behaviour and your life in general, being extremely specific is best. Saying 'I want to be a better person' may be true but it doesn't give enough information to be getting on with. The detail is what matters. See Chapter 8 for more on goal setting.

Try out Worksheet 14-13. Do it now, and then do it again, after reading or re-reading Chapter 8.

Worksheet 14-13	My Specific Areas for Self-improvement
What emotional problems do I want to overcome?	
How would I like to feel differently? (see Chapter 6 on finding your feelings)	
What aspects of my behaviour do I want to change?	
How would I like to behave differently?	
In which specific situations would I like to behave and feel differently?	
How will changing the way I feel and behave in these situations be of benefit to me (think short, medium, and long term)?	
Which aspects of my life circumstances do I want to improve?	
What action do I need to take to initiate these improvements?	
What steps can I take – and when – to help me make basic changes to my circumstances?	

Embracing personal responsibility

Other people or world/life events don't wholly mess us up. No. The meanings we assign to these events do a far more thorough and comprehensive job of that.

Poor Rajesh is tired! He's working hard on his own issues. Try Worksheet 14-14 on your own to discover your personal meanings We think you'll survive.

Worksheet 14-14	My Personal Responsibility Reckoning Record
What happened? (Be clear and precise!)	
What personal meanings am I ascribing to the situation/event?	
Am I making any thinking errors that lead me to feel unhealthy emotions?	
What (if anything) did I do that was poor or bad in context of the situation?	
How can I attempt to make amends if appropriate or necessary?	
How can I take a compassionate view of myself in light of the circumstances? (Think of what you would say to a close friend or loved one.)	
Am I wholly responsible for the event?	
Who else may have some degree of responsibility for the event?	

When you take *appropriate* responsibility for your behaviour and your emotions you're much more able to make effective changes. When you blame other people or life conditions/events for your disturbed emotions or self-destructive behaviour, you're giving up your power to make things better.

Regularly Reviewing Reasons for Self-Acceptance

Self-acceptance takes practice. Sometimes you may find believing in and acting according to your new attitudes easy and at other times doing so is more difficult. Worksheet 14-15 may help you to see the sense of self-acceptance attitudes when your conviction is waning.

Review the work you've done in this chapter and record whatever answers you find the most persuasive in this final worksheet.

Worksheet 14-15	Your Reasons for Self/Other Acceptance
My self/other acceptance attitude:	
Why does it make sound logical sense to hold this attitude?	
Why is this attitude true? (How does this attitude fit with reality?)	
In what specific ways is it helpful/ useful for me to hold this attitude?	
How does holding this attitude positively benefit my mood?	

You can use Worksheet 14-15 as a crib sheet. Carry it with you and consult it every so often (or when you feel a self-battering coming on) to keep the concepts fresh in your mind.

Chapter 15

Maintaining Relationships

Your ability to get along with others depends on your ability to be accepting of them and to experience healthy negative emotions instead of unhealthy ones such as rage, hate, and fury. (Take a look at Chapter 6 for an explanation of healthy and unhealthy negative emotions.) Unhealthy anger is a common reason for relationship problems. Another common cause of interpersonal difficulties is low self-opinion. In this chapter we help you to work out what type of anger you most often experience and to get better at being healthily angry. We also give you a few exercises to strengthen your acceptance of yourself and others – thereby increasing your chances of developing satisfying and functional relationships.

Overcoming Outrage

Everyone does it from time to time – loses their cool, blows their top, throws a wobbly, goes berserk. Some behave in this way more often than others, though. Losing your temper can cause problems in your romantic life, family relationships, friendships, and work life.

Recognising whether or not unhealthy outrage is the type of emotion you're experiencing is the first step in overcoming it. This section helps you to discern the difference between irrational rage and appropriate annoyance.

Recognising healthy anger

Let's have a look at the aspects of healthy anger. When you're healthily angry you tend to be thinking in a balanced and accepting way about others. You recognise that someone has stepped on your toes or violated one of your personal rules without deciding that they really *mustn't* do so. You still feel in control of yourself and you behave in an assertive but non-threatening manner.

Choose a recent or typical example when you got angry, and use the checklist in Worksheet 15-1 to identify aspects of healthy anger that apply to your thoughts, behaviours, and physical reactions.

Worksheet 15-1	Aspects of Healthy Anger Checklist

Thinking Aspects

- ❑ Holding strong preferences about how others/ the world behave
- ❑ Allowing others to live according to their own personal rules
- ❑ Strongly preferring that others treat you well and neither disrespect nor ridicule you
- ❑ Desiring that other people and life conditions don't get in the way of you pursuing your goals
- ❑ Thinking realistically about whether or not other people have deliberately acted badly toward you
- ❑ Considering that both you and the other person may be right and wrong to some degree
- ❑ Making an effort to understand the other person's point of view

Action Aspects

- ❑ Asserting yourself respectfully
- ❑ Staying in the situation and trying to resolve any disagreement
- ❑ Asking the other person to modify their behaviour whilst respecting their right to disagree with you
- ❑ Looking for evidence that the other person may not have behaved with malicious intent

Physical Aspects

- ❑ Some degree of muscular tension
- ❑ Minor shaking or trembling
- ❑ Feeling a bit hot or flushed
- ❑ Slightly raised heart rate

Seeing aspects of unhealthy anger

Anger of the unhealthy variety is typified by certain ways of thinking and acting plus certain physical sensations. Generally, unhealthy anger means that you're thinking in very harsh ways about someone else and behaving in an intimidating manner (that you *may* later regret). The sensation usually feels pretty uncomfortable and all consuming.

As a rule, *unhealthy anger* lasts longer and is more intensely uncomfortable than its healthier version.

Think of a recent or typical example of a time when you became angry. Use the checklist in Worksheet 15-2 to tick off the aspects of unhealthy anger that apply to you.

Worksheet 15-2	Aspects of Unhealthy Anger Checklist

Thinking Aspects

❑ Rigid demands or rules about how other people/the world must or must not behave

❑ Insisting that others must not disrespect or ridicule you

❑ Demanding that others and life conditions do not get in the way of you getting what you want, when you want it

❑ Assuming that other people have deliberately acted in an undesirable or unpleasant way toward you

❑ Taking the stance that you're totally right and others are totally wrong

❑ Refusing to consider the other person's point of view or opinion

Action Aspects

❑ Either actually attacking or wanting to attack another person verbally and/or physically

❑ Getting back at the other person in subtle ways such as sabotaging their job or relationship (which is known as passive aggression in psychological terms)

❑ Venting your anger on innocent parties such as other people in your life, animals, or objects

❑ Fantasising about and plotting revenge

❑ Sulking or freezing the other person out

❑ Looking for evidence that the offence was both malicious and is likely to be repeated

Physical Aspects

❑ Muscular tension

❑ Trembling or shaking

❑ Clenched jaw

❑ Feeling hot and flushed

❑ Raised heart rate

Having had a look at the difference between healthy and unhealthy anger through using the checklists, you may now be in a better position to decide which type of anger you most frequently experience.

Counting the Cost of Losing Your Cool

Getting unhealthily angry can have negative consequences on your relationships and your life in general. Sometimes you may think that your rage has positive benefits that healthy annoyance wouldn't bring about. You're probably wrong. Usually you're more articulate and effective at making your points if you're not fumin with hostility.

Paul hates other people telling him what to do. He tells himself that he can't stand it when other people try to assert control over him. Even if his girlfriend makes a minor request he sees it as an imposition and becomes very defensive. Paul also has trouble at work because he thinks his boss is belittling him if he's anything other than complimentary about his work. He's lost many jobs as a result of his angry outbursts. Recently Paul had a serious row with his girlfriend because she disagreed with him about holiday plans. He shouted at her and accused her of 'treating him like an idiot' for questioning his choice of destination. During the row he pushed her forcefully against a piece of furniture, badly bruising her back. As a result, Paul's girlfriend has refused to go on holiday with him and is re-thinking the future of their relationship. Paul now feels guilty for hurting his girlfriend and is kicking himself for his behaviour. Paul used Worksheet 15-3 to count the cost of his unhealthy anger.

Worksheet 15-3   Paul's Counting the Cost of Losing His Cool Worksheet

Recall a recent or typical situation in which you became unhealthily angry:	My girlfriend disagreed with me about where to go for our summer holiday.
Who or what were you angry with?	My girlfriend, for challenging my opinion and plans.
What did your unhealthy anger lead you to do?	I shouted at her and called her rude names. I threatened her and pushed her into the bookshelf.
What effect did your unhealthy anger have on the other person involved and/or your relationship with them? (Think both short and long term)	She cried, looked hurt and frightened, and ran out of my flat. She now won't come on holiday with me and is thinking seriously about breaking up with me.
What effect did your unhealthy anger have on the situation/problem? (Think both short and long term)	It made the problem much more serious than it needed to be and has created a really upsetting and painful situation between myself and my girlfriend. The holiday is totally off.
What effect did your unhealthy anger have on you? (Think both short and long term)	I felt really out of control at the time of the row. I now feel guilty for hurting my girlfriend and am very worried that she'll dump me for being so violent.

Use Worksheet 15-4 to help you count the cost of losing your cool.

Worksheet 15-4   My Counting the Cost of Losing My Cool Worksheet

Recall a recent or typical situation in which you became unhealthily angry:	
Who or what were you angry with?	
What did your unhealthy anger lead you to do?	
What effect did your unhealthy anger have on the other person involved and/or your relationship with them? (Think both short and long term)	
What effect did your unhealthy anger have on the situation/problem? (Think both short and long term)	
What effect did your unhealthy anger have on you? (Think both short and long term)	

Chapter 8 contains a Cost–Benefit Analysis (CBA) form that you may find helpful for further weighing up the costs and benefits of both healthy and unhealthy anger.

Lengthening Your Fuse

Okay, so perhaps you're realising that you often feel unhealthily angry and that it has some pretty negative results. So what's next? Dealing with your anger may be challenging, but if you want to enough and are prepared to put in some serious hard work, you can do it.

If you have strict rules that you demand others and the world adhere to at all times then you're prone to unhealthily anger if they break your rules. Giving others the right to hold and voice their own opinions is a good first step toward experiencing healthy anger. Also having preferences for how others behave but not insisting that everyone do as you wish helps you to avoid unhealthy outrage.

Paul used the questions in Worksheet 15-5 to work toward a healthier version of anger.

Worksheet 15-5	Paul's Fuse-lengthening Formula
Recent or typical situation in which I became unhealthily angry:	My girlfriend disagreed with me about where to go for our summer holiday.
What was I demanding of the other person/situation?	She must agree with me and she must not challenge me about where to go.
Was I insisting that I was right and the other person was wrong? What about?	I was insisting that I was right about where to go on holiday and that she was wrong to question my choice.
Was I refusing to allow the other person to disagree with me or to hold a different opinion or set of values to my own?	Yes, I completely discounted her opinion and ideas. I shouted her down and got very aggressive.
What is a more flexible and tolerant attitude I can hold about the other person/situation?	I'd rather that my girlfriend agreed with me about holiday plans but there's no reason that she has to. I can stand her disagreement and it doesn't mean that I'm weak or ineffectual if she disagrees with me.
How might holding this new attitude help me to resolve the problem?	I'd probably listen to her and not become loud and unpleasant. She may have a valid point and I might be wise to listen to her point of view. Also, if I hadn't gone totally ballistic we may still be going on holiday together and she may not be thinking about breaking up with me.
How might holding this new attitude benefit the other person involved?	My girlfriend wouldn't be afraid, insulted, and physically injured. She may feel appreciated and understood rather than bullied and abused.

When completing the worksheets in the remainder of this chapter, certain questions may not apply to you. Their relevance depends on whether you're unhealthily angry with another person or with the world/life conditions.

Following Paul's example, use the questions in Worksheet 15-6 to help you turn your unhealthy anger producing demands into flexible preferences that lead to healthy anger.

Worksheet 15-6	Your Fuse-lengthening Formula
Recent or typical situation in which I became unhealthily angry:	
What was I demanding of the other person/situation?	
Was I insisting that I was right and the other person was wrong? What about?	
Was I refusing to allow the other person to disagree with me or to hold a different opinion or set of values to my own?	
What is a more flexible and tolerant attitude I can hold about the other person/situation?	
How might holding this new attitude help me to resolve the problem?	
How might holding this new attitude benefit the other person involved?	

Embracing Effective Assertion

Learning to be assertive takes a lot of practice, so give yourself permission to get it wrong a few times before you get it right. The best recipe for assertion is to accept both yourself and the other person as flawed human beings who can make mistakes. Then listen to the other person and really think about what you want to say in response. This process is especially relevant if you're in the throes of disagreement or on the receiving end of critical comments.

Healthy assertion is about getting your point across and standing up for your rights when others are treating you unfairly or poorly. Unlike aggression, assertion doesn't mean proving to another that you're right and they're wrong. Assertion is intended to be a civil exchange with the aim of resolving a difference and/or reaching a compromise. When you're being assertive you tend to do the following things:

✔ Speak respectfully to the other person without name calling or using offensive or abusive language

✔ Avoid intimidating, unduly upsetting, or diminishing the other person

✔ Give the other person a chance to tell you their views

✔ Refrain from any violence or threat of violence

✔ Engage in discussion with the other person rather than trying to score points or win an argument

✔ Strive to resolve differences if possible or agree to disagree on a point

When resolving a disagreement, you need to find an environment private enough to talk when both of you have time. Keep in mind that conditions don't have to be perfect for you to discuss issues with another person but it helps to minimize possible distractions. If it's a work issue, you may wish to book an appointment to speak to your collegue or boss.

You can use Worksheet 15-7 . to help you to work through a disagreement with another person and review the benefits of using the assertion principles discussed in this section.

Worksheet 15-7	My Assertion Action Plan
Before the Meeting	
What time and place have I set for the discussion?	
What specific points do I want to voice? How can I both stick to my point and be respectful when doing so?	
Can I remind myself to take responsibility for my feelings rather than blaming or condemning the other person/situation?	
After the Meeting:	
In what ways can I learn from or use any constructive criticism or feedback from the other person?	
Is there a grain of truth in what the other person is saying about me, my behaviour, or the situation?	
How can following these steps potentially benefit both me and the other person involved?	

Putting Yourself on a Par with Your Peers

Low self-opinion can lead to all sorts of social difficulties. Viewing yourself in this way can lead to unhealthy anger, as described in the previous sections. It can also lead you to compare yourself negatively and harshly with others. You may feel socially anxious because you fundamentally believe that others won't like you or accept you just as you are.

One of the very best ways (if not the *only* way) to truly enjoy social interaction, make friends, and maintain relationships is to consider yourself equal in human worth to all others. Holding this opinion may sound pretty easy, but like many CBT principles, putting it into practice is considerably harder. fYour sense of equality involves giving up your need to be *superior* in order to not *feel inferior*. It also involves being your *true* self and allowing others to like or dislike you on that basis – and vice versa. Considering yourself equal also involves being able to accept, embrace, and even rejoice in your own ordinariness. *Most* of us are *mostly* average in *most* respects. And that situation's normal and just fine. If you only let it be so.

Simone believes that she must be liked and approved of by others at all times. If she senses that someone doesn't wholly like her, she becomes depressed or hurt. Simone tells herself that being disliked or rejected proves that she's a totally unlikable person. Because of her demands to be liked and approved of, Simone goes out of her way to please other people. Sometimes she pretends to be interested in things she knows little about in an attempt to impress others. Simone craves social contact but because she's so afraid of being disliked she often feels very anxious in social situations. Recently Simone was invited to a friend's wedding. Prior to the wedding she became very anxious about her appearance and whether she would know the other guests. During the wedding supper Simone was placed at a table with five other guests, none of whom knew each other very well. The other guests chatted and got to know one another over the meal. Simone was so focused on what they might be thinking about her that she lost a lot of the conversation and tripped over her words a bit. Finally she withdrew from the conversation altogether and berated herself for being a 'social freak'. One man at Simone's table was very outgoing and made a lot of jokes. He made a few good-natured remarks about how quiet Simone was during the meal. Simone felt hurt by his remarks and resented him for drawing attention to her. 'What an insensitive creep,' she thought, 'how *dare* he call attention to me.' Simone felt low for a few days after the wedding and continued to put herself down for being awkward. She also blamed her friend for placing her on that table with that 'horrid man' who had 'ruined' her evening. Simone used Worksheet 15-8 to get to grips with the crux of her self-opinion problem and her tendency to blame others for her bad feelings.

See Chapter 14 for much more about self-acceptance and how to develop it!

Worksheet 15-8	Simone's Putting Herself on a Par Page
When do I typically put myself down (or cite a recent example)?	At my friend's wedding, when I got anxious and awkward during the supper.
What are some good reasons for believing in my inherent human worth?	I'm a fallible, complex, and ever-changing human being. I can make mistakes like anyone else. My social unease is only one part of my whole self. Being rejected or disliked isn't nice but it's also not a sign that I'm totally unlikable. I can't be a hit with everyone and trying too hard to please others ends up costing me a lot of energy. I can like myself even if I don't always get obvious approval from others within a social group.

(continued)

Am I allowing myself to be an individual without trying too hard to impress or please other people?	No. In this wedding situation I was utterly focused on making a good impression and avoiding any negative judgements from the other guests. My personality took a back seat.
Am I accepting others as individuals and allowing them to have their own personalities, tastes, and idiosyncrasies whether I agree with them or not?	No. I totally blamed the outgoing man at the table for making me feel anxious. I also called him a creep and a horrid man (in my head) because I didn't like his way of socialising.
Am I devaluing or putting down others in order to feel better about myself?	Not really, but I suppose that by putting the loud man down I made myself feel less responsible for my own social anxiety.
Am I taking myself too seriously?	Definitely! How important is a wedding supper in the grand scheme of things anyway? So I was anxious and it showed. Why am I making such a big deal about it days after the event?
Am I taking the opinions/actions of others too seriously?	Definitely! I'm still worried and obsessing about what the other five guests are thinking about me days after the event. They probably have forgotten about me by now or are certainly more focused on their own lives than on my social awkwardness.
Am I taking the situation too seriously?	Yes. It wasn't a life or death situation, for heaven's sake. I was one guest out of hundreds.
How can I get myself to lighten up and let the laughter leak out?	I could laugh at my ridiculous way of thinking at the time and for the few days following. I could appreciate that the loud man was only being friendly and trying to get me to relax. It's kind of funny now to think about how nutty my thinking was at the time. It's laughable to assume that those five people spent most of the supper (or the days after) concentrating on my social problems. Surely they have their own lives!

Now do the same exercise as Simone in Worksheet 15-9 and see if it helps you to readjust your self-opinion for the better! Also see if you can recognise where you may be missing an opportunity to laugh at yourself or the situation.

You can give 'yes' or 'no' answers to the questions in this worksheet. Giving yourself specific examples for each question will be more helpful to you, though.

Worksheet 15-9	My Putting Myself on a Par Page
When do I typically put myself down (or cite a recent example)?	
What are some good reasons for believing in my inherent human worth?	
Am I allowing myself to be an individual without trying too hard to impress or please other people?	
Am I accepting others as individuals and allowing them to have their own personalities, tastes, and idiosyncrasies whether I agree with them or not?	
Am I devaluing or putting down others in order to feel better about myself?	
Am I taking myself too seriously?	
Am I taking the opinions/actions of others too seriously?	
Am I taking the situation too seriously?	
How can I get myself to lighten up and let the laughter leak out?	

Hopefully you'll now be more equipped to nurture your relationships with others and to deprive your unhealthy anger attitudes of further fuel.

Part IV
Forging into the Future

The 5th Wave   By Rich Tennant

"I think she's getting better. She bought three 'Life is Good' T-shirts yesterday."

In this part . . .

This part helps you to look at long-standing beliefs and ways of thinking that may affect you in the present. We help you challenge old and unhelpful beliefs about yourself, others and the world at large. We give you the tools to make new beliefs more permanent, and to focus on further personal development.

We can't ignore the possibility of relapse, so we give you a chance to plan for and troubleshoot possible problem recurrence. We finish up by helping you to live in a positive way even after you've largely defeated your initial problems.

Chapter 16

Examining and Changing Long-Standing Beliefs

. . . .

In This Chapter

▶ Linking early experiences with present beliefs

▶ Getting to know your core beliefs

▶ Creating healthy new beliefs

. . . .

*P*ast experiences and early childhood situations can influence the way you think about yourself and others, and how you make sense of the world in your present life. You learn certain messages from your parents, other relatives, teachers, and peers. Sometimes these messages are helpful and other times they are not. As you get older you often reassess the validity and usefulness of some of your early beliefs and ideas. At other times you don't re-evaluate ideas you took as gospel truth in your early life and continue to live according to these philosophies and beliefs. In this chapter we introduce you to some techniques to help you unearth your core beliefs and to replace unhelpful inaccurate beliefs with new and helpful ways of thinking.

Uncovering Your Core Beliefs

In CBT long-standing enduring beliefs about yourself, people, or the world are called *core beliefs*. Core beliefs are generally global and absolute in nature. So usually you consider that your core beliefs are 100 per cent true at all times and you may thus ignore or misinterpret evidence that contradicts them. If you think of core beliefs as being at the very *heart* (or *core*) of your belief system – and the way you understand yourself and all the things around you – you can begin to see how important they are to your mental and emotional health.

Beliefs adopted in early life tend to be very tenacious and difficult to shift. Even if you know that you hold an unhelpful belief about yourself such as 'I'm ugly' or 'I'm unlovable' or 'I'm weak', refraining from thinking and acting according to that damaging self-belief can be very difficult. Identifying and understanding the ways in which your past experiences have influenced the beliefs you *still* hold is a useful first step to overcoming negative core beliefs.

Sorting out the three types of core beliefs

Core beliefs are ways of thinking about and making sense of the world around you and the people in it – yourself included. Healthy positive core beliefs help you adjust to negative circumstances, promote positive self-opinion, and contribute to you forming rewarding relationships. Many people develop reasonably rational and healthy core beliefs in childhood or update and change their ways of thinking as they grow older.

Core beliefs are generally formed in childhood and early life; they are often influenced by repeated messages you received from others and/or your environment. Similar and repeated experiences are called *themes*. Negative early experiences like poor parenting, death of loved ones, abuse, illness, injuries and accidents, bullying at school or at home, rejection from peers or family, or growing up in an area with a lot of poverty and crime contribute greatly to the development of unhealthy core beliefs. Unhealthy negative core beliefs impede your ability to problem solve and adjust to negative circumstances, undermine self-esteem and may cause relationship problems.

Your core beliefs determine how you conduct yourself in relationships and in your overall life. They inform what you expect the world to be like and how you expect others to treat you. Your core beliefs influence your *personal rules* (demands that you put on yourself for your behavior) and your *automatic thoughts* (thoughts that just seem to pop into your head in certain situations)

Core beliefs fall into three main camps:

- ✔ Beliefs about *yourself* inform the way you understand your own worth.

  If you experienced harsh criticism, neglect or abuse as a child, you may have learnt to think of yourself as weak or inadequate, for example.

- ✔ Your beliefs about *other people* also frequently have their roots in early life.

  Again, if you suffered traumas or very negative treatment from others you may adopt the belief that people are dangerous or untrustworthy.

- ✔ Your beliefs about life in general and how the world operates help determine your general attitudes. If you grow up in a deprived or unpredictable environment you may develop negative beliefs about the world and life. Beliefs that the world/life is dangerous, cruel, or unfair are examples of the kinds of beliefs negative life conditions may give rise to.

  Healthy core beliefs about the world, yourself and other people may include 'the world is mostly a good place' or 'most people are decent' and 'I'm a worthwhile person'. Positive early experiences of life conditions, parents and other family are likely to give rise to healthy core beliefs.

Mary's mother was an alcoholic and very unpredictable in her moods. Sometimes she would be violent towards Mary. Mary's mother would often leave her alone in the house at night. As a result Mary formed the core belief about herself 'I'm unlovable' because it seemed to make sense of her mother's neglect and abuse. Mary also developed a core belief that 'other people are unreliable' and that 'the world is a scary and lonely place'. Because her core beliefs are so deeply entrenched they impact greatly on how Mary makes sense of her current experiences.

Recently Mary's boyfriend of six months broke up with her. He explained to Mary that he didn't think they were well suited and that he wasn't ready for a long-term relationship with her. Mary used Worksheet 16-1 to examine how her core beliefs determine her understanding of the break-up.

Worksheet 16-1	Mary's Core Belief Breakdown
My core beliefs about myself:	I'm unloveable
My core beliefs about others:	Other people are unreliable
My core beliefs about the world/life:	The world is frightening and lonely

Recent situation/event:	My boyfriend ended our six month relationship
My negative automatic thoughts about the event: (How my core beliefs determine what the event means to me)	He was right to break up with me. I'm not good enough to keep a boyfriend interested in me for long. I deserve to be alone. Other people will abandon me and leave me alone.
My personal rules and demands: (How do my core beliefs lead me to act in future based on this event/ experience?):	I should not rely on other people to stay with me. I must not allow myself to be abandoned again. I must try harder to be loveable or I'll always be alone. I should not give others any reason to be displeased with me.

You can see that Mary's unhealthy negative core beliefs lead her to make some extreme conclusions about herself, other people, and the future based on the recent break up.

Use Worksheet 16-2 in the same way Mary did to see if you can identify your core beliefs and how they may be influencing your understanding of a recent event in your life. Getting familiar with your beliefs and their effects is the first step in changing them to healthy more positive alternatives.

Worksheet 16-2	**My Core Belief Breakdown**
My core beliefs about myself:	
My core beliefs about others:	
My core beliefs about the world/life:	
Recent situation/event:	
My negative automatic thoughts about the event: (How my core beliefs determine what the event means to me)	
My personal rules and demands: (How do my core beliefs lead me to act in future based on this event/experience?)	

Bringing past relationships into the light of the present

Your relationships with your family members, and in particular your parents, have a lot of influence over the ideas you develop about yourself. Other important people in your early life, such as neighbours, extended family, siblings, friends, first loves, teachers, or religious leaders, can also have a significant impact on the beliefs you form.

Lester is the middle child. His parents were loving but often overlooked Lester because his older brother was very intelligent and charming and his younger sister had learning difficulties. Lester was an average child, but very responsible and capable, so his parents could rely on him to get on with things on his own. Lester often felt like an outsider in his own family. At school Lester did well but his teachers often compared him to his intelligent older brother or told him how lucky he was not to struggle like his little sister. He had friends, but Lester had trouble making lasting relationships. As a teenager, Lester's first real girlfriend eventually broke up with him to date a more popular boy. Another girl went out with Lester for a while but it turned out that she was more interested in his older brother and they ultimately broke up. In his adult life, Lester has assertion problems at work and occasional episodes of depression. He is often jealous and suspicious in his romantic relationships.

Lester used Worksheet 16-3 to help him better understand the role events and individuals played in the early development of his core beliefs.

Worksheet 16-3	Lester's Early Experiences Worksheet
Who were the most significant people in my life during childhood, teenage, and early adult years?	My parents, brother, and sister. My maths teacher, who I really liked. My first and second girlfriends. My classmates.
Were there recurring themes to some of my early experiences?	My parents often gave me less attention than my brother and sister. Teachers compared me to my brother and sister, even my maths teacher, who told me that I should study more to be as good at maths as my brother. My first girlfriend left me for a boy that I thought was more popular and likeable than me. My second girlfriend preferred my brother to me.
What beliefs did I learn from these experiences?	That I am easily overlooked and less important than other people like my brother and sister. I learnt that I am lucky to get any positive attention from others. I suppose I also believe that women will only stay with me until they find someone better.

Through the worksheet Lester is beginning to get an idea of how his past influenced his present way of thinking and how it contributes to some of his current emotional problems.

Although you may be able to accurately attribute certain core beliefs you hold to events and/or the actions of people from your past, this is *not* an exercise in assigning blame. If you blame your past or your parents for your current problems as an adult, you are likely to stop yourself from moving on and getting better. Past aspects of your life may have *contributed* to the unhelpful ways you think and act in the present. However, you are the one who now has the choice to revamp your ideas and live in a new and more fruitful way. Don't let yourself get sucked into the quicksand of your past. Instead review your past with the purpose of better understanding and improving your present life.

Worksheet 16-4 can help you to understand which significant people in your life have contributed to your core beliefs. Also recording recurring experiences in your life (or themes) can help you recognize how specific events may have further contributed to the core beliefs you hold.

Use Worksheet 16-4 to record some of your early formative experiences.

Worksheet 16-4	**My Early Experiences Worksheet**
Who were the most significant people in my life during childhood, teenage, and early adult years?	
Were there recurring themes to some of my early experiences?	
What beliefs did I learn from these experiences?	

Lester's analysis of his past relationships helped him fill in the Three Camps of Belief Record in Worksheet 16-5 to better understand what fundamental beliefs he holds in these three areas.

Worksheet 16-5	Lester's Three Camps of Beliefs Record
What are my core beliefs about myself?	I am unimportant. I am inadequate.
What are my core beliefs about other people?	Others are superior to me. People will leave me eventually.
What are my core beliefs about the world/life?	Life is difficult. The world is against me.

Giving some thought to the way you make sense of yourself, others, and the world is useful. Consider the types of core beliefs you may hold in these three areas. By getting to grips with your core beliefs, you're in a good position to challenge some of them.

Use Worksheet 16-6 to record your considerations. Show your record to your CBT therapist if you're working with one.

Worksheet 16-6	My Three Camps of Belief Record
What are my core beliefs about myself?	
What are my core beliefs about other people?	
What are my core beliefs about the world/life?	

Catching your core beliefs interacting

Your core beliefs don't exist in isolation. Rather they tend to interact and reinforce one another. If you hold a core belief about yourself 'I'm weak' and that 'others are strong and dangerous' and believe 'life is harsh and difficult' you can see how you may easily become depressed and feel powerless to solve problems. Looking more closely at how your core beliefs interact can help you see why you might keep having the same kinds of problems.

Lester asks a girl from work on a date but she declines because she is already in a relationship. Lester makes sense of this rejection according to his three camps of core beliefs. Worksheet 16-7 provides a look at how Lester's core beliefs play off one another.

Worksheet 16-7	Lester's Belief Interaction Chart
Core Belief	*Effect on Meaning Assigned to the Situation*
Self: I am unimportant and inadequate.	Molly is too good for me. Her boyfriend is more important than I am as a person. If I were a more adequate person she might have agreed to date me.
Others: Others are superior to me. People will leave me eventually.	Molly is better than me and so is her boyfriend. I could never keep the interest of a girl like Molly anyway. Someone else would take her from me.
World/life: Life is difficult. The world is against me.	It took a lot of courage to ask Molly out and it was all in vain. Romance never works out for me.

Hopefully, you can see with Lester's example that his beliefs in all three areas influence the meanings he assigns to being turned down by Molly. Also you can probably see that the beliefs he holds about himself, others, and the world are reinforced by one another. Looking at this Worksheet 16-7 it becomes easier to understand how Lester became quite depressed over this rather minor rejection.

Now try working out how your beliefs interact with each other in Worksheet 16-8. Think of a recent situation in which you became emotionally disturbed. Fill in your beliefs on the chart (you can refer to Worksheet 16-6) and then think about how they may have contributed to the meaning you assigned to the event.

Worksheet 16-8	My Belief Interaction Chart
Core Belief	*Effect on Meaning Assigned to the Situation*
Self:	
Others:	
World/life:	

Digging Up Your Core Beliefs

Sometimes, unearthing your precise core beliefs can be tricky. Often you may not hear your core beliefs in their absolute form. Usually you are more aware of your negative automatic thoughts (or NATs, which we talk about in Chapter 3). For example, if you held a core belief of being a failure you may not actually say this to yourself very often. More likely perhaps you say things to yourself like 'here I go screwing up again' or 'I never do anything right'. These sections offer more exercises that can help you to really pin down the nature of your core beliefs if you're having trouble.

Doing a downward arrow

The downward arrow technique is really quite simple. Start by identifying a situation or event in which you felt an unhealthy negative emotion – such as guilt, shame, or depression (Chapter 6 talks about healthy and unhealthy negative emotions). What happened and who else was involved? The emotions you feel in response to adverse events are more likely to be unhealthy ones (like deep depression rather than healthy intense sadness) when your core beliefs are unhealthy negative ones. Next, ask yourself what the situation *means* about you, others, or the world. Your answer will probably be a negative automatic thought. Keep asking yourself what your answers *mean* to you until you finish with a global label or statement. The statement you finish with is your core belief. You can also do a downward arrow for all three types of core beliefs separately.

Worksheet 16-9 shows how Lester did a downward arrow on his situation of being turned down by Molly when he asked her for a date. He used the technique to arrive at his core belief about himself.

Worksheet 16-9   **Lester's Downward Arrow**

> **Situation**
> Molly turned me down when I asked her for a date.

↓

> **What does this mean about me:**
> Molly doesn't think I'm good enough for her.
>
> **Others:**
>
> **The world:**

↓

> **What does this mean about me:**
> She'd rather go out with someone interesting like her current boyfriend.
>
> **Others:**
>
> **The world:**

↓

> **What does this mean about me:**
> I'll never have a decent relationship with a girl I really like.
>
> **Others:**
>
> **The world:**

↓

> **What does this mean about me:**
> No girl will ever find me attractive.
>
> **Others:**
>
> **The world:**

↓

> **What does this mean about me:**
> I'm inadequate.
>
> **Others:**
>
> **The world:**

 You may need to complete the downward arrow a few times until you arrive at a core belief.

You can use the downward arrow technique to boil down your thinking about any type of situation, past or present, until you arrive at a core belief.

Use Worksheet 16-10 to get yourself started.

Worksheet 16-10	My Downward Arrow

Situation

↓

What does this mean about me:

Others:

The world:

↓

What does this mean about me:

Others:

The world:

↓

What does this mean about me:

Others:

The world:

↓

What does this mean about me:

Others:

The world:

↓

What does this mean about me:

Others:

The world:

Taking note of themes

Another way of journeying to the core of your beliefs involves tracking familiar themes in your thinking. You can review your ABC forms in Chapter 3 to find recurrent themes that point to a core belief. Themes include ways of thinking about yourself, others, and the world that you tend to revisit over and over. So if you often have thoughts about yourself that seem to boil down to the same *theme* such as inadequacy, failure, or insignificance, this gives you a strong clue to what your core belief is about yourself.

Lester notes that he often thinks thematically consistent things about himself, others, and the world in lots of different negative situations. Take a glance at Lester's list of thinking themes in Worksheet 16-11.

Worksheet 16-11	Lester's Thinking Themes
About myself:	My opinions don't really count.
	Other people are more capable at work than I am.
	I don't succeed socially.
	I am lucky to get any positive attention from others.
About other people:	People are better at things than I am.
	I shouldn't upset other people by voicing my opinions or disagreeing with them.
	People always leave me for someone better.
About the world/life:	I never seem to get the good things in life that other people get.
	Other people seem to negotiate life more easily than I do.

By looking at his list of thinking themes, Lester can begin to take an accurate guess at what core beliefs he holds.

Use Worksheet 16-12 to see whether you can recognise themes in your thinking.

Worksheet 16-12	My Thinking Themes
About myself:	
About other people:	
About the world/life:	

Forming a Formulation

In this section, you put all your hard work together on one handy form. Pulling all this information together reminds you where your core beliefs may have sprung from, how they lead you to think in everyday situations, and what behaviours they promote. Your formulation can also serve to remind you of the beliefs that you want to change and reasons why.

Follow these steps to complete your formulation form in Worksheet 16-13.

1. **In the first box, record early events or past experiences that you think contribute to the development of your core beliefs.**

2. **In the second box, write down your unhelpful core beliefs about yourself, others, and the world/life.**

3. **In the third box, record the rules, demands, or codes that you expect yourself to live by or other people and the world to live by.**

   These assumptions are formed *due to* your core beliefs. For example, Lester's rules include: 'I must not assert myself' and 'Other people must not reject me'.

4. **In the fourth box, list things you do to avoid triggering your core beliefs or unhelpful things you do to cope with your core beliefs.**

Worksheet 16-13	My Formulation Form

FORMULATION OF MY BELIEFS AND RULES

RELEVANT EARLY/ PAST EXPERIENCES		CORE UNHELPFUL BELIEFS I am . . ., The world is . . ., Other people . . .	RULES/ ASSUMPTIONS If . . . then . . ., Demands about self, the world, others.
	→		

AVOIDANCE AND COMPENSATORY BEHAVIOURS Situations you tend to avoid or things you do excessively as a consequence of your beliefs/rules	WHAT I'VE GOT GOING FOR ME List your personal strengths and assets

Creating Constructive Core Beliefs

Well, identifying your core beliefs has been a trifle bleak, hasn't it? Happily, though, you are now ready to change those beliefs and adopt new ones. Consider good (and more balanced) ideas you have that contradict your negative beliefs, and think about how you can use this information to construct new ways of viewing yourself, others, and the world. Especially remind yourself of positive experiences you've had with other people, traits and characteristics you like about yourself, and anything you've experienced that suggests the world has many good things to offer. Then scribble down a few of those better, more accurate beliefs.

You may find it helpful to make a list of life experiences and personal attributes that contradict your unhelpful core beliefs. Remember to include positive experiences with others. Then use your list to develop more balanced and accurate core beliefs.

Lester listed his more constructive beliefs in Worksheet 16-14.

Worksheet 16-14	Lester's Constructive Core Beliefs
Information that Contradicts My Negative Core Beliefs	*More Helpful/Constructive Beliefs I Can Adopt*
My work colleagues often ask my opinion on procedures and seek my input during meetings.	Self: I am basically okay and on a par with other people.
I have two friends that have stuck by me even when I have been depressed.	Others: People are as worthy as me, no more and no less. Some people have been my friends for a long time.
A girl who works in the coffee shop near work often flirts with me.	World/life: Life can be difficult but it also can be good. Good things do happen to me.
I have a decent job and a comfortable home that I obtained through my own efforts.	
I am generally polite and kind to others.	
Other people are often friendly toward me.	
My boss gave me a pay rise last year.	

Now rejig your core ideas using Worksheet 16-15, keeping in mind that your constructive core beliefs should be statements about yourself, others, and the world that you can *genuinely* imagine eventually *truly* believing in.

Worksheet 16-15	Your Constructive Core Beliefs
Information that Contradicts My Negative Core Beliefs	*More Helpful/Constructive Beliefs I Can Adopt*
	Self:
	Others:
	World/life:

Changing your negative core beliefs isn't tantamount to sugar-coated positive thinking. So be wary of replacing a negative belief such as 'I'm inadequate' with something over the top like 'I'm fantastic!' Firstly, no one is totally fantastic. Nor is anyone totally inadequate. Both are global statements. Secondly, if you've spent years thinking of yourself in a negative way, you're highly unlikely to believe in an overly positive view of yourself. Instead try to come up with reasons why your negative core beliefs are not 100 per cent true. Work on generating *balanced*, *optimistic*, and *realistic* alternative views.

Assigning New Meanings to Old Events

As a child, young adult, or even later in life, you may have given idiosyncratic meanings to certain life events and experiences. These meanings are often the foundation of negative core beliefs. Fortunately you can now reassess the meanings you attached to these events and assign new and more accurate meanings to them. In doing so, you can further your work toward generating healthier beliefs.

Lester attached the meaning 'I'm unimportant and inadequate' to the experience of his parents overlooking him and attending to his brother and sister. He attached the same meaning to the event of his teachers comparing him to his siblings. Lester used the Meaning Sheet in Worksheet 16-16 to challenge and change these meanings and thus create healthier core beliefs.

Worksheet 16-16 Lester's Meaning Sheet about Himself

Event: Parents ignoring me and giving more attention to my siblings.

Old Meaning	New Meaning
I must not be as important to my parents as my brother and sister.	My parents may not have been aware of ignoring me. My brother was very gregarious and commanded a lot of attention. My sister had problems and it is pretty understandable that my parents devoted much of their attention to her. It may have been more a case of circumstances that I ended up overlooked rather than a true reflection of my importance to my parents.
Old Core Belief	**New Core Belief**
I am unimportant and inadequate.	I have importance just like everyone else. I am adequate just like everyone else.

When Lester was rejected by two girlfriends, he attached the meaning 'other people are superior to me' and 'people will leave me' to the events. He used Worksheet 16-17 to confront and revamp his beliefs about other people.

Worksheet 16-17 Lester's Meaning Sheet about Others

Event: My first girlfriend breaking up with me to date a popular boy. My second girlfriend having a crush on my older brother.

Old Meaning	New Meaning
My brother and other boys are better than me. There must be something about them that makes my girlfriends prefer them to me. People I get close to will leave me for someone else eventually.	Okay, so I had bad luck with my first couple of girlfriends. They may have left me for other people or fancied my brother but that doesn't mean that other people are better than me. It just means that those two girls preferred other people. That can happen to anyone, not just me. Just because I lost my relationships with two girlfriends doesn't mean that everyone I get close to will leave me. Some may and some may not. I have already survived rejection and I can survive it again if it happens.
Old Core Belief	**New Core Belief**
Others are superior to me. People will leave me eventually.	I am equal in worth to other people. Not everyone I get close to will leave me.

You can also use this worksheet to form new beliefs about the world/life. We haven't provided an example here, but you complete it in exactly the same way.

Give the Meaning Sheet your best shot and grapple those grisly beliefs to the ground, using the blank Worksheets 16-18, 16-19, and 16-20.

Worksheet 16-18	My Meaning Sheet for Myself

Event:

Old Meaning	*New Meaning*

Old Core Belief	*New Core Belief*

Worksheet 16-19	My Meaning Sheet about Others

Event:

Old Meaning	*New Meaning*

Old Core Belief	*New Core Belief*

Worksheet 16-20	My Meaning Sheet about the World/Life

Event:

Old Meaning	New Meaning

Old Core Belief	New Core Belief

Well done! You are now on your way to changing the way you feel and act (for the better) by changing your core beliefs.

The more negative your life experiences, the more extreme the beliefs you developed are likely to be. You can use the techniques described throughout this chapter to confront and deal with any life event, even very traumatic or long-lasting ones. We don't expect your experiences to mirror Lester's. We only use him as an example to show you how to use the worksheets. Everyone is different and has different backgrounds, including you.

Chapter 17

Consolidating Conviction in New Core Beliefs

So, you've done a lot of work thus far and now you've got yourself a set of healthy beliefs that you want to strengthen (Chapters 1, 2, 3, and 16 cover healthy beliefs in detail). Learning to live with a new set of beliefs takes yet more work. You need to reprogramme your brain to make sense of situations in a new way. Unhelpful core beliefs tend to be very rigid and long held. Thus a fair bit of retraining is necessary for your new healthy beliefs to become second nature. Persistence and patience are also needed. Most people we see for CBT can fairly readily recognise the self-defeating nature of their unhealthy beliefs, come up with better ways of thinking, and understand that their new beliefs make sense. But very often we hear patients say, 'I know these new beliefs will help me but I just don't *really believe* them yet.' In CBT parlance we call this division between what you *know* to be true and helpful and what you actually *believe*, the 'head–heart' or 'head–gut' issue. This chapter is devoted to helping you resolve the 'head–heart' conflict.

You've probably been living according to your unhealthy core beliefs for many years – maybe most of your life. That your thinking automatically veers that way when you encounter a negative life event is thus understandable. But habits *can* be broken – even if doing so is difficult and feels awkward at first. Imagine that you break your dominant arm badly – the one you write with and use for most tasks. As the doctor puts you in plaster from your wrist to your shoulder, you realise that you'll have to rely on your other arm for several weeks. At first it feels very weird and uncomfortable, everything is difficult, and you doubt that you will be able to brush your teeth and hair until your arm is mended. But over time your brain adjusts to your altered circumstances and before you know it you're doing things relatively easily. Changing your belief system is a bit like this example.

Spotlighting Beliefs You Want to Strengthen

Healthy beliefs have the following characteristics:

✔ **They are *flexible and preference based*.** Instead of insisting that you must meet certain criteria, you prefer a specific outcome or desire to achieve a specific goal but you also accept the possibility of failing to do so. You leave room for normal human error and for random life events. So instead of 'I *must* not fail!' you may have the healthy belief 'I'd *prefer* not to fail but there is no reason that I absolutely *must* not'.

✔ **They include a sensible *if-then* statement.** Instead of concluding extreme negative things about yourself, others, or the world based on a singular event, you can put the event into a healthy perspective. So rather than '*If* I fail at something, *then* it proves that I am a total failure' you may believe '*If* I fail, *then* it's bad but not terrible and just means that I am a normal fallible person'.

✔ **They include a positive and realistic general truth.** Rather than assigning global negative ratings to yourself, others or the world you allow for the co-existence of good, less good, neutral, and bad elements. So in place of a belief such as 'I'm worthless' and 'the world is terrible' you may have 'I am basically okay' or 'the world is complex and has both good and bad parts'.

The first step is to make note of the beliefs that you want to take on board for each of three main categories:

✔ **Yourself:** Your self-opinion and ideas about your worthiness.

✔ **Other people:** Your view of others and how you expect them to behave generally or toward you specifically.

✔ **The world/life:** Your expectations of how the world will treat you, how life is likely to unfold for you and/or others.

Chapter 16 discusses these three types of core beliefs in depth.

Preparing a Portfolio of Persuasive Arguments

A good way of generating lots of sound arguments to support your new beliefs is to create a portfolio of good sound reasons that they make sense. All you need to do is record your ideas about why your new healthy beliefs make sense, reflect reality and help you to function.

Make your beliefs hold to these basic guidelines:

✔ **True and consistent with reality:** Ensure that your new beliefs or philosophies don't distort the facts of any given situation or event nor deny the actual situation or event.

✔ **Flexible and preference based:** They leave a margin for error. They recognise that you and other humans are fallible and capable of both success and failure at any given task or endeavor. They acknowledge that life is full of random events and that complete certainty is rarely possible.

✔ **Balanced and non-extreme:** You resist using judgmental, absolute, harsh labels to describe yourself, others, or the world. Instead strive to use descriptive terms that include the complexity and changeability of you, other people, and life itself.

✔ **Sensible and logical:** Construct new beliefs that make good sense and are logically sound.

✔ **Helpful to you:** Your new beliefs should be ways of thinking that can assist you in reaching your goals and lead to mental/emotional health.

Agatha has a core belief that she is a failure. She is very hard on herself and gets depressed at the slightest sniff of failure. Agatha works very hard to avoid failing at anything she does because to her any failure or mistake means that she is a total failure as a person. Often she avoids experiences such as taking her driving test and going for new jobs because she is too terrified of the possibility of failure. Agatha has worked hard to change her belief that she is a failure. She used Worksheet 17-1 to help increase her conviction in a healthy alternative belief about herself.

Worksheet 17-1	Agatha's Portfolio of Persuasive Arguments
Healthy core belief about myself:	I prefer not to fail but there is no reason that I must not do so. Failing at things means that I am a normal person, capable of both succeeding and failing.
What reasons show that my belief is true?	Anybody can fail sometimes, even at important things, and so can I. If failing at one or more things meant that I was a total failure, then I would never be able to succeed at anything. The truth is that I have succeeded at lots of things in my life. It's true that I prefer not to fail but it's also true that no reason exists why I should not fail from time to time. Even people that I respect have failed at things. For example, my best friend failed her driving test three times and I don't think that she's a total failure.
How does my belief reflect reality?	Reality shows that I can (and do) make mistakes and fail sometimes. So if I insist that I must not fail, I am denying reality. My new belief reflects reality because it accepts the possibility that I can potentially both fail and succeed at tasks. It is normal for people to fail and my new belief acknowledges this point.
In what ways is my belief flexible?	My new belief allows me to prefer to succeed and to strive to reach my goals but it also allows me to accept the possibility of failure. After all, to err is human and I'm human. My new belief makes it possible for me to fail at important (or less important) things without deciding that I'm a total failure and becoming depressed.
In what ways is my belief balanced and non-extreme?	My new belief is balanced because it is realistic and desirable to not fail but it's not the end of the world if I do. I also do not have to put myself down in extreme and nasty ways if I do fail at something.
What reasons show that my belief is sensible and logical?	It makes sense to prefer not to fail but it is illogical to insist that therefore I must not fail. Just because I want to succeed it doesn't follow logically that I must succeed. When I do fail at something it makes sense to feel disappointed because it's a negative event. But it also makes sense to review possible reasons for my failure and to try again if it's appropriate. It makes logical sense that one failure does not make me a total failure as a person.
How will holding this new belief be helpful to me?	I will feel disappointed or sad when I fail but not depressed and full of self-loathing. I'll probably enjoy life more because I won't see everything I do as a test of my overall worth. I'll be more likely to take some risks and try new things because I won't be so worried about getting it wrong.

Agatha now has a comprehensive portfolio of arguments that support her new core belief. She can use this portfolio to help her when she struggles with resurgence of her old, unhealthy belief system. Agatha can also review her portfolio regularly to help resolve the head–heart issue.

You can use Worksheet 17-2 to generate arguments in defence of your new core beliefs about others and the world at large, as well as about yourself as Agatha does!

Worksheet 17-2	Your Portfolio of Persuasive Arguments
Healthy core belief :	
What reasons show that my belief is true?	
How does my belief reflect reality?	
In what ways is my belief flexible?	
In what ways is my belief balanced and non-extreme?	
What reasons show that my belief is sensible and logical?	
How will holding this new belief be helpful to me?	

You can repeat this exercise if you find yourself feeling emotionally disturbed in response to a particular life event. Emotional disturbance (see Chapter 6) is a reliable indicator that you are thinking in a rigid and unhealthy manner. You may wish to do an A-B-C form (Chapter 3) on the event and then repeat this worksheet to renew your conviction in your healthy beliefs.

If At First You Don't Succeed, Try and Try Again

Finding yourself thinking and acting according to your old negative core beliefs, even after a lot of effort on your part to embrace new ones, can be pretty discouraging.

Remind yourself that doing so is a normal part of change and resume your efforts. In this section we give you some additional arsenal for aiming the big guns at your unhelpful beliefs.

If you find yourself faltering in your attempts to change your beliefs, take a moment to reflect on what you have discovered about yourself thus far. Also think about positive changes (no matter how small) you have made. Record them for future reference on Worksheet 17-3.

Worksheet 17-3	My List of Positive Changes

Acting accordingly

One of the best ways of truly embracing new beliefs and ways of thinking is to behave as if you already *really* believe them. The way you act or behave has a big impact on your thinking. So if you deliberately act *against* your negative core beliefs you are simultaneously eroding them and building up your new beliefs. We call this process the *acting as if* exercise. This exercise is extremely helpful, so practice it often. Here are some steps to help you get acting 'as-if':

1. **Record you healthy new belief on a bit of paper.**

2. **Consider what the people in your life would notice if they could see positive changes in you. Think how your behaviour would be different if you truly believed in your new way of thinking about yourself, others, and/or the world.**

    Think of people that you know who seem to hold the healthy core belief that you wish to strengthen, how do they behave in ways that reflect that way of thinking?

3. **Identify times that you can devote to test driving behaviors that match your new core belief.**

Let's take a look at Agatha again. Her core belief (of old) is that she is a failure.

Now have a look at how Agatha got into acting *as if* exercise using Worksheet 17-4.

Worksheet 17-4	Agatha's 'As If' Actions
New core belief:	I prefer not to fail but there is no reason that I must not do so. Failing at things means that I am a normal person, capable of both succeeding and failing.
If I truly believed this, how would I act/behave?	I'd start driving lessons. I'd take on new tasks at work. I'd approach my boss about a promotion. I'd join the local pub quiz team. I'd shake off minor failures and refuse to condemn myself.
When can I practise these healthy actions?	I'll book driving lessons on Monday. I'll speak to my boss after the staff meeting on Wednesday. I'll go to the pub and join the quiz team tonight.

Take a leaf from Agatha's book and do Worksheet 17-5 for yourself.

Try to be specific about times when you can act in line with beliefs that you want to strengthen. Doing so will help you to move from intention to action.

Worksheet 17-5	My 'As If' Actions
New core belief:	
If I truly believed this, how would I act/behave?	
When can I practise these healthy actions?	

Now get out there and act in the ways you have identified!

You can also use Worksheet 17-5 to identify ways of acting according to healthy beliefs about others and the world. For example, you may think of behaviours that go with a belief such as 'other people are mostly decent and trustworthy' or 'life includes both bad and good events'.

Digging out and defeating doubts

Having some doubts or reservations about the truth of your new core beliefs and associated behaviours is natural. When you first start acting according to new ways of thinking you may feel as though you're going against the grain.

You need to really look at any doubts you may have about making changes. That way you can deal with them before you are in a tricky situation and your old beliefs are triggered. Facing your misgivings, qualms, or niggling worries about your new beliefs helps you to strengthen them. The Zig-Zag technique is a useful way of digging out and defeating doubts. Here are the steps for using this technique and filling in Worksheet 17-7.

1. **Record the belief that you want to strengthen in the top left-hand box. Rate how strongly you believe it is true from 0 per cent to 100 per cent.**

2. **In the next box record one of your doubts or arguments *against* your healthy belief.**

3. **In the third box record an argument that challenges your doubt and *defends* your healthy belief.**

4. **In the fourth box record another one of your doubts and *attack* your healthy belief again.**

5. **In the fifth box, again record an argument that challenges your doubt and *defends* your healthy belief.**

6. **Repeat this process of attacking and defending your healthy belief until you have dealt with all your doubts.**

   Make sure you stop on a defence of the healthy belief not on an attack!

7. **Re-rate how strongly you believe in the new core belief from 0 per cent to 100 per cent.**

   The strength of your conviction in your new belief is likely to go up after using this technique. If it hasn't, you may need to repeat the process or defend your belief more vigorously. If you are seeing a CBT therapist, you can show them your Zig-Zag and they can help you to see where you may have missed good defences.

Agatha knows that she really *wants* to start living according to her new core belief. But in her heart she has some residual thoughts about whether or not her new way of thinking about herself is actually true.

Agatha used the Zig-Zag form to confront her troublesome thoughts in Worksheet 17-6.

Worksheet 17-6   **Agatha's Zig-Zag Form**

HEALTHY BELIEF

> I prefer not to fail but there is no reason that I must not do so. Failing at things means that I am a normal person, capable of both succeeding and failing.

Rate conviction in Healthy Belief <u>30%</u>

THE
ZIG-ZAG
FORM

ATTACK

> But if I fail at a lot of things or at all really important things, such as work or relationships, then that must mean that I am a total failure.

DEFENCE

> No, it doesn't! It may be more inconvenient and disappointing to fail at important things but it still doesn't make me a total failure. Even if I fail many times it is still possible that I will succeed at some of the things I try. If I were a total failure, the I would only be able to fail and that is not what has happened in reality. Lots of people fail at things that are important to them – not just me. So failing really just means that I am a normal human being.

ATTACK

> But if I hold this new belief, I will stop working so hard to succeed and I'll become lazy and complacent.

DEFENCE

> Allowing myself to fail without putting myself down will help me to take risks and do new things. I will still be motivated to work hard because I prefer to do well. Instead of being driven by a fear of failure, I'll push myself to do things that are important to me because they are worth doing.

ATTACK

> But if I try to do something and fail at it, other people will think that I'm a loser. I'll make a fool of myself. If other people think that I'm a total failure, it must be true.

DEFENCE

> First of all, I don't know for sure what other people think of me. Even if others do think that I'm foolish to try something or that I'm a failure – that doesn't make it true. I can't control what other people think of me but I can decide how to think about myself. If I constantly worry about other people's opinions of me, I'll never try anything. If other people treated me like I were a failure it would be hard to cope with but I can choose to disagree with them. At the end of the day, I can survive the discomfort of being ridiculed or criticised by other people.

Re-rate conviction in Healthy Belief <u>80%</u>

Agatha increased her conviction in her healthy belief to 80%, which is a solid percentage to be getting on with. The type of doubts she recorded are very common and often obstruct positive change.

Do your own Zig-Zag on one of your healthy new core beliefs about yourself, other people, or the world. You can use the form in Worksheet 17-7 again and again, so make some copies before you get started.

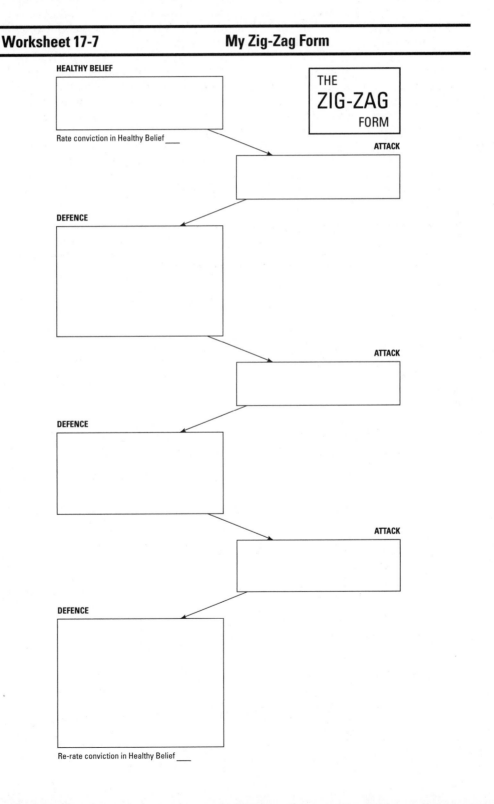

Practising what you preach

If you're trying to endorse a new belief about yourself, then applying the same rule to other people and vice versa makes sense. So, if like Agatha you're trying to give yourself permission to fail sometimes, give others the same permission too. Or if you're trying to believe that you are basically likable (warts and all!), then consider that other people are basically acceptable and worthy despite their individual flaws or shortcomings. If you are overly harsh on yourself, you may find that you are sometimes overly critical of others. Or the other way around – beliefs about yourself and others can sometimes be a double-edged sword.

Give some thought to any double standards you may be holding, adding *specific* suggestions that you can put into practice immediately. If others are allowed to fail and mess up, then why aren't you? If you are allowed to behave thoughtlessly occasionally, then why aren't your friends given the same liberty? Use Worksheet 17-8 to commit to ways in which you can practise what you preach on a daily basis.

Think of clear and definite examples of when you can practise what you preach. Also clearly identify (and list) other people to whom you can apply your new beliefs, and list specific situations in which you can do so.

Worksheet 17-8 **My 'Practising What I Preach' Plan**

How can I treat myself according to my new belief?

When?

Where?

How can I treat others according to my new belief?

Who?

When?

Where?

How can I live in the world according to my new belief?

When?

Where?

Who else may be involved?

Considering what you'd want your child to believe

Another method for increasing your belief in a new healthy way of thinking is to ask yourself what you want someone that you truly love to believe. Would you want your child, niece, cousin, best friend, or partner to hold your new healthy or old unhealthy belief? Hopefully you'd recommend your healthy belief to anyone that you care deeply about. So think about why. These reasons are likely to be good arguments that will help to further your conviction in the truth and usefulness of your new way of thinking.

Agatha thought about her three-year-old son and what attitude she would like him to have toward failure. She used Worksheet 17-9 to highlight the reasons she wants her son to hold a healthy core belief about failing at things in his life.

Worksheet 17-9	Agatha's Belief for Her Beloved
Who is someone that I really love and care for?	Max, my three-year-old son.
What is my healthy core belief?	I prefer not to fail but there is no reason that I must not do so. Failing at things means that I am a normal person, capable of both succeeding and failing.

(continued)

What are the reasons that I rec-ommend this way of thinking?	I love Max no matter whether he succeeds or fails. I'd never want Max to think he was a total failure – even if he failed every exam he ever took! I want him to consider failure a normal part of life and not a huge catastrophic event. I also want Max to be happy with who he is and not always be judging himself according to how well he does. I'll never think of Max as a failure and I certainly don't want him to torture himself about mistakes and short-comings in the way that I have tortured myself. I think Max will lead a fulfilling and satisfying life if he holds this healthy belief.
How will this belief help my loved one?	It will prevent Max from becoming depressed about failures. He will also be able to try new things and push himself to give his best effort rather than being paralysed by fear of failure. It will save him from anxiety and worry prior to exams, job interviews, asking people out on dates and so on! This belief will help Max to have a robust sense of his own intrinsic self-worth. Max will also be less affected by the negative judgements of others if he holds this healthy belief about himself. This belief will ultimately help Max to pursue his goals in life.

Perhaps the best way of imparting healthy self-belief and well-balanced world views to your children (or other loved ones) is to model them!

You can use Worksheet 17-10 to make your own arguments for passing a healthy belief on to others in your life. If the belief makes sense for them, it makes sense for you.

Worksheet 17-10	**My Belief for My Beloved**
Who is someone that I really love and care for?	
What is my healthy core belief:	

What are the reasons that I recommend this way of thinking?	
How will this belief help my loved one?	

Nurturing Nice New Beliefs

After you develop new healthier beliefs and start acting according to them, it can be very useful to keep a record of the benefits you and the people in your life reap as a result. Doing so not only further consolidates your conviction in your new ways of thinking but also gives you a turbo boost should your enthusiasm wane or old beliefs raise their ugly heads. Take a bit of time to thoroughly record the positive effects of acting on new beliefs and to acknowledge positive responses from other people.

Worksheet 17-11 provides a format for getting going.

Worksheet 17-11	**My Positive Data Log**
My healthy core belief:	
What recent experiences have I had that support this belief?	
What positive reactions have I had from other people when acting according to this new belief?	
What positive changes to my life (however small) have occurred as a result of acting according to this new belief?	
What other evidence do I have that this new belief is helpful to me? (include positive effects on your emotions and behaviours)	
Are there any ways in which holding this new belief has been helpful to other people in my life?	

Chapter 18

Delving into Personal Development

In This Chapter

▶ Anticipating setbacks and relapse

▶ Recovering from a relapse

▶ Developing yourself

▶ Looking ahead

*Y*ou need to nurture the positive changes you're making to your thinking, behaviour, and emotions. A common reason for problems reappearing is complacency.

Constantly practising your new ways of thinking and related behaviours and not taking your improved mental health for granted can help to prevent relapse. For example, if you make changes to your thinking but then return to old unhealthy ways of behaving, you put your gains at risk. Consistently acting in line with your new beliefs (see Chapter 17 for tips on how to do that) and moving toward your goals (peek at Chapter 8 for advice on getting goal-directed) helps you to stay on track.

Unfortunately, despite your best efforts setbacks can and often do occur. One of the best ways of dealing with relapse is to be prepared for it – forewarned is forearmed! In this chapter we offer you guidelines for making a relapse prevention plan and on pursuing *personal development*, thereby making serious setbacks less likely.

Being Realistic about Relapse

It would be nice if the road to recovery were a straight and sure path with no detours. In reality you can expect to have difficult periods and to experience setbacks when trying to overcome your psychological problems. To some extent, relapse is a normal part of recovery.

Panicking or *catastrophising* (taking a relatively minor event and imagining nightmare scenarios resulting from it) about setbacks can often lead to a more serious return of symptoms. Try to view setbacks as disappointing but not disastrous. You can use them as an opportunity to further consolidate your understanding of core CBT techniques. Be compassionate with yourself when in the grip of a relapse rather than giving yourself a hard time about it. Have a look at Chapter 23 for inspiration.

Use Worksheet 18-1 to get started on your relapse prevention plan.

When completing the worksheets in this chapter you may wish to review work you've done from other chapters to jog your memory.

Worksheet 18-1	Your Problem/Goal Review

What were my original target problems?

Emotional problems:	
Behavioural problems:	
Practical problems:	

What are my goals in relation to these problems?

Emotional goals:	
Behavioural goals:	
Practical goals:	

What positive changes/progress have I made thus far?

Emotional progress:	
Behavioural progress:	
Practical progress:	

What are the benefits of positive changes I've made thus far?

Emotional benefits:	
Behavioural benefits:	
Practical benefits:	

Ideally this exercise reminds you how far you've come and renews your motivation to continue the good work.

An ounce of prevention

This step in your relapse prevention plan is about, you guessed it, *prevention* – or troubleshooting. First, recall the ways of thinking, feeling, and acting that maintained or worsened your target problems. Now try to imagine scenarios that may come up in the future and trigger off these old unhealthy ways of thinking, behaving, and feeling. Next imagine yourself coping successfully with your trigger situation by thinking and acting in constructive healthy ways. The 'A pound of cure' section coming up next has further advice on troubleshooting potential difficulties.

You can use Worksheet 18-2 to structure your troubleshooting. The idea is to help you spot potential setbacks before they truly take hold. You may wish to revisit Chapters 16 and 17 to help you better use this worksheet. These chapters discuss core beliefs and how to replace old destructive beliefs with new constructive ones in depth.

Worksheet 18-2   **My Troubleshooting Tableau**

What negative core beliefs have I been working on eroding?

Self:

Others:

World:

What healthy alternative core beliefs have I been working on strengthening?

Self:

Others:

World:

What thinking errors do I typically make?

What types of situations or conditions typically trigger my unhealthy core beliefs/thinking errors?

Past environmental triggers: (Include illness, financial worry, work hassles, seasonal changes, household bills, moving house, and so on)

Past interpersonal triggers: (Include relationship conflicts with family, friends, colleagues, and so on)

What possible triggers can I look out for in the future?

Environmental triggers:

Interpersonal triggers:

What destructive behaviours have I used in the past to try to cope with my problems?

What early warning signs can I look out for that may signal my problems returning?

Unhealthy negative emotions:

Negative changes to my thinking:

Negative changes to my behaviour:

If you've been working with a CBT therapist, involving him or her in drawing up your relapse prevention plan is a good idea. Your therapist is likely to provide valuable input.

A pound of cure

Often we hear our patients say things such as 'I really hope I don't get depressed again' or 'I'm keeping my fingers crossed that I stay well'. These sentiments are utterly normal and understandable. But our advice is 'don't leave staying well to chance!' Don't ignore early warning signs – nip your recurring problem in the bud! Be confident that whatever strategies you used to get better in the first place are more than likely to work again.

For example, if some of the strategies described in Chapter 5 really helped you to manage your negative thoughts, record your preferred strategies and remind yourself to use them again if your symptoms return. If sticking to an activity schedule helped you to overcome depression (Chapter 12) then note that down and use it again when you notice a dip in your mood. Or perhaps the behavioural experiments found in Chapter 4 helped you to confront your anxieties, make a note to of these too.

Worksheet 18-3 provides a convenient reminder of helpful strategies you've used before and can re-use anytime you need them.

Chapter 21 offers tips for finding and working with professionals.

Worksheet 18-3	**My Pound of Cure Compendium**
What areas do I most need to keep working on in order to maintain my gains?	
Which specific CBT strategies aid me most in overcoming my emotional/ behavioural problems?	
What helpful beliefs and attitudes do I want to keep practising and strengthening?	
What are the most helpful behavioural techniques I have used to overcome my problems?	
Who can I go to for additional support if I start to struggle?	
Professionals:	
Friends:	
Family:	
Support groups:	

If you've been prescribed medication before and found it beneficial, speak to your doctor in the event of relapse. Sometimes the right medication at the right time can prevent a more serious resurgence of symptoms.

Never self-medicate. Don't restart left-over medication from previous prescriptions. Always consult your doctor about any medication.

Getting Back to Your Personal Values and Hobbies

Another way of keeping yourself on the straight and narrow is to think about what is important to you. Sometimes emotional problems take up so much of your attention that you can lose sight of your own personal values. Now that you're on the road to recovery you can turn your attention to the kind of world you want to live in. Perhaps you value polite conduct, racial and cultural equality, or environmental initiatives to name but a few possibilities. Your personal values may be specific to your home life or apply more broadly to your community, city, and the planet.

People tend to be most content when they're involved in meaningful, absorbing activities. Because CBT focuses on goals regarding your problems, it also recognises the benefit of working toward broader goals based on what's important to you. Acting in line with your personal values and engaging in activities that you enjoy or consider worthwhile helps you to stay psychologically healthy.

Take a minute now to make a note of your personal values in Worksheet 18-4.

Worksheet 18-4	My Personal Values
What values do I hold for myself, my family, and my friends?	
What broader values do I hold for my community, the human race, and the planet?	

Filling your life with meaningful activities consistent with your values can help keep your mood on an even keel.

Acting consistently

After you assess your personal values, you can identify ways of putting them into practice more often. We're not suggesting that you make it your mission to single-handedly rid the world of crime or stop global warming – not necessarily. But we do suggest living in a manner that reflects what's important to you. Doing so can promote a sense of wellbeing and of involvement with the world around you – good news for your continued mental health.

Pinpoint particular ways (however small) in which you can strive to act consistently with your values. Use Worksheet 18-5 for each of your identified values. Include simple value-based tasks such as reading to your children, recycling, donating to a charity, and eating fair trade foods.

Worksheet 18-5	My Value-based Activities
One of my personal values:	
What specific action can I take to promote this value?	
Where?	
When?	
With whom?	
How often?	

Reinstating personally significant practices

Your hobbies and interests may have been neglected due to your psychological problems. Now is the time to reintroduce practices that you used to enjoy and that gave you a sense of achievement. Activities such as gardening, recreational study, religious/spiritual practice, reading, visiting art exhibitions are all valid ways of filling up your life. Now that you have more time for enjoying yourself, you may want to start new projects or take up new hobbies.

Jot down some ideas on Worksheet 18-6.

Worksheet 18-6	My Personally Significant Practices
What activities did I use to enjoy and would now like to reintroduce?	
What activities would I like to start?	

Looking At Your Lifestyle

Striking a balance between your personal life and your work life is part of keeping emotionally and physically well. Keeping the different aspects of your life fairly balanced helps to ensure that you don't overdo some things and neglect others.

Use Worksheet 18-7 to take stock of your current lifestyle. Base your answers on a weekly average over the past three to four weeks.

Worksheet 18-7	My Current Lifestyle Check-up
Question	*Answer*
How many (if any) days have I worked later than usual or taken work home with me?	
How many times have I been out socially?	
How many evenings/weekends have I allocated to spending time with friends and/or family?	
How often have I taken some form of exercise?	
How many hours/days have I spent on hobbies or activities that interest me?	

Question	Answer
How much time have I allocated to taking care of household duties?	
How do I usually relax in the evenings?	
How much time have I spent on self-help or continued CBT practice?	
What other activities have I spent time on?	
Which activities could I benefit from devoting more time to per week?	
Which activities could I benefit from spending less time on per week?	
Which times/days can I allocate to neglected activities in the coming week?	

Look at your answers to worksheet 18-7. Is your time roughly divided between various activities (both work and play) or is it concentrated in one or two particular areas such as work or household duties? Are you devoting enough of your time to activities that help keep you emotionally and mentally healthy such as socialising, relaxation, and exercise? Everyone's life circumstances are different and therefore there are no hard and fast rules about how much time you should dedicate to any singular activity. However, relaxation is very important because it gives your body and mind a chance to recharge. Relaxation activities can include pretty much anything that helps you to chill out and unwind. Walking, reading, meditating, sitting down with a cup of tea and looking out the window, listening to music, or chatting to a friend are all fine examples of relaxation activities. You benefit from spending at least one hour each day doing something relaxing.

Exercise is also good for both physical and mental health but most of us don't get enough of it. Aim to increase your exercise wherever you can. Walk to the shops instead of getting the bus or driving and take the stairs instead of the lift. Raising your heart rate through exercise for 20 minutes a minimum of three times per week is acceptable. Bear in mind however, the more exercise you take the better.

Try to spend at least a couple of hours at the weekend or in the evenings on hobbies like gardening, painting, cycling or whatever you're interested in doing. Spend a minimum of one evening or day each week with your family and/or friends.

Aim to spend a minimum of two hours per week reviewing the CBT strategies that helped you overcome your problems. Practice is key to staying well. You can plan to practise self-help techniques at various times during your week instead of doing all your practice in a two-hour chunk.

In general, strive to keep work duties confined to office hours. Not everyone works 9 to 5 but the principle is to stick to working during the hours you're contracted and paid to do so.

Obviously you'll have times when work or family responsibilities, for example, temporarily require most of your energy and attention. During times of crisis, you naturally and appropriately have to concentrate on the issue and not on yourself. Just remind yourself to restore the balance afterwards.

If you're wondering where you'll find the time to do more exercising, studying, or socialising – in fact, any of the activities that you're currently not doing enough of – try slotting these pursuits into times when you're usually just watching television or working late.

Going Boldly Where You've Not Gone Before

Let's assume that you've largely overcome your problems and have an eye out for possible relapse risks. You've taken up some hobbies and value-based activities and are managing to maintain a pretty balanced lifestyle. Great. Well done. Perhaps you may now wish to think about your goals for the future. Think about longer-term personal development goals such as furthering your career, changing career, moving house, travelling, and so on.

Fill in Worksheet 18-8 to help you clarify any goals you may have for the future and what steps you need to take in order to realise them. (Chapter 8 shows you how to set effective goals.)

Worksheet 18-8	My Future Goals
My personal development goals	*Steps I need to take to achieve my goals*
In the next 6–12 months:	
In the next 1–2 years:	
In the next 5 years:	

Chapter 19

Rupturing Roadblocks to Recovery

● ●

In This Chapter
▶ Getting past emotions that obstruct recovery
▶ Asking for a little help
▶ Keeping up with positive practices

● ●

*O*n your way to overcoming your psychological problems, you're likely to stumble once, twice, or even thrice – doing so isn't unusual (Chapter 18 offers tips on regaining your footing). You may strike a brick wall, which can be discouraging.

Obstacles to positive change come in several forms: Sometimes you may unwittingly block your own progress through faulty thinking leading to unhelpful emotions such as shame or guilt. Other times you may be aware of deliberately (or almost deliberately) practising self-sabotage. Why? Well, any change (even positive change) can be daunting, risky, hard work, and even frightening. You may find yourself putting obstacles in your way because staying as you are seems temporarily more attractive than putting yourself through a lot of effort and discomfort to overcome your problems.

Whatever the reasons for getting stuck, this chapter focuses on how to rupture roadblocks on your route to a robust recovery.

Exorcising Emotions that Bind You

A common roadblock to recovery is *secondary emotional problems*, a term used to describe feeling bad about your original, or *primary*, problem. Examples could be feeling guilty about being depressed or feeling ashamed of *having* panic attacks. Guilt or shame often mean that you're putting yourself down for having psychological difficulties. Guilt, shame, and pride are three of the most common types of secondary emotional problems:

✔ **Guilt** often emerges as a secondary emotional problem in depression. Depression can lead you to withdraw from others and avoid social contact. You may believe that you're neglecting your loved ones because of your depression and make yourself feel guilty. When you're depressed, everyday tasks can feel overwhelming and you may not be able to function effectively. You may make yourself feel guilty about letting tasks build up or failing to fulfill obligations. It's common for depressed people to berate themselves for being unproductive. Secondary guilt about the effects of your depression can worsen your mood.

✔ **Shame** is often a secondary emotional problem for people with anxiety disorders such as panic attacks or OCD. If you think that your anxiety problem means that you're weak or foolish, you're probably making yourself feel ashamed about experiencing anxiety. Because OCD typically involves unwelcome intrusive thoughts and images that you find unacceptable, it's very possible that you feel shame about having these OCD symptoms in the first place.

Shame can stop you from talking to others about your problems or seeking professional treatment.

⮑ **Pride** attends many emotional problems. Often people think that they should be able to overcome their emotional problems without any outside support. Especially if you consider yourself 'someone who copes', value your independence, and/or see psychological problems as unacceptable weaknesses, you may be too proud to admit to yourself or others that you need help. Pride can even prevent you from embarking on a course of self-help because you believe that you should know all the answers yourself without needing to consult books.

Secondary problems can really stop you in your tracks. These types of unhealthy emotions may prevent you from talking to other people about your situation or from seeking valuable professional help. They can also frequently lead to unhelpful behaviours such as avoidance and denial and actually worsen the symptoms of your primary problem.

Silas has obsessive-compulsive disorder (OCD). He experiences unwanted thoughts about harming children and animals. (See Chapter 13 for more about OCD.) Silas thinks that nobody would understand his problem and that his thoughts mean that he's a bad person. He feels very guilty about having intrusive upsetting thoughts.

Silas used Worksheet 19-1 to shed light on his secondary emotional problem.

Worksheet 19-1	Silas's Secondary Emotions Sheet
My primary problem:	I have been diagnosed with OCD. I have lots of really unpleasant thoughts about hurting children and small animals.
Unhealthy negative emotions I have about this problem: (my secondary emotional problem)	I feel guilty about the thoughts I have but I can't control them. I feel like a bad and nasty person for having such dark and unacceptable thoughts.

See Chapter 6 for clarification about healthy and unhealthy negative emotions.

You can use Worksheet 19-2 to put your finger on any secondary emotional problems you may be experiencing.

Worksheet 19-2	My Secondary Emotions Sheet
My primary problem:	
Unhealthy negative emotions I have about this problem: (my secondary emotional problem)	

If, like Silas, you've identified either guilt or another unhealthy negative emotion about your primary problem, your next step is to work on overcoming these obstructive feelings.

Giving up on guilt

Sometimes your disorder may lead you to think in ways that aren't in keeping with your morals, as in the case of Silas in the preceding section. His OCD means that he thinks about hurting the very creatures he believes deserve protection. Or your depression may impede your ability to do things that you consider to be important such as caring for your family or performing well at work. Making yourself feel guilty about your illness is all too easy. But guilt only serves to make you feel worse and delay your improvement.

Instead of solely focusing on the negative effects of your illness on others and on what you're unable to do as a result of your problems, try being more understanding and compassionate with yourself. The person who suffers most from your OCD, depression, anxiety, or other problem is *you*. Remind yourself that you're only human and that although your psychological problems may be negatively impacting on others in your life, making yourself guilty about this reality won't fix anything. You're not neglecting your duties or family deliberately out of malice; this is just a regrettable side effect of many different psychological problems. In Chapter 6 we discuss the differences between healthy and unhealthy negative emotions like guilt.

Silas's primary problem is having OCD-intrusive thoughts about harming children and small animals, which lead to feelings of guilt. He used Worksheet 19-3 to help him let go of guilt and move in a goal-directed direction.

Worksheet 19-3	Silas's Giving Up On Guilt Guide
Guilt-producing Thoughts	*Guilt-removing Arguments*
I should not be having these thoughts.	Unwanted thoughts are a feature of OCD.
These thoughts mean that I'm bad.	Thoughts aren't actions. These thoughts mean that I'm ill, but they don't mean anything else about me.
Decent people don't think like this.	Everyone has unwanted thoughts from time to time.
My thoughts are dangerous.	I certainly don't like having these thoughts and I wish I didn't. But the only person who is suffering from my OCD is me. I'm not inconveniencing, harming, or damaging anyone else by having unpleasant and intrusive thoughts.

In Worksheet 19-4 Silas records ways giving up on guilt can help him in his recovery from OCD. Use Worksheet 19-5 to highlight the benefits of giving up your own guilt about your emotional problem. Consider about how guilty thinking may be eating up your time and worsening your mood. How would you be acting differently if you were guilt-free?

Worksheet 19-4 **Silas's Guilt-Free Benefits**

How giving up on guilt will be helpful to my recovery:

I'll be more able to focus on getting treatment for my OCD. I'll be willing to talk to other OCD sufferers about their experiences and share my own. I still won't like the thoughts but I won't feel so devastated about having them in the first place. I won't be judging myself as a bad person for having thoughts that I don't want. I'll believe that I deserve to get help and to get better.

You may find that you need to work hard to generate convincing and credible arguments in opposition to your guilty feelings. Having to make a big effort is *not* a sign that your guilt is appropriate; rather, it's a side effect of thinking in a self-punishing way for a long time.

Now use Worksheets 19-5 and 19-6 to exorcise your guilty thoughts and feelings about your primary problem.

Worksheet 19-5 **My Giving Up On Guilt Guide**

My Primary Problem:

Guilt-producing thoughts	*Guilt-removing arguments*

Worksheet 19-6 **My Guilt-Free Benefits**

How giving up on guilt will be helpful to my recovery:

Refusing to play the shame game

Shame is a slimy little emotion that can get you stuck. Heave out humiliation and shame by giving yourself permission to be both human and fallible. Instead of ridiculing, belittling, or denigrating yourself for having psychological problems, try being a bit more compassionate and understanding with yourself. Remember that as a human being you don't expect to never become physically ill or to be injured in some way. So why should you expect yourself to always be in tip top mental and emotional shape?

It makes sense to dislike having psychological difficulties, but if you make yourself ashamed of your problems then you're telling yourself that you must not have them. That just doesn't make sense.

Think of as many reasons as you can to counteract your shame. Try reminding yourself that however uncomfortable and undesirable your problem is, this is a normal part of being human and there is no reason that you shouldn't be experiencing psychological difficulties.

You may be surprised by the support and concern you receive from other people in your life, too. You may expect to be rejected on the basis of your problems when in reality people want to help. Be prepared to be pleasantly surprised by some of the reactions you get from those who care about you.

Neha has panic attacks. She finds it very difficult to go into supermarkets or other busy shops. Neha is ashamed of her problem and therefore tries to hide her anxiety from people. She hasn't told anyone about her problem because she thinks it makes her weak and that other people will also think her weak and pathetic if they know. (Glance at Chapter 9 for more on anxiety and panic and how to treat them.)

Neha put her shame-provoking thoughts about her panic attacks down on paper in Worksheet 19-7 and disputed them using evidence against them.

Worksheet 19-7   Neha's Heaving Out Humiliation Worksheet

My primary problem: *Panic attacks.*

Shame-producing thoughts	*Shame-disputing arguments*
Only weak people and wimps panic for no reason.	All the literature I've read and Web sites I've seen show that all sorts of people from all walks of life have anxiety disorders. Panic attacks are actually very common.
People will think less of me if they find out that I suffer panic attacks.	Some of my friends or colleagues may also have a similar problem. People like me for lots of reasons and my panic is just one small part of who I am.
I should be able to stop my panic.	In time I can learn to overcome my panic attacks. If I tell myself that I must not panic and beat myself up when I do, I just make the problem worse. Obviously, I'd much prefer not to panic, but there's no earthly reason that I absolutely should not have panic attacks. I'm human and not a robot.

Neha then used Worksheet 19-8 to list how saying goodbye to her shame could help in overcoming her panic attacks.

Worksheet 19-8   Neha's Heaving Out Humiliation Benefits Worksheet

How heaving out humiliation and shame will help in my recovery:

Shame leads me to try to hide/stop my anxiety symptoms, which makes me even more anxious and likely to panic.

Humiliation stops me from going outdoors and socialising, which means that I feel isolated and lonely.

If I stop making myself ashamed about having panic attacks I'll undertake exposure exercises and get some support.

Now you can give the shame and humiliation your primary problem produces the heave-ho by working through Worksheet 19-9.

Worksheet 19-9   My Heaving Out Humiliation Worksheet

My primary problem:

Shame-producing thoughts	*Shame-disputing arguments*

Use Worksheet 19-10 to list how sending shame scurrying can help with your recovery.

Worksheet 19-10	My Heaving Out Humiliation Benefits Worksheet

How heaving out humiliation and shame will help in my recovery:

_____

_____

_____

_____

Paralysing problematic pride

You may be surprised to realise that your pride can indeed put paid to progress. If you tell yourself that you should be able to get better on your own or know all the answers to your problems, you may be too proud to get professional help. Your pride may also stop you from confiding in others about your problems for fear of appearing weak or flawed. You may even be reluctant to admit your problems to yourself and instead exhaust yourself trying to mask them or insist that you 'pull yourself together'.

Pablo has a pride problem. Actually he's depressed and has been for several months, but he keeps telling himself to 'pull himself together' and 'get over it'. Unfortunately, Pablo just feels worse about himself when he can't get over his depression on his own. Simultaneously, he also thinks that self-help techniques won't work for him and that he should know how to get over his depression instinctively. Pablo used Worksheet 19-11 to petrify his paralysing pride problems connected to his depression.

Worksheet 19-11	Pablo's Prevailing Over Pride Page

My primary problem: *Depression.*

Pride-based Thoughts	*Balanced Thoughts*
I'm intelligent so I should be able to work this problem out on my own!	Even the brightest people need help and guidance with things outside their knowledge base occasionally. Depression can happen to anyone no matter how smart they are.
I'm a strong person and I can fight this on my own.	Depression is not a sign of weakness. Ultimately I will be the one who fights my own depression but that doesn't mean that I can't seek help or guidance to do so.
If I thought self-help techniques would work, I'd have done it a long time ago!	Actually I can't really help myself without knowing how to. Maybe professional advice would put me on the right track.

Pablo then considered how overcoming his pride could help him conquer his depression in Worksheet 19-12.

Worksheet 19-12   **Pablo's Putting Pride Aside Benefits**

How putting aside my pride will aid my recovery:

I may actually research depression more fully and see what's out there in terms of treatment.

I may be more inclined to talk to my doctor about my situation and maybe even take medication for a while.

I'll tell the people closest to me how I'm feeling rather than shutting them out and avoiding them. They might understand me and give me some extra support.

Is pride getting in the way of owning up to your primary problem or seeking help to overcome it? If you think so, put pen to paper and fill in Worksheet 19-13.

Worksheet 19-13   **My Prevailing Over Pride Page**

My primary problem:

Pride-based Thoughts	*Balanced Thoughts*

Now use Worksheet 19-14 to record how letting your pride go can bring big benefits.

Worksheet 19-14	My Putting Pride Aside Benefits
How putting aside my pride will aid my recovery:	

Letting Others Help to Bear the Burden

You get by with a little help from my friends – or do you? After you've dealt with some of your problematic secondary emotions, can you elicit a little support from others? We hope so because sorting out your problems on your own is a lonely old business.

A big (and not so very rare) obstacle to recovery is hiding your problems away and refusing to let others in on how you're feeling. You may conceal your problem as a result of shame, guilt, pride, or fear of burdening others. We urge you to take the risk of approaching others. Even if your friends or family don't totally understand your particular problem, they may well be willing to try.

Other people may be far more understanding, compassionate, and empathetic than you give them credit for when you're feeling low.

Whilst thinking that everyone in your life will be ready and willing to give you a bit of support or care in your time of need is nice, that isn't always the case. If you're already at a low ebb, talking to someone who is unlikely to give you the kind of attention you need right now makes little sense. So if your best friend is great to go out dancing with but has very little patience or no understanding about anxiety problems, then she may not be the ideal candidate to talk to about your panic attacks. Looking for support from unsuitable sources can give you a poor experience of opening up and might put you off the idea altogether. So give some thought to who you think is suitable to lend you support.

Make a list of the people in your life that you may be able to talk to openly and honestly about your emotional and/or behavioural problem. Worksheet 19-15 walks you through identifying contacting sympathetic family and friends and recording the type of support you can expect from each. Don't forget about professional people and well-established support groups.

A doctor or psychiatrist can prescribe appropriate medication and refer you for therapy. A friend may be able to empathise with your problems because they have been through a similar experience. Another friend may be more able to give you financial advice and help you to develop strategies for resolving practical problems. Your mum may give you tea and sympathy but really not understand your problem. Your siblings may be able to give you some much needed child care or help around the house. The possibilities entirely depend upon your own circumstances and the people in your life. The point is to think about the different types of support you need and who in your life is most likely to be able to provide such support.

If you're afraid of their reaction, ask yourself how you'd react if they came to you with the same problem. Chances are you'd be very willing to help them however you could. So take the plunge and lean on others a little.

Worksheet 19-15	My Suitable Sources of Support Sheet
Who in my life is most likely to understand my current problem?	
What specific forms of support do I most need right now?	
Which specific friends or family members can I seek support from? (List names)	
What kind of support am I most likely to get from each of the people listed?	
Who can I approach for professional help?	
What support groups can I join or look into?	

Look to the people in your life to give you the kind of support you think they are most likely to be able to provide.

Persisting with Practice

Practice may be tedious, but it's absolutely essential. If you really want to bust through blockages you have to persevere. Most people find sticking to difficult and uncomfortable tasks hard – even when they know that they're in their long-term best interest. But you *can* overcome your effort and discomfort intolerance in the short term if you seriously consider why doing so is worthwhile. Very often, *doing* something about your problem is actually easier than *thinking* about it.

Worksheet 19-17 helps you to stick with goal directed action (Chapter 8 covers goals). It also gives you a chance to review techniques that have helped you to get better. Chapter 3 describes the A-B-C Form Mortimer found helpful. Chapter 12 gives you advice on beating depression, and Chapter 9 addresses anxiety. You may also have used strategies offered in Chapter 13 to overcome your obsessional problems. Use the worksheet to further plan and persist with your recovery.

Mortimer has social anxiety. He rehearses what he says before he says it, leaving little room for spontaneity. He replays social events in his head once they are over and looks for gaffs he may have made. Mortimer also pays very close attention to how others are responding to him during a social interaction. If he thinks he has made a poor impression, Mortimer berates himself harshly and calls himself a selection of deeply horrid names for being socially awkward. He often drinks too much to quell his nerves and then finds that he regrets it the next day because he worries that he has behaved badly when drunk. Mortimer has been working hard to overcome his social anxiety but hit a wall recently when he thought he'd done enough and didn't want to push himself any further.

Mortimer used Worksheet 19-16 to help him get back on the road to recovery and to persuade himself to persist with goal-directed practices.

Worksheet 19-16	Mortimer's Persistence Policy
What is my primary problem?	Social anxiety
What are my goals for my primary problem?	To feel concerned but not anxious about my performance socially.
What techniques have helped me thus far?	Fixing my attention on other people and my environment.
	Listening to what others are saying and responding without preparing a speech.
	Sitting or standing in a central position during a social outing.
	Using an ABC form.

(continued)

What is my helpful attitude/belief about my primary problem?	I'd prefer not to make social errors but there is no earthly reason why I must not. If I do make a gaff, it simply means that I made a social error like anyone else can do. I can still think of myself as a worthwhile and like-able person in the face of social unease.
In what ways do I need to push myself in order to advance my progress?	I should really go to the Christmas party at work and try to stand in the middle of the room. I need to make conversation without pre-planning it when I go out with friends. I ought to try to talk to people that I think are above me or wouldn't like me when I am out and see what happens. Even if they reject me, I'll live.
Why is it worth pushing toward overcoming my problem? (Be specific,)	I'll get rid of this social anxiety and feel appropriately nervous or concerned about social outings in the long run. I'll be more able to make friends and socialise rather than sit at home alone. Ironically, I'll probably appear more interesting and attractive to others when I'm socially relaxed than when I'm freaking out about what they might be thinking about me. I might get up the nerve to ask a girl I really fancy at work out for a drink. And if I do ask the girl in question out for a drink, I'll be able to talk to her normally without having to go to the toilet every five minutes because I'm so anxious!
How can I be compassionate with myself about setbacks and my reluctance to carry on?	As anyone with social anxiety knows, deliberately going into social situations that you could otherwise avoid is terrifying. I'm doing well to keep trying. Even if I screw up on one occasion, I can learn from it. I'm only human and born to make mistakes. Everyone has setbacks, and I am no different. I'm a whole, complex, changing individual and my social unease is only one small part of who I am in total. And anyway, I'm not the only person in the world with social anxiety! Lots of people have it. So I don't need to beat myself up about it.

What behaviours do I most need to resist in order to overcome my problem?	Monitoring myself for signs of anxiety such as shaking, blushing, and sweating.
	Planning what to say before I open my mouth.
	Sticking to safe areas such as the sides of the room, the bar, or my seat.
	Talking only to people I know and feel reasonably comfortable with.
	Drinking too much too quickly in an attempt to quell my nerves.
	Replaying the social event and battering myself for any minor social gaffs.
What behaviours do I most need to foster in order to overcome my problem?	Going out more often.
	Inviting myself along to after-work drinks.
	Keeping my attention trained outward on other people and my environment.
	Speaking without preparing in advance.
	Making small talk with people I don't know well.
	Drawing a line under any social outing after it has ended and resisting the urge to review it and judge my performance.
	Monitoring my alcohol intake closely during a social event and not allowing myself to have a drink solely for the purpose of relieving my anxiety.
When can I allocate time to practise CBT, both behavioural and thinking based?	I can think in a healthy way about social unease and social blips every day — especially before I enter the office and during any social banter throughout the working day.
	I can go out every Friday night with people from work.
	I can join a club that interests me and force myself to meet new people (one that meets weekly).
	I can practise saying hello to people in the street, the bus driver, and shop assistants on a daily basis and remind myself that though I'd really like them to respond in kind, they don't have to! I'm likeable even if I get a poor response from others sometimes.

Now that you've seen how Mortimer has renewed his commitment to his goals and revived his general 'get up and go', see if you can use Worksheet 19-17 to the same effect for your own problems.

You may want to review some of the previous chapters to help you get to the guts of your given problem. Have a flick through the index and look at the chapters that you think might be most relevant to you right now.

Worksheet 19-17	**My Persistence Policy**
What is my primary problem?	
What are my goals for my primary problem?	
What techniques have helped me thus far?	
What is my helpful attitude/belief about my primary problem?	
In what ways do I need to push myself in order to advance my progress?	
Why is it worth pushing toward overcoming my problem? (Be specific)	

How can I be compassionate with myself about setbacks and my reluctance to carry on?	
What behaviours do I most need to resist in order to overcome my problem?	
What behaviours do I most need to foster in order to overcome my problem?	
When can I allocate time to practise CBT, both behavioural and thinking based?	

Chapter 20

Putting into Practice Principles of Positive Living

· ·

In This Chapter

▶ Taking appropriate responsibility and worthwhile risks

▶ Getting involved with life through holding healthy attitudes

· ·

*L*ife holds more than overcoming psychological problems. Once you've sustained recovery from your difficulties for a while, it may be time to look at how you live your life and see whether you can do so more positively. In this chapter we briefly outline the types of personal principles and attitudes that can help you to get the most out of life. We include seeking out positive experiences and also dealing effectively with negative ones.

Receiving Your Ration of Responsibility

Obviously, bad things do happen and often you can do little about changing them. But you can try to identify where you may have some responsibility for what happened or for how you respond to the event. Taking responsibility isn't about blaming yourself or others for a negative event or situation. You're not fault finding as such. Rather, taking responsibility is about empowering yourself to either change a negative situation by problem solving (if possible) or alternatively adapting and adjusting to conditions.

Patrick is very sensitive to rejection from females. He isn't very confident about his attractiveness to the opposite sex. Patrick finds it hard to imagine that any girl would be interested in him. A barmaid called Susan at Patrick's local pub caught his eye a few months ago. Although he hangs around the bar in order to be near Susan, Patrick freezes up whenever she attempts to make conversation with him. As a result Patrick seems aloof and disinterested. A mate of Patrick's called Jack also likes Susan. Patrick compares himself negatively to Jack and considers Jack far more attractive and charming than himself. Last weekend Jack asked Susan out for dinner and she agreed. Patrick is furious with Jack for callously moving in on his love interest. He's also very hurt that Susan agreed to date Jack and sees it as a huge personal rejection and as further proof of his unattractiveness. Patrick used Worksheet 20-1 to see if he could take some responsibility for what happened with Jack and Susan. Using the worksheet also helped him to see how his reactions to the negative event were making things worse for himself.

Worksheet 20-1	Patrick's Responsibility Ration Record
Identified negative event or situation:	Jack asked out Susan and she said yes. They had dinner together last weekend.
Which people or conditions contributed to the negative event/situation occurring?	Jack, Susan, the local pub environment, and my failure to make a move before Jack did.
Can I take a degree of personal responsibility for what occurred?	I suppose my fear that Susan would reject me if I expressed my interest in her led me to appear aloof. I didn't ask her out even though I had plenty of chances, and I didn't even speak to her much when she tried to talk to me. I didn't tell Jack how much I like Susan, so he didn't know that I'd be upset if he asked her out.
How can I take personal responsibility for my emotional and behavioural responses to the negative event/situation?	I'm getting angry with Jack for something he doesn't know he did to offend me. Not talking to him or going to the pub with him as punishment is a bit off. I'm basically sulking but not telling Jack why I'm angry. I'm making myself all hurt and wounded about Susan going out with Jack but she hasn't betrayed me. She doesn't even know that I like her. Comparing myself negatively to Jack and deciding that I'm a geek and he's totally cool is just making me feel really depressed and hopeless. Jack's a good looking, nice guy but he's not superman.
How might taking appropriate personal responsibility help me to resolve the event/situation or adjust healthily to it?	It will help me to stop taking the whole thing so personally and stop making myself angry, hurt, and depressed.

I will be more able to talk to Jack and let him know my feelings for Susan. I'll be more able to recognise that I've perhaps missed my chance with Susan and accept that she and Jack are now dating.

It may help me to stop comparing myself to Jack and instead accept that we're two different people, with different traits and personalities.

I will be more able to move on and look for someone else that I like and try to overcome my social unease in order to ask her out. |

Now that Patrick has shown you the ropes, take a swing yourself in Worksheet 20-2.

Worksheet 20-2	My Responsibility Ration Record
Identified negative event or situation:	
Which people or conditions contributed to the negative event/situation occurring?	
Can I take a degree of legitimate responsibility for what occurred?	
How can I take personal responsibility for my emotional and behavioural responses to the negative event/situation?	
How might taking appropriate personal responsibility help me to resolve the event/situation or adjust healthily to it?	

If someone has violated your human rights or you've been traumatised by an accident or a tragic life event, you're *not* responsible for what has happened. However, you can still take personal responsibility for the rest of your life and how you'd like to live it. To a degree, you can choose how you emotionally respond to very negative life events.

Finding that Flexibility Feeds Fun

Often being 'stuck in your ways' indicates rigid and unyielding ways of thinking about life. The more rigid your personal rules about yourself, others, and the world, the more vulnerable you are to experiencing emotional disturbance and life problems. Rigid thinking limits your ability to creatively adapt to changing life circumstances. This attitude also leads you to avoid taking risks of any kind.

If you want to change from rigid to flexible thinking, you need to acknowledge that 'want' does not equal 'have to get'. So if you *want* to succeed at a task but don't insist that you *have to* succeed, then you're thinking flexibly and leaving room for error.

If you want to have fun, you have to be flexible! Otherwise you'll never try anything new or a bit risky, even when it's worth doing so. Consider Patrick and his unexpressed adoration of Susan from the preceding section. Look at how Patrick got to grips with his rigid thinking in Worksheet 20-3.

Refer to Chapter 2 for more on thinking errors and demands. Also check out Chapters 16 and 17 for more on core beliefs about yourself, others, and the world. Go to Chapter 6 for explanation about healthy and unhealthy negative emotions.

Worksheet 20-3	Patrick's Finding Flexibility Form
What situation/event (past, present, or future) am I thinking rigidly about?	Jack and Susan going out together for dinner. My not asking Susan out first or telling Jack that I liked her.
What specific rigid demands am I making?	Self: I must be attractive to the opposite sex. I must not be rejected by Susan. Others: Jack must not ask out Susan. Susan must not reject me for Jack. World: The Jack–Susan situation is totally unfair and it should not be happening!
How is my rigid thinking negatively impacting on my emotions? (List any unhealthy negative emotions)	Anger, depression, and hurt.
How is my rigid thinking negatively impacting on my behaviour? (List any destructive or self-defeating behaviours)	Sulking with Jack and refusing to spend time with him. Comparing myself negatively to Jack and putting myself down as unattractive. Being sullen with Susan and giving her the cold shoulder.
What are more flexible attitudes I can adopt about the situation/event that may help me to feel less disturbed and act more constructively?	Self: I'd rather be attractive to the opposite sex but I don't have to be! I don't want to be rejected by Susan but there's no reason she mustn't reject me. If I am rejected by Susan, or any other girl, it means that those girls didn't fancy me. It doesn't mean that I'm wholly unattractive or unlikable. Others: It would be better if Jack didn't ask out Susan but there's no reason he shouldn't. I'd prefer it if Susan chose me over Jack but she doesn't have to! Neither Jack nor Susan have to do what I want them to do. World: The Jack–Susan situation is unfortunate and disappointing but not so very unfair. It's the way it goes and I can deal with it if I choose to do so!

Flexible thinking generally leads to healthy negative emotions in the face of negative events and to effective problem solving.

Here's your chance to go from rigid to flexible in one simple worksheet – Worksheet 20-4!

Worksheet 20-4	My Finding Flexibility Form
What situation/event (past, present, or future) am I thinking rigidly about?	
What specific rigid demands am I making?	Self: Others: World:
How is my rigid thinking negatively impacting on my emotions? (List any unhealthy negative emotions):	
How is my rigid thinking negatively impacting on my behaviour? (List any destructive or self-defeating behaviours):	
What are more flexible attitudes I can adopt about the situation/event that may help me to feel less disturbed and act more constructively?	Self: Others: World:

Understanding Uncertainty and Lack of Control as Unavoidable

Trying to control events that aren't within your control and to gain certainty about things that you can't be certain about is pretty dis-empowering. The truth is that you, along with the rest of the human race, live with uncertainty and limited control over life events every single day, whether you choose to acknowledge it or not. No one, not even you, is all-knowing and all-powerful. So try as you might to get absolute certainty about future events or to control random events and other people, you just can't do it. Accepting uncertainty and limited personal control can help you to overcome anxiety and enjoy life fully.

Patrick confronts his demands for certainty and control by using Worksheet 20-5.

Worksheet 20-5	Patrick's Uncertain, Uncontrollable, and Unavoidable Record
Negative situation/event (past, present, or future):	Jack and Susan dating.
What aspect of the situation am I trying to control?	Susan being attracted to Jack and vice versa. Jack asking Susan out in the first place.
What aspects of the situation am I trying to gain certainty about?	I was insisting on being certain about how Susan felt about me before asking her out. I tried to be certain that Susan would not reject me. I insist on certainty that people (like Susan) think as much of me as they do of others (like Jack).
Are these aspects of the situation within my range of control?	No. I can't control what other people feel, think, and do. Jack and Susan can act however they choose to act, no matter how hard I insist that they do what I want them to do.

Is it possible to be certain about these aspects of the situation?	No. Even if Susan reassured me that she liked me as much as Jack, she can always change her mind in the future. I can't be certain that Susan will not reject me, and if I never ask her out, I'll never know. Also Susan may not reject me today, but I can't be totally certain that she won't reject me at some point in the future. Rejection is a risk no matter who I date. I spend a lot of time searching for clues about how other people feel about me and guessing what they're thinking about me. But even a well-researched guess is not a guarantee.
How are my attempts to gain control and certainty affecting my ability to adjust to the situation/event?	In general I feel very anxious in social situations. I get very self-conscious in situations that I either can't control or in which I can't be certain that I'm making a good impression. My demands for certainty and control have stopped me from asking Susan out. My demands for certainty and control have also led me to feel angry and hurt about Jack and Susan dating.

Use the same questions in Worksheet 20-6 regarding your own situation to see where you may be demanding (in vain) that you get certainty or control.

Worksheet 20-6	My Uncertain, Uncontrollable, and Unavoidable Record
Negative situation/event (past, present, or future):	
What aspect of the situation am I trying to control?	

(continued)

What aspects of the situation am I trying to gain certainty about?	
Are these aspects of the situation within my range of control?	
Is it possible to be certain about these aspects of the situation?	
How are my attempts to gain control and certainty affecting my ability to adjust to the situation/event?	

Letting Life Be Unfair

Life is a jumble of positive, negative, and neutral events. Moreover, life isn't always fair. Sometimes things happen that are undeserved. Life just doesn't seem to stop and consider who deserves a good or bad thing to happen to them at any given time. Rather, life events seem to occur in a pretty random way.

Imagine you experience a negative event and conclude that life is unfair and that you've been victimised. Thinking in this way may be understandable, but dwelling on unfairness can ensnare you in unhealthy emotions and prevent you from making things better for yourself. Sometimes taking a second to consider whether what you're experiencing is truly 'unfair' or more accurately 'bad', 'unfortunate', or even 'tragic' is worthwhile. We're not saying that unfair things don't happen, because they most certainly do. However, life is unfair to everyone from time to time, not just to you.

Patrick challenged his victim mentality by asking himself the questions in Worksheet 20-7 about the Jack and Susan situation.

Worksheet 20-7	Patrick's Letting Life Be Unfair List
Negative situation/event:	Susan and Jack dating.
Aspects of the situation/event that I think are unfair:	Jack asking out the girl I like. Susan agreeing to date Jack before I got a chance to ask her out myself. Jack always gets the girl. Everyone always likes Jack more than me because he's so charming. It's unfair that I'm not a social butterfly like Jack. It's not fair that I'm a social moth!
Am I mislabeling any aspects of the situation as 'unfair' when to view them as 'bad', 'unfortunate', or 'tragic' is more accurate?	It's unfortunate that I was too anxious to ask Susan out before Jack did. It's bad that she agreed to date him when I wanted to go out with her. It's not unfair that Jack is socially skilled and I'm anxious in social situations. We're different, that's all. If Jack had known that I liked Susan and asked her out anyway, he may have been acting unfairly. I still think it's unfair that Jack always gets the girl!
What arguments can I use to convince myself that accepting life's potential to be unfair is in my best interest?	If I keep thinking that life is unfair only to me, then I'll just give up. I can do something to improve my social skills and to overcome my social anxiety. But if I think of my problems as 'unfair', then I'm less likely to bite the bullet and make some changes. It may be unfair that Jack gets the girls and I don't. But that's life and if I start taking some risks by talking to girls, then I might level the playing field a bit more. Lots of guys have trouble approaching women, not just me. So if social anxiety is an example of life's unfairness, then I'm not the only one affected! By accepting that life can and will be unfair from time to time, I'll be more able to problem solve because I'll spend less time being hurt, resentful, and whining.

Think of a recent negative and/or unfair life event that you've experienced. See if you can use Worksheet 20-8 to help you take a more proactive stance on resolving it, if possible, or at least adjusting to it.

Worksheet 20-8	My Letting Life Be Unfair List
Negative situation/event:	
Aspects of the situation/event that I think are unfair:	
Am I mislabeling any aspects of the situation as 'unfair' when to view them as 'bad', 'unfortunate', or 'tragic' is more accurate?	
What arguments can I use to convince myself that accepting life's potential to be unfair is in my best interest?	

Taking Risks and Making Mistakes

Sometimes mistakes are well worth making and risks well worth taking. The trick is to be able to 'go for it' when you think doing so is in your best interests *and* to believe you're able to cope with the consequences of any mistakes, poor outcomes, or bad decisions. If you believe that making mistakes is unacceptable, then you'll be unlikely to take any form of risk for fear of failure. Accepting yourself as a fallible human being capable of both success and failure can help you to take worthwhile risks.

Patrick recognised some personal risks he's been avoiding because he fears rejection. To Patrick, rejection means that he's an unattractive and unlikable person overall. He used Worksheet 20-9 to help him weigh up personal risks and to be more compassionate with himself.

Worksheet 20-9	Patrick's Risk Assessment
Risks I'd like to take but am avoiding:	Asking a girl out on a date.
Why am I avoiding taking action?	I'm afraid of being rejected. It would prove to me that I'm unattractive.
Realistically, what's the worst thing that could happen if I take this risk?	I could be rejected in an unpleasant way. I'd make myself feel depressed.
Can I imagine surviving the worst possible case scenario?	I suppose being rejected would be bad but not as terrible as I've been telling myself. I could decide to take it on the chin and resist putting myself down as an unattractive loser. You win some, you lose some. I can choose to feel sad about being rejected but not depressed. Rejection means that someone doesn't want to date me; it doesn't make me an ugly loser.
Is it worth it to me to take this risk even if I don't get my desired outcome? If so, why?	Yes. Even if a girl I like declines my invitation to go out, I'll at least have tried. It's good practice for me to talk to girls and take the risk of asking them out. I also get the chance to become more robust about rejection. It would help me to believe that I can survive rejection.

Write up your own risk assessment using Worksheet 20-10.

Worksheet 20-10	My Risk Assessment
Risk I'd like to take but am avoiding:	
Why am I avoiding taking action?	
Realistically, what's the worst thing that could happen if I take this risk?	
Can I imagine surviving the worst possible case scenario?	
Is it worth it to me to take this risk even if I don't get my desired outcome? If so, why?	

Choosing Self-Acceptance Over Other-Approval

Having other people think well of you is nice. Being approved of by others is a good thing, most of the time. Wanting to be liked is okay, too. However, *nobody* can be a hit with *everybody*.

If you believe that you've *got* to be approved of by everyone you meet, then you'll run into emotional trouble. You'll probably spend a lot of time worrying about what others think of you, try so hard to please others that you surrender your own needs and opinions, be a bag of nerves in social settings, lose your spontaneity, or act in ways that you think will impress others.

You stand a far better of chance of enjoying social interaction, making meaningful relationships, and expressing your own unique personality if you regard approval from others as a bonus rather than a dire necessity. Accepting yourself doesn't mean becoming vain or arrogant and disregarding the opinions of others completely. Self-acceptance means seeing yourself as an equal to others and being comfortable in your own skin. We cover the concept of self-acceptance in detail in Chapter 14.

Have a look at how Patrick uncovered some of his approval-seeking attitudes in Worksheet 20-11.

Worksheet 20-11	Patrick's Other-Approval Account
Broad description of situation/ event: (Think of a specific recent or typical event in which you sought other people's approval.)	Recently I wanted to ask Susan out on a date and let her know that I liked her.
Whose approval am I seeking in this situation?	Susan's.
What specific type of approval am I seeking from this person/ persons?	I wanted her to find me attractive and think of me as cool and intriguing.
Am I putting myself down about any specific aspects of myself when I sense that I'm not getting approval?	Yes. I decide that I'm ugly, dull, and a total loser with girls.

(continued)

What arguments can I use to convince myself that accepting myself is a good idea even in the absence of approval from this person/persons?	If I accept myself, then I'll be able to ask girls like Susan out. Even if I get turned down, I won't put myself down so viciously. Accepting myself as a basically worthwhile person (whether Susan fancies me or not) will probably help me to relax around her and behave more like myself. Accepting myself will help me to reach my goal of being able to socialise with girls I find attractive. Accepting myself feels a lot better because I'm not making myself depressed by putting myself down.
What arguments can I use to convince myself that though I want this person's approval, I don't have to get it?	It doesn't make sense that because I really want Susan to fancy me that she has to do so. Just because I want something very much, it doesn't logically follow that I must get it. If Susan prefers Jack to me then that's disappointing, but it won't kill me. I can survive not getting what I want. I really like Susan and I really want her to like me back. But if she doesn't, I can still go on to lead a happy and fulfilling life. I don't need Susan's approval to get on with life. If Susan absolutely had to fancy me she'd be deprived of her own free will. In reality, she has the ability to either fancy me or not. She has her own mind and will decide how she feels about me for herself.

Now complete Worksheet 20-12 to address how you seek the approval of others.

Worksheet 20-12	My Other-Approval Account
Broad description of situation/ event: (Think of a specific recent or typical event in which you sought other people's approval):	
Whose approval am I seeking in this situation?	
What specific type of approval am I seeking from this person/ persons?	
Am I putting myself down about any specific aspects of myself when I sense that I'm not getting approval?	
What arguments can I use to convince myself that accepting myself is a good idea even in the absence of approval from this person/persons?	
What arguments can I use to convince myself that though I want this person's approval, I don't have to get it?	

Putting the principles outlined in this chapter into regular practice will help you to become emotionally healthy and to stay that way.

Part V
The Part of Tens

In this part . . .

It wouldn't be a *For Dummies* book without a Part of Tens, now would it? This part contains handy top ten tips for working with professionals, getting some sleep, and renewing your motivation to get better.

Chapter 21

Ten Tips for Working with Professionals

In This Chapter

▶ Where to look for professional help

▶ Making the most of professional treatment

Despite your best efforts to get better using self-help methods like this workbook, you may find that you need to seek out some professional input. Possibly your problems are interfering with your ability to put self-help into practice or you may feel that seeing a therapist will give you an added boost. Whatever your reasons for seeking out professional help, this chapter offers useful advice on choosing the best treatment strategy for you and useful tips on making the most of your therapy.

Choosing the Right Therapy for You

Psychiatrists and doctors are increasingly recommending CBT treatment because scientific research proves its effectiveness. Its problem-solving approach and emphasis on helping you to become your own therapist also reduces relapse.

However, you may encounter many other types of therapy. You may wish to try out a different sort of therapy even if you found CBT beneficial. Perhaps you want to focus more on your past experiences or on your relationships, for example. A few of the more common types of therapy include: Psychoanalytical, psychodynamic, person centred, systemic, and interpersonal therapy. We can't fully describe these different types of treatment in this chapter but we offer a few brief points about each:

- ✔ **Psychoanalytical therapy** was developed by Sigmund Freud. It involves free association and places emphasis on your childhood relationships, particularly family dynamics. You are likely to be asked to commit to attending therapy sessions more than once a week for at least a year.

- ✔ **Psychodynamic therapy** looks at how your past experiences and relationships influenced your development. This therapy places a lot of emphasis on the past. It also tends to require long-term treatment.

- ✔ **Person centred therapy** was developed by Carl Rogers and focuses very much on the relationship or *alliance* between client and therapist. A person centered therapist doesn't direct the sessions but expects to be lead by you.

- ✔ **Systemic therapy** is often used for work with couples and families. It focuses on family systems and the roles individuals play within their relationships with others.

- ✔ **Interpersonal therapy** is a short-term therapy often used to treat depression. The treatment focuses on how you relate to others and ways to enhance and improve your relationships and social activity.

And there are many other schools of therapy out there.

We recommend that you thoroughly research whatever type of therapy you choose and ensure that it is a genuine treatment protocol recognised by a professional body. You can ask for advice from your doctor, psychiatrist, or regulating bodies for psychotherapies such as the United Kingdom Council for Psychotherapy (UKCP) in the UK. You can visit their Web site at www.psychotherapy.org.uk.

Knowing Who's Who in the Psychology World

Many different types of mental health professional are able to offer general counselling. General counselling can be helpful, but if you have a specific disorder such as depression, OCD, or post-traumatic stress, seeing a fully qualified therapist with experience of dealing with your type of problem is best. Some counsellors are specifically trained in a therapeutic orientation such as CBT but asking clearly about specialist qualifications is still worthwhile.

Any CBT therapist you decide to see should hold a degree, diploma, or ideally a Masters qualification, in CBT from a university or recognised training institute.

Following is a brief run down of different professionals and the type of help they can offer:

- **Clinical and counselling psychologists** usually have studied a broad range of therapies and have a basic knowledge of applying them to specific problems. Often they have counselling training. Many may have knowledge of CBT but not all have advanced training.

- **Counsellors** generally are trained in listening and helping skills. They may hold a certificate in basic counselling or are trained to deal with certain types of problems such as grief or addictions. Not all counsellors have a psychology degree or particular knowledge of psychological problems.

- **Psychiatric nurses and nurse therapists** have a more in-depth knowledge of psychology and psychological problems than general nurses. Increasingly nurses in the UK are training to specialise in CBT.

- **Psychiatrists** are medically trained doctors who specialise in psychological disorders. Some are trained in CBT or another type of psychotherapy but more often they conduct assessments and then refer you to a suitable therapist. They can prescribe medication and know more about the drugs used to treat psychiatric problems than general practitioners.

- **Psychotherapists** usually specialise in a school of psychotherapy such as CBT. Many have a psychology degree and in-depth knowledge/experience of psychological problems. The level of training and experience can vary widely, however.

Asking the Right Questions

If you ask yourself certain questions, such as the ones we list here, you may be clearer about what you want to ask your potential therapist.

✔ What do I want help with? What are my problems?

✔ How often do I want sessions? Weekly? Fortnightly?

✔ Do I prefer a female or male therapist?

✔ How much can I afford to pay?

✔ How far am I prepared to travel?

✔ How many sessions am I prepared to have?

Don't be worried about asking a potential therapist as many questions as you like, either during your first session or during initial telephone contact. Ensuring that you have your questions answered before you agree to start treatment is best. Sometimes a therapist may find it difficult to answer certain questions conclusively prior to assessment, such as how many sessions you are likely to need, but most will be able to give you a rough idea at least.

Looking in the Best Places for a Therapist

Recommendations from doctors and psychiatrists are probably the most reliable sources for finding a therapist. Most medical professionals only refer to therapists that they know and have referred to before. Recommendations from friends can be good too, but check out that they have a similar problem to yours or that you're looking for the same things from a therapist as they want.

You can also look on Web site directories for accredited or licensed CBT therapists. In the UK, properly trained therapists are accredited by the British Association for Behavioural and Cognitive Psychotherapy (www.babcp.com) or the UKCP or both.

Vetting Your CBT (or other) Therapist

Unfortunately, some people advertise themselves as counsellors or psychotherapists without any professional training or qualifications.

Any therapist worth their salt will not take offence to any questions you ask about their experience or training. In fact, most professional psychotherapists will expect you to do so. Ask your prospective therapist, CBT or otherwise, which professional bodies they are accredited or registered with, where they studied, and how long they have been practising. Novice therapists can be very competent but they may not have extensive experience of dealing with your type of problem, so asking about this is worthwhile. If you are considering a CBT therapist, ask specifically about the extent and nature of their CBT training.

All professional psychotherapists in the UK are required to undertake regular clinical supervision from a more advanced or equally experienced therapist. Ask your therapist about their supervision arrangements. Supervision strives to ensure that all accredited professional therapists are practising according to their therapeutic orientation.

If you have some background information about your therapist and have checked to see that they are licensed or accredited, you are in a better position to lodge a complaint if you have concerns about your treatment.

Remaining Open Minded About Medication

You may not be terribly keen on the idea of taking medication to help you overcome your psychological or emotional troubles. Many people don't like taking medication and prefer to try to overcome their problems solely through therapy. Often this approach can work and very frequently CBT on its own is enough to help you beat depression or anxiety, for example. But sometimes even your best efforts are not sufficient to resolve your problems.

Medication can help relieve some of your symptoms and enable you to more fully engage with and benefit from therapy. Even a low dose of the right type of medication can help take the edge off symptoms that may be blocking your progress with CBT.

If you couldn't fight off an infection you'd probably go to your doctor for antibiotics. Your mental health is not so very different to your physical health in this regard. So don't overlook the power of the pill.

Your doctor may be able to prescribe the kind of medication best suited to your description of your problem. If you are not sure what medication you need, ask to be referred to a psychiatrist as these doctors have specialist knowledge of this type of medication.

Working on Stuff Between Sessions

Your CBT therapist is likely to work with you to devise specific between-session tasks that help to further your understanding of core concepts. These tasks can also help you to face your fears, overcome your problematic behaviours, and strengthen healthy ways of thinking. Carrying out between-session work and reporting any problems with it (or positive results from it) to your therapist is in your best interest.

Therapy sessions are usually only one hour or even 50 minutes long. You can make the most of treatment by working between sessions and preparing your thoughts before sessions.

Record results of your between-session work. Think about any doubts, reservations, or confusion you may have about either therapy itself or your between-session work and discuss them in the next session.

Discussing Issues During Sessions

Therapy can only really be of benefit if you're prepared to talk openly and honestly to your therapist. Although trained and experienced in all sorts of psychological problems, therapists aren't mind readers. We rely on you to provide us with the information we need to understand your difficulties.

You may feel a bit embarrassed or worried about telling your therapist about some of your thoughts or behaviours. Try to remember that your therapist is not there to judge you but to try to understand and offer you recognised techniques for dealing with your problems. Most experienced therapists are relatively unshockable. Remind yourself that your therapist has trained for years and met many people with problems very similar to your own.

Above all, your therapist is a human being first and a professional mental health worker second. Many of the thoughts and behaviours that you may wish to discuss are common human experiences. Making a list of issues you feel you need to address prior to your first session may help. Then, if words fail you at the time, you can simply read out your list or hand it over to your therapist to read.

Use Worksheet 21-1 to write down issues that are leading you to seek therapy.

Worksheet 21-1	My Issue List
What are the key issues in my life that I want to discuss in therapy?	

Preparing Prior to Sessions

In addition to working on therapeutic tasks between sessions and being open to discussing your issues during sessions, you can further prepare prior to sessions. Although you probably define your problems and goals with your therapist in the first few sessions, life can throw some unexpected things your way, and you may find that your circumstances have changed since your first session. You can prepare for sessions by making brief notes about any changes in your circumstances, problems, or goals that your therapist may need to be told about. Keeping all your therapy paperwork in a file or folder so that you can easily bring it to sessions and review your work with your therapist can also be useful.

Getting Yourself Goals

CBT is a goal-directed therapy. Expect your therapist to listen to your description of your problems in the initial sessions and to ask you what your goals are regarding them. Thinking about not only your specific problematic emotions and behaviours but also about how you want to change is a good idea. So you may decide, for example, that you want to be more confident about your appearance, more assertive with your partner, sad but not depressed about the loss of your job, or nervous but not anxious about entering social situations. See Chapter 8 for more guidance on goal setting.

Use Worksheet 21-2 to record a list of goals in relation to your problems. Bring the completed list with you to your first therapy session.

Your therapist can help you to establish appropriate, realistic, and achievable goals.

Worksheet 21-2	My Goals Sheet
What are my problems?	
What are my goals for these problems? How do I want to feel/act differently?	

Chapter 22

Ten Tips for Getting a Good Night's Sleep

Many common psychological problems can lead to sleep disturbance of one kind or another. You may find it difficult to get off to sleep or perhaps you frequently wake in the night and are unable to get back to sleep. Sleep disturbance of any kind is unpleasant. In this chapter we include some tips to help increase your chances of getting a good night's rest.

Wear Yourself Out with Exercise

Perhaps you're an exception to the rule, but most of us don't get enough daily exercise. Exercise is important not only because it keeps you physically fit but studies also show that it has a real positive impact on mental fitness too. When you exercise (especially quite vigorously) your brain releases 'feel good' chemicals called *endorphins*. These little fellas are good news for your general mood and can help promote relaxation.

Perhaps you've had the experience of spending a day gardening, at the seaside, or hiking and felt very physically tired afterward. Chances are you slept well that night. The combination of fresh air and physical exertion is a great recipe for restful sleep.

Try to increase the amount you exercise each day. Even small changes such as walking to the station instead of driving or taking the stairs instead of the lift can make a difference. Ideally you want to increase your heart rate (and really work up a sweat) through cardiovascular exercise such as running, swimming, or cycling at least three times per week.

Doing your more vigorous exercising early on in the day is a good idea, otherwise you may thwart yourself by exercising too close to bedtime and getting yourself physically 'pumped' instead of relaxed. Suitable gentle exercises for the evening include yoga, Pilates, or walking.

Establish a Schedule

If you aren't sleeping well at night you may be tempted to try to 'catch up' on your sleep by either getting up later or taking naps during the day. But ultimately doing so can cement bad sleep habits rather than help to get your sleeping back on track.

If you're trying to restore a pattern to your sleep, try getting up and *out* of bed at the same time every day for at *least* two weeks, even weekends! This routine means *not* hitting the snooze button on the alarm clock. Also steadfastly resist napping during the day no matter how poorly you slept the night before. The idea is that your body will begin to feel sleepy at a regular time each night because you're getting up at a regular time and staying awake all day. You'll probably also find that (eventually) you fall asleep more readily when your head hits the pillow. You may feel uncomfortably tired for the first few days after you start sticking to a sleep schedule. In the long run, however, you'll benefit from establishing a better sleep pattern.

If you know that you tend to feel sleepy and want to nap at a certain point during the day, plan to be doing something active at this time.

Use Worksheet 22-1 to schedule your getting up time and nap avoidance strategies.

Worksheet 22-1	My Sleep Schedule
My regular time for getting up and out of bed each day:	
Times I most often feel like napping:	
Things I can do instead of napping:	

Don't Lie in Bed Tossing and Turning

If you find it difficult to get to sleep or wake in the night and can't readily get back to sleep, you'll gain little from lying in bed bemoaning the fact. Give yourself 10 to 15 minutes to fall asleep and if you don't succeed, then get up.

Try doing something not overly stimulating (in fact doing something boring or monotonous is recommended). Sorting the laundry, ironing, reading a dull book, or doing something repetitive such as knitting are some ideas. Avoid alcoholic or caffeinated drinks. Have a cup of herbal tea or a warm milky drink instead. Try not to return to bed until you are genuinely sleepy and your eyelids are getting heavy.

You may feel more tired the next day if you've been up a lot in the night or got to sleep late. However, over time your sleep pattern will stabilise. Lying in bed tossing and turning can build up unhelpful associations of sleeplessness whilst you're in bed.

Monitor Your Caffeine and Stimulant Intake

Some people are more sensitive to caffeine than others. Caffeine can stay in your system for a long time. So even if you don't think that you're very sensitive to it, avoiding caffeine and other stimulants can be a good idea. Many energy drinks contain substances such as matte and guarana, which are stimulating. Try cutting out all these types of drinks from mid to late afternoon onwards.

Bed in a Bedtime Routine

If you were trying to soothe a child to sleep you'd probably take away his noisy toys, give him a warm bath, put him in some comfy pyjamas, read him a story or sing him a lullaby by the light of a soft lamp, then tuck him up and say 'sweet dreams'. Wouldn't you? Try giving yourself a similarly soothing bedtime routine. Many adults make the mistake of jumping into bed without giving themselves a chance to wind down.

Particularly if you're having sleep problems, using your bed *only* for sleeping in is important. Working on a laptop, watching TV, or even reading are activities you're best off doing elsewhere. The one obvious exception to this rule is sex. You can keep doing that in bed. The idea here is to build associations of getting into bed and going to sleep (either before or after making whoopee) rather than associations of doing your tax return (not a relaxing activity for most people!).

Try reading or listening to soothing music or a sedate radio programme in a comfortable chair near your bed. But only get into bed when you feel ready for sleep.

Put pen to paper and properly plan out your peaceful pre-bedtime procedure in Worksheet 22-2. Getting into a soothing bedtime routine can really help your body and mind to recognise that the day is done and it's time to shut down.

Worksheet 22-2	My Bedtime Routine
Regular time to start my bedtime routine:	
Relaxing and unwinding activities I can indulge in pre-bedtime:	

Cozy Up Your Sleeping Area

Is your bedroom a sleep inducing place to be? If not, get cozying. Ideally your bedroom should hold strong associations for you of (surprise, surprise) sleeping! Remove excess clutter from your bedroom, keep your bed linen fresh and clean, invest in some comfortable (even sumptuous) sleepwear, keep the temperature comfortable, and take telephones out of the room. Think about how you might arrange a child's sleep area. Apply the same basic principles to your own bedroom – and get out your favorite teddy.

Apply Some Oils

It's a proven fact that smells carry strong associations. Some studies show that olfactory cued memories are the most powerful. So give some thought to the kind of smells that give you a sense of wellbeing or peacefulness.

Some people prefer woody or spicy smells and others are partial to fruity or floral aromas. Luckily there is probably an essential oil (or oil combination) that is nigh on perfect for you. Research different oils online and then visit a shop so that you can actually smell the oils and decide which ones you most like. Some more popular oils reputed for their relaxation effects include lavender, clary sage, geranium, chamomile, and patchouli.

You can add oils to your bath, scent rooms with them by burning them in a specially designed oil infuser, or get them in spray form to fragrance your linen and clothing.

Always get professional advice on how to properly use essential oils. They are very potent and should not be used undiluted. Also consult your doctor before using oils if you're on medication, suffer from allergies, or are pregnant.

Treat yourself to an aromatherapy massage as often as you can afford to do so. Massage can be very therapeutic, de-stressing, and promote a sense of wellbeing. Again, always see a properly trained and qualified person for a massage.

Shed a Little Light on the Subject

Lighting can have a significant effect on mood. Soft lighting tends to promote relaxation, so building in subdued lighting to your pre-bedtime routine can help encourage your body and mind to wind down. Low energy light bulbs give a softer light than traditional bulbs, so try using these in the bathroom and bedroom. Downlighting as opposed to overhead or uplighting also tends to lend a 'chilled out' atmosphere to a room. So a few hours before bedtime try using lamps or fairy lights to light your rooms. You may also wish to use candles in the bathroom or bedroom. Just be sure to use suitable candle holders and be mindful of fire hazards.

Set Sensible Sleep Expectations

Despite your efforts to set the scene for bedtime, you may find your thoughts working against you. This point is very important because the pressure you may be putting on yourself to sleep well or the expectations you may have about sleeping poorly can really affect your actual sleep outcome. If your sleep has been disturbed for some time, it is understandable that you may have thoughts such as 'I've *got* to get some sleep tonight' or 'I'll be up all night again' or 'I can't cope on so little sleep any longer'. Unfortunately these types of thoughts can become self-fulfilling prophesies.

Many of the tips in this chapter are designed to help you set the optimum conditions for relaxation and sleep inducement, but sleep itself is something that you're best off not forcing. No matter how uncomfortable it is, many people do cope on little or poor quality sleep without disaster. So try challenging your negative sleep expectations by telling yourself something such as, 'I don't know how I'll sleep tonight so I'll just see how it goes' or ' If I don't sleep well tonight, then I'll be tired tomorrow but I will cope'.

In reality, sleep is your body's natural response to fatigue. In fact, sleep is such a natural and automatic process that you needn't *try* to get to sleep, you're best off just letting it happen spontaneously.

Recording your negative expectations or demands about your sleeping can be helpful. Then you can generate some more sensible sleep expectations to take the pressure off and allow sleep to come of its own volition. Try using Worksheet 22-3 to replace unhelpful thoughts with more helpful ones.

Worksheet 22-3	My Sensible Sleep Expectation Sheet
What are my negative sleep expectations/demands?	
What are some more realistic and constructive ways of thinking about my current sleep problems?	
What are my sensible sleep expectations?	

Leave Your Cares at the Bedroom Door

Throughout history, very few people have put the world to rights whilst in bed. Bedtime is not the best time to embark on problem solving. A lot of people with sleep disturbance unwittingly use bedtime as 'worry time'. Since worrying isn't a relaxing activity it tends to seriously impede sleep. Putting your thoughts on hold for the night can be very difficult but with practice you can train yourself to do it.

Try setting aside half an hour (or less) before bedtime to run through preparations for the next day or to deal with any residual concerns from the current day. Then tell yourself to draw a line under your concerns until the next day. If worries return during sleep time, remind yourself that now is not the time to deal with them and that you will sort it out during daylight hours. You can even use a little imagery exercise if you're so inclined: Stand in front of your bedroom doorway and do a brief shaking action – imagine that you're shaking off your workaday worries before getting into bed and snuggling down.

Chapter 23

Ten Reasons to Never Give Up

In This Chapter

▶ Keeping your motivation moving forward

▶ Preserving an optimistic perspective

*W*e wrote this workbook to equip you with core skills and techniques to help you overcome your personal problems. We fully expect that if you use the worksheets in this book you will benefit. That said, there are times when all your best efforts seem not to be enough. Don't despair! It is entirely normal and human to feel demotivated and disheartened from time to time. Many psychological problems are disruptive, consuming and very stubborn opponents. This chapter contains advice and encouragement to keep you on the road to recovery.

Setbacks Are Not Exceptional

Setbacks, relapses, and symptom reappearance are *normal.* In fact, if you recovered from anxiety, depression, an eating disorder, an addiction, OCD, or virtually any psychological disturbance *without* a setback, *that* would be exceptional.

It is important to remember that change is not linear. By this we mean that recovery from an emotional, behavioural or psychological problem rarely (if ever) goes steadily upward in a straight line. Sure it would be nice if you just got better and better every day until you achieved full recovery, but that just ain't the way it normally works. And actually, that's ok. You might as well expect the occasional hiccup- forewarned is forearmed!

Given that setbacks are normal and that change isn't linear, it is a good idea to accept the possibility of setbacks rather than living in fear of them. Try taking the following attitude toward possible setbacks: 'I'd really prefer not to have a setback *but* there is *no* reason that I shouldn't have one and *if* I do, I *will* get through it and back on track'.

Have a go at using Worksheet 23-1 to help you surmount setbacks.

Worksheet 23-1	**My Surmounting Setbacks Sheet**
List the techniques that you used to overcome your problem. (The same techniques that worked the first time round will work for setbacks!)	
List the progress you have made so far. Include changes to your daily activities and changes in your thinking and mood. (It is easy to forget how far you have come!)	
Take a moment to give yourself credit for your efforts thus far. When you're facing a setback is when you most need to pat yourself on the back. List at least three of the harder things you have done in order to help yourself get better.	
List a minimum of three people you can go to for support. Try to include at least one professional person like a doctor or therapist.	
Rate your current problem severity on a scale of 1 to 10. Next rate the severity of your problem *before* you started working on overcoming it. Compare the two ratings. (Even if your problem is only a few points less severe than when you first began, you have improved!)	
Current rating:	
Rating at start of treatment:	

Point difference:	
Review your relapse prevention plan in Chapter 18. List three things from your plan that you can put into practice. For example, you may consider restarting or increasing medication if it has helped you before (with your doctor's advice of course!).	

Setbacks do not mean a return to square one. What often determines how long a setback lasts is how quickly you take action to arrest it. A realistically optimistic attitude toward overcoming setbacks also makes a big difference. That's why the above sheet and a relapse prevention plan are useful tools to have in your belt.

Recovery Requires Practice, Patience, and Persistence

We've been in this therapy game a long time and we've never seen anybody get better overnight. Rome wasn't built in a day and we'd be prepared to bet that it took a darn sight longer than a couple of months to construct. Yet there it is, a whopping great city. So if you follow the 3 P's (practice, patience, and persistence), you'll get there. After all, Rome did.

Small Achievements Add Up

Every little bit of progress you make counts in large amounts! Take notice of the small positive changes to your life. Have another look at step 2 on the Surmounting Setbacks Sheet. When you are feeling disheartened it's all too easy to discredit your achievements. So try making a fair and accurate assessment of your progress to date. Small changes can be very significant.

You Have Value in the World

However you may be thinking about yourself during your low times, the world needs you! Every time you act in a socially responsible way you are enhancing your environment. Be it smiling at a shopkeeper, recycling your rubbish or something grander, your positive input adds to the world you live in. Do not underestimate your individual value and contribution to the world. Also remember that when you feel depressed or guilty or otherwise emotionally disturbed, you are probably not the best person to judge your value. Reserve your judgement for another day when you may have a more balanced and realistic view of yourself. Pay a visit to Chapter 14 for more info on how to accept yourself just as you are.

Nobody is Perfect

Well ain't that the truth? No one is perfectly happy, healthy or perfect in any other way. As human beings we are fundamentally designed to be fallible. That means that humans are prone to make mistakes, to sometimes behave self-destructively and to occasionally do bad things. Rather than condemning yourself on the basis of your human imperfection, try treating yourself with some compassion and understanding as you would a friend. Perfection is an unachievable goal. Focus instead on selecting specific and realistic aspects of yourself for improvement. Do this *whilst* accepting yourself as perfectly *imperfect.* Just like everybody else.

You May Feel Differently Tomorrow

Bear in mind that the way you *feel* influences the way you *think.* If today you are feeling depressed, anxious or angry for example, it is highly likely that you will be thinking negative, threatening or anger provoking thoughts. Your negative feelings can temporarily taint your view of life. Tomorrow you may feel differently and may see the world in a much more favourable light.

If you are tempted to make a decision today (especially a major decision!) based on your current negative feelings, try holding off for a while. You may feel better tomorrow or next week and be more able to make a balanced, informed decision based on facts rather than on feelings.

You Can Always Try Other Options

Even if you have tried very hard to get past your problems and still the payoffs seem meager, you can try other things. It may be that self help isn't enough for you right now. You may want to try out some of the following options:

- **Medication:** It can help. Speak to your doctor or psychiatrist and see what they have to say on the subject. Often medication can take the edge off your symptoms and enable to more fully engage with either self help or therapy sessions.

- **Support groups:** There are many different types of support groups available in the community for a host of different types of problems. There are also on-line forums and websites that may be able to give you additional support.

- **Individual therapy:** Seeing a therapist for regular sessions may give you the extra boost that you need. Self help does often work but frequently people find that seeing a therapist as well makes a big difference.

- **Other therapies:** Sometimes other types of therapy apart from CBT can be useful. Clearly we think that CBT is highly effective but that doesn't mean that other schools of therapy don't have value. Investigate your options by looking stuff up on the Internet, speaking to professionals and asking for recommendations from friends.

Any therapist you decide to see should be able to tell you their qualifications and be accredited with a recognised professional body. Accept nothing less.

✔ **Holistic therapies:** Massage, reflexology, acupuncture, and osteopathy are growing in recognition and can be used as adjuncts to CBT Massage and reflexology can promote relaxation. Acupuncture is frequently used to help minimise cravings in addiction treatment. Osteopathy is a sophisticated muscular and skeletal treatment that may help resolve chronic pain and can promote overall well-being. Again, always be sure to see someone with a professional qualification.

Talking to Others Often Helps

If you are feeling discouraged with your progress the temptation can often be to clam up and tell no one. But talking to others about it can help in the following ways:

✔ Friends or family may be able to offer much needed encouragement.

✔ Others may be able to offer you practical help.

✔ Talking to others can give you different perspective on your situation.

✔ Friends or family may help you to normalise your feelings and experiences by sharing some of their own.

Use Worksheet 23-2 to list people you can count on for support (you can list more than three!)

Worksheet 23-2	People I Can Turn to if the Going Gets Tough
1.	
2.	
3.	

You Are Not Alone

Nope. You're not the only one. You're in this life gig with all the rest of us. No matter how on your tod you may be feeling other people feel the same way too. We can guarantee it. Everybody struggles from time to time, even doctors, therapists and psychiatrists. That's because we are people first and professionals second (or third, fourth or fifth . . .). If you really were the only one with psychological problems these books we've been writing wouldn't be selling so well and in fact, neither of us would have a job. So rather than putting yourself on an island-come back to the mainland and rejoin the human race.

Change is an On-going Process

Recovery is a process not a one off event. You'll be far better off considering your efforts to triumph over your difficulties as a lifestyle shift rather than as a finite endeavour. We humans all have to make an on-going concerted effort to keep emotionally well. So whilst it is a very good thing to establish clear goals and to put a time frame around achieving them, be prepared to be flexible. It helps to make a distinction between long, medium and short term goals. You can have a look at Chapter 8 for more on goal setting. But the main message here is that you are a vibrant, ever-changing, complex creature. There will always be more fun and exciting things to work on. Enjoy the journey!

Index

• D •

• E •

Notes

Notes

FOR DUMMIES®

Making Everything Easier!™

UK editions

BUSINESS

Bookkeeping For Dummies
978-0-470-97626-5

Leadership For Dummies
978-0-470-97211-3

Starting & Running a Business All-In-One For Dummies
978-1-119-97527-4

REFERENCE

British Politics For Dummies
978-0-470-68637-9

DIY For Dummies
978-0-470-97450-6

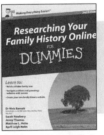

Researching Your Family History Online For Dummies
978-0-470-74535-9

HOBBIES

Growing Your Own Fruit & Veg For Dummies
978-0-470-69960-7

Allotment Gardening For Dummies
978-0-470-68641-6

Electronics For Dummies
978-0-470-68178-7

Asperger's Syndrome For Dummies
978-0-470-66087-4

Basic Maths For Dummies
978-1-119-97452-9

Boosting Self-Esteem For Dummies
978-0-470-74193-1

British Sign Language For Dummies
978-0-470-69477-0

Cricket For Dummies
978-0-470-03454-5

Diabetes For Dummies, 3rd Edition
978-0-470-97711-8

English Grammar For Dummies
978-0-470-05752-0

Flirting For Dummies
978-0-470-74259-4

IBS For Dummies
978-0-470-51737-6

Improving Your Relationship For Dummies
978-0-470-68472-6

Keeping Chickens For Dummies
978-1-119-99417-6

Lean Six Sigma For Dummies
978-0-470-75626-3

Management For Dummies, 2nd Edition
978-0-470-97769-9

Neuro-linguistic Programming For Dummies, 2nd Edition
978-0-470-66543-5

Nutrition For Dummies, 2nd Edition
978-0-470-97276-2

FOR DUMMIES®

A world of resources to help you grow

UK editions

SELF–HELP

978-0-470-66541-1

978-1-119-99264-6

978-0-470-66086-7

STUDENTS

978-0-470-68820-5

978-0-470-74711-7

978-1-119-99134-2

HISTORY

978-0-470-68792-5

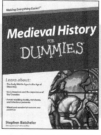

978-0-470-74783-4

978-0-470-97819-1

Origami Kit For Dummies
978-0-470-75857-1

Overcoming Depression For Dummies
978-0-470-69430-5

Positive Psychology For Dummies
978-0-470-72136-0

PRINCE2 For Dummies, 2009 Edition
978-0-470-71025-8

Project Management For Dummies
978-0-470-71119-4

Psychometric Tests For Dummies
978-0-470-75366-8

Reading the Financial Pages
For Dummies
978-0-470-71432-4

Rugby Union For Dummies, 3rd Edition
978-1-119-99092-5

Sage 50 Accounts For Dummies
978-0-470-71558-1

Self-Hypnosis For Dummies
978-0-470-66073-7

Study Skills For Dummies
978-0-470-74047-7

Teaching English as a Foreign Language
For Dummies
978-0-470-74576-2

Time Management For Dummies
978-0-470-77765-7

Training Your Brain For Dummies
978-0-470-97449-0

Work-Life Balance For Dummies
978-0-470-71380-8

Writing a Dissertation For Dummies
978-0-470-74270-9

**Available wherever books are sold. For more information or to order direct go to
www.wiley.com or call +44 (0) 1243 843291**

FOR DUMMIES®

The easy way to get more done and have more fun

LANGUAGES

978-0-470-68815-1
UK Edition

978-1-118-00464-7

978-0-470-90101-4

MUSIC

978-0-470-97799-6
UK Edition

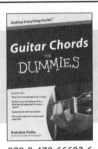

978-0-470-66603-6
Lay-flat, UK Edition

978-0-470-66372-1
UK Edition

SCIENCE & MATHS

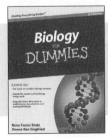

978-0-470-59875-7

978-0-470-55964-2

978-0-470-55174-5

Art For Dummies
978-0-7645-5104-8

Bass Guitar For Dummies, 2nd Edition
978-0-470-53961-3

Criminology For Dummies
978-0-470-39696-4

Currency Trading For Dummies,
2nd Edition
978-1-118-01851-4

Drawing For Dummies, 2nd Edition
978-0-470-61842-4

Forensics For Dummies
978-0-7645-5580-0

Guitar For Dummies, 2nd Edition
978-0-7645-9904-0

Hinduism For Dummies
978-0-470-87858-3

Index Investing For Dummies
978-0-470-29406-2

Knitting For Dummies, 2nd Edition
978-0-470-28747-7

Music Theory For Dummies, 2nd Edition
978-1-118-09550-8

Piano For Dummies, 2nd Edition
978-0-470-49644-2

Physics For Dummies, 2nd Edition
978-0-470-90324-7

Schizophrenia For Dummies
978-0-470-25927-6

Sex For Dummies, 3rd Edition
978-0-470-04523-7

Sherlock Holmes For Dummies
978-0-470-48444-9

Solar Power Your Home
For Dummies, 2nd Edition
978-0-470-59678-4

Available wherever books are sold. For more information or to order direct go to
www.wiley.com or call +44 (0) 1243 843291

FOR DUMMIES

Helping you expand your horizons and achieve your potential

COMPUTER BASICS

978-0-470-57829-2

978-0-470-61454-9

978-0-470-49743-2

DIGITAL PHOTOGRAPHY

978-0-470-25074-7

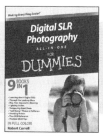

978-0-470-76878-5

978-1-118-00472-2

MICROSOFT OFFICE 2010

978-0-470-48998-7

978-0-470-58302-9

978-0-470-48953-6

Access 2010 For Dummies
978-0-470-49747-0

Android Application Development
For Dummies
978-0-470-77018-4

AutoCAD 2011 For Dummies
978-0-470-59539-8

C++ For Dummies, 6th Edition
978-0-470-31726-6

Computers For Seniors For Dummies,
2nd Edition
978-0-470-53483-0

Dreamweaver CS5 For Dummies
978-0-470-61076-3

iPad For Dummies 2nd Edition
978-1-118-02444-7

Macs For Dummies, 11th Edition
978-0-470-87868-2

Mac OS X Snow Leopard For Dummies
978-0-470-43543-4

Photoshop CS5 For Dummies
978-0-470-61078-7

Photoshop Elements 9 For Dummies
978-0-470-87872-9

Search Engine Optimization
For Dummies, 4th Edition
978-0-470-88104-0

The Internet For Dummies,
12th Edition
978-0-470-56095-2

Visual Studio 2010 All-In-One
For Dummies
978-0-470-53943-9

Web Analytics For Dummies
978-0-470-09824-0

Word 2010 For Dummies
978-0-470-48772-3

WordPress For Dummies, 4th Edition
978-1-118-07342-1

Available wherever books are sold. For more information or to order direct go to www.wiley.com or call +44 (0) 1243 843291